Mirrors of a Disaster

Mirrors
of a
Disaster

The Spanish Military
Conquest of America

Gérard Chaliand

With a new introduction by the author

Translated by A.M. Berrett

Transaction Publishers
New Brunswick (U.S.A.) and London (U.K.)

Library of Congress Catalog Number: 2004066084
ISBN: 1-4128-0471-X
Printed in the United States of America

Library of Congress Cataloging-in-Publication Data

Chaliand, Gérard, 1934-
　　[Miroirs d'un désastre. English]
　　Mirrors of a disaster : the Spanish military conquest of America / Gérard Chaliand ; with a new introduction by the author.
　　　　p. cm.
　　Originally published: Watertown, Mass.: Blue Crane Books, 1994.
　　Includes bibliographical references and index.
　　ISBN 1-4128-0471-X (pbk. : alk. paper)
　　1. Mexico—History—Conquest, 1519-1540. 2. Peru—History—Conquest, 1522-1548. 3. Guatemala—History—To 1821. 4. Indians—History—16th century. I. Title.
F1230.C513 2005
972'.02—dc22
　　　　　　　　　　　　　　　　　　　　　　　　　2004066084

For André and Jean-Claude

*This book is dedicated to Bernardino de Sahagun
and Francisco de Vitoria.*

"The most important event in history since the creation of the world, excepting the incarnation and death of its Creator, is the discovery of the Indies."

Francisco Lopez de Gomara
General History of the Indies

"Accustomed to a long slavery under the domination of their own sovereigns as well as under that of the first conquerors, the natives of Mexico patiently suffer the vexations to which they are frequently exposed from the whites. They oppose to them only a cunning veiled under the deceitful appearances of apathy and stupidity. As the Indian can very rarely revenge himself on the Spaniards, he delights in making common cause with them for the oppression of his own fellow citizens. Harassed for ages and compelled to a blind obedience, he wishes to tyrannize in his turn. The Indian villages are governed by magistrates of the copper-colored race; and an Indian *alcalde* exercises his power with so much the greater severity because he is sure of being supported by the priest or the Spanish *subdelegado*. Oppression produces everywhere the same effects, it everywhere corrupts the morals."

A. von Humboldt

CONTENTS

MAPS

INTRODUCTION TO THE TRANSACTION EDITION

THE CONQUISTADORS
MEXICO—PERU

The conquests of Mexico and Peru took place during the first part of the sixteenth century, a period when Spain was at the height of its power and glory. Christopher Columbus' discovery of the continent may date back to 1492, but it was, in effect, conquered in 1521 when Hernan Cortez claimed Mexico. A dozen years later, Francisco Pizarro, with unprecedented audacity, would overthrow the Incan empire of Peru.

Rarely has the notion of culture shock been as palpably illustrated as in the confrontation between the Spaniards and the Indians of Mexico and Peru. A similar phenomenon took place during the nineteenth century when newly industrialized Europe brutally invaded the Afro-Asian world.

The West today is stirred by the plight of the victims, in a similar manner to which, in the past, its people were solely preoccupied with the glory of the conquerors. Victims now tend to be considered sacred, while conquerors are demonized. These two visions are lacking in nuance, and, more importantly, are anachronistic; they judge an event from the past under present criteria. Why then not utterly condemn Aristotle for not having denounced slavery, or Plato for his very inferior vision of women in the City?

The culture shock between pre-Columbian civilizations—Aztec and Inca in this case—and Spanish conquistadors could only end with the Indians' defeat. This in no way lessens the remarkable exploits of Cortez, Pizarro, and their companions. Their triumphs remain exceptional, and are part of history's major military conquests, especially in Cortez's case. Had they been vanquished, another wave of conquistadors would ultimately have overcome their opponents.

The vast cultural difference, including issues of religion and technology, was too immense for the Indians to ever have had a chance at victory against the Spaniards.

Aztecs and Incas were defeated for many reasons, the main one being the global inferiority of their development. This in no way detracts from the dazzling artistic creativity of pre-Columbian civilizations, which, with no proper alphabet, created absolute masterpieces. There is no doubt that at a very initial stage, which greatly benefited the Spaniards, their arrival captivated the Aztecs, and most notably their almighty sovereign, Montezuma. The foremost vulnerability of the Aztecs was one of mind and soul. Did they first imagine that the Spanish were gods announcing the end of the world, therefore allowing the conquerors to penetrate Mexico with such ease? Or could this simply be the easiest explanation for the string of events preferred by the Indians when looking back on the past? The Aztec defeat was more than just a military collapse; it was an absolute disaster that they just could not face.

Four centuries earlier, Crusaders and Muslims met and battled for Jerusalem. Neither of these two civilizations had any self-doubt nor uncertainties regarding the superiority of one religion over another; they both considered themselves to be entirely equal. This is absolutely not the case in the conquest of America, which foreshadows the colonial era.

The three pieces of work published here give a precise reflection of the conquest of the continent, especially Mexico. From the conquerors' perspective, we have at hand not only dispatches illustrating Cortez's skillful and clever strategy in conquest, but also one of the world's most beautiful chronicles, Bernal Diaz's account of events.

Born in Castile around 1495, Diaz grew up in a very modest family, and his studies were cursory at best. He arrived in Cuba at the age of approximately twenty, and immediately joined the first two expeditions to the new continent, before joining Cortez. After having taken part in the Mexico campaign, Diaz settled in Guatemala as one of its leading citizens, and, already of a certain age, undertook the writing of *The Conquest of New Spain*. His objective was to give Cortez's companions their rightful role in the events, a reaction to having read with indignation the publication in Spain of an account entirely focused on Cortez. It took Bernal Diaz over fifteen years to write his journal of events, which was not to be published during his lifetime, and yet it is one of the most remarkable accounts of the conquest of Mexico. His feel for narrative, his acute sense of observation, and his open mind make it what I consider one of the greatest tales of conquest and exploration related by a direct witness (all different styles of literature included).

The chronicles of the conquest of Peru are nowhere near as detailed and abundant. However, the discovery and conquest of Peru, as described by Pedro Pizarro, one of conquistador Francisco Pizarro's nephews, does give the reader an accurate and vivid vision of the trials and tribulations of this siege, which was more complex than that of Mexico.

Cortez was born in 1485 in the town of Medellin in Estramadur, a province that at the time was fertile in adventurous men. The son of a hidalgo, born into a modest family, his short law studies in Salamanca were quickly interrupted when he left for Cuba, where he lived for over fifteen years, making quite a fortune for himself. Yet his appetite was not sated, and when the time came he was made captain of an expedition to the new continent. Cortez left Cuba for Mexico on February 18, 1519, in command of a small fleet that included a hundred sailors, five hundred soldiers, sixteen horses, and fourteen pieces of artillery. However, the governor of Cuba, who had named him the leader of the expedition, appeared to be having second thoughts, which caused Cortez to hastily leave the island without waiting for a definitive agreement. Therefore, from the start, he had no choice but to succeed, despite the fact that several members of his troops were partisans of the governor of Cuba. A short time later, with the help of his own followers, Cortez took down the masts of his ships so that they could not turn back. Furthermore, through his dispatches, he ably pleaded his case in an attempt to obtain legitimacy.

Upon his approach to Mexico, Cortez managed to obtain some fragmentary information from two previous successful expeditions as some members of his crew were veterans of these events. The conquistadors were actually entering unknown land. As luck would have it, Cortez immediately found two interpreters: a Spanish captive who had survived a shipwreck and who spoke Mayan, the language used on the Yucatan coastline, and a young Indian woman that the Spanish named Marina—called *Malinche* by the Mexicans— daughter of an Aztec Chief, who had been sold as a slave and was offered to Cortez. She spoke her native language of *Nahuatl* and quickly learned Spanish, becoming Cortez's interpreter and his mistress, and, later on, bearing him a son. Thanks to her, the Spaniards gained insight into their opponents' thoughts and strategy, a decisive advantage the Aztecs never had.

Cortez entered battle only when absolutely necessary, but, when choosing to do so, he acted in an extremely audacious manner, with a superiority conferred on him through his possession of horses (an animal that was unknown in North America at that time), the quality of his weapons, and the cohesion of his troops. Cortez preferred to negotiate and create alliances; diplomacy was his favored method. He soon became aware of the fact that the Aztecs' recent domination over nearly all of central Mexico, from the valley of Mexico-Tenochtitlan onwards, was resented by the other nations, who were made to pay heavy taxes while the Aztecs abducted young men and women for sacrificial ceremonies to their gods.

Four civilizations had preceded the world in which the Aztecs lived, which, along with other nations, was destined to disappear at a date set at the time of Creation. The Sun, created at the time of the original sacrifice of the gods, had to be provided with human blood in order to stay its course, thus explaining the holocaust of prisoners and other nations. "Human sacrifice is a transmutation through which we create life with death," explains Jacques Soustelle in *The Four Suns*. When discovered, these human sacrifices repelled the Spanish, as did the acts of cannibalism and sodomy also in practice.

Despite the Aztecs' reluctance, Cortez decided to enter Mexico sooner rather than later. Through his acts of diplomacy and, when necessary, war, he managed to create relationships of friendship or submission with various nations.

On November 3, 1519, approaching the towns surrounding Mexico City, Cortez was greeted by Montezuma, the indisputable authority and ruler of all Aztecs, who apparently was much impressed by the Spaniard. The Spanish troops, dazzled by the lakeside citadel, were able to enter Mexico peacefully following one of the embankments. Despite Montezuma's welcome, however, the small unit—400 men at most—felt the situation to be insecure, the citadel being heavily populated and surrounded by embankments. Cortez, accompanied by his general staff, visited Montezuma and then ordered him to remain permanently at the Spanish headquarters. The sovereign agreed to this without calling for his guards. This decision of Montezuma's is one of the main causes of the Aztec's defeat.

Shortly after he gained control over Montezuma, Cortez learned of the Cuban governor's plan to send over 1,000 men to capture him and his troops. He managed to intercept the Cuban expedition before its arrival in the citadel, and to prevent the force from accomplishing its mission with promises of gold and other treasures. Meanwhile, a revolt against the Spaniards broke out in Mexico, resulting in the death of Montezuma in the throes of the insurrection. When the situation became insufferable for the Spaniards, the only possible solution was for them to flee. On June 30, 1520, taking advantage of nightfall, the Spaniards withdrew—alas, word of their withdrawal spread, and as a result Cortez lost half of his men during what came to be called somberly, *La Noche Triste* (The Sad Night). A week later, the Spaniards were forced to fight a final battle in order to retreat. On horseback and surrounded by a few faithful men, Cortez managed to save the day by killing the enemy chief, thereby provoking the Aztecs to abandon the battlefield, despite their greater number of troops.

The Aztec concept of war clearly explains their defeat. Their concept was coded, battles were planned in advance and announced with no element of surprise whatsoever, and, more importantly, consisted less in killing enemies than in taking prisoners. The capture of four prisoners was sufficient reason for a simple soldier to be considered an elite warrior. Aztec weapons included inept bows used with arrows with obsidian heads, or wooden arrows hardened by fire, short javelins with obsidian tips, long spears, wooden cudgels strengthened with obsidian tips, and dangerous slings manipulated with an immense amount of precision by the warriors. Obsidian is extremely sharp, but is also infinitely more fragile than the steel used for Spanish rapiers.

War was of a completely different nature for the Spanish. Their intent was to defeat their opponents through total warfare, and to conquer them once their backs were up against the wall. All members of the Spanish troops knew that their only choice was to conquer or die. Their purpose was to obliterate their opponent's will and take complete control, guided by their unbridled faith, the backing of the Crown, and their desire for wealth and glory. Spanish weaponry was obviously of a far greater quality than that of the Indians. The role of firearms during battle was much more psychological than physical; the crossbow was more efficient than a wooden bow but took much longer to reload. The main advantages held by the Spanish, who were considered to be among the best European troops at the time, included the amazing strength of their horses and the cohesion and discipline of an infantry based on offense. Basi-

XVIII   MIRRORS OF A DISASTER

cally, once it was deprived of its head, a highly hierarchical civilization such as that of the Aztecs or Incas could only collapse and fall
into total disarray. In America, at the time, the nations that put up a
stronger resistance during a longer period of time were those that
had no truly established political state, such as the Chichimec Indians of North Mexico or the Araucans of Chile.

Defeated but not overcome, Cortez decided to continue with his
mission. His allies, those peoples that had suffered the Aztec oppression or feared their hegemony, never betrayed him. He received
more backup, and, with the help of his allies, prepared to continue
the war, with Mexico City as his target. Meanwhile, having been
brought over to the new continent by the Spaniards, smallpox pro-
liferated, becoming a huge epidemic in Mexico, and eventually striking down Montezuma's successor.

Because Mexico City was a lakeside citadel, Cortez decided to
attack it through a pincer strategy, by land and water. He had his
men build small boats that were transported in spare parts, and eleven
months after the *Noche Triste*, he began the siege of the citadel.

What could the Aztec population have numbered at that time:
300,000? This means that maybe 75,000 men were available for
battle, compared to the thousand or so Spaniards and the few thousand Indian allies that made up the Spanish side.

The aqueduct, from which drinking water was brought into the
citadel, had been sabotaged, and after a series of dramatic and trying incidents, the encircled and starved Aztecs, suffering from smallpox and cholera, were at the end of their tether. The final assault
took place on August 13, 1521: after two and a half months of siege,
Mexico City fell, and the Aztec world began to unravel. Having
conquered their enemy—the worshipers of idols—the Spaniards had
no choice but to destroy their world as well, believing spiritual power
belonged only to the Sacred Church. Seeing what price had been
paid, the Spaniards believed that while souls were being saved, the
Crown's authority should be firmly established.

The estimations regarding the number of inhabitants of Mexico
at the time of the conquest have varied widely during the last fifty
years, from less than 10 million to over 30 million, this last number
being provided by the University of California at Berkeley. This
figure appears to be highly improbable, since it would place the
population of sixteenth-century Mexico at the same level as that of
China, a country with highly developed agricultural resources based
on fertile land and extremely industrious farmers.

Whatever the real number of people, the fact is that, due mainly to disease, the population in both Mexico and Peru collapsed very quickly. Yes, the conquest was cruel and the exploitation of Indians, especially in the mines of Peru, was atrocious. Yes, sixty years after the invasion, Mexico's estimated population was 3 million, and, yes, one century later, it was 1,600,000 million, but this tragic decline was not only due to the Spanish intention to annihilate the Indians, which would have been a genocide. Due to the epidemics, simple contact was absolutely devastating. It should also be noted that the Spanish did not have the human means to obliterate the great mass of Indians, their workforce, had they chosen to do so.

The debates in Spain on the treatment of Indians, though not our subject here, clarified the Crown's intentions and the Church's position. Two men were very much ahead of their time in that they urged the recognition of Indian rights and the "people's rights." Francisco de Victoria contributed admirably, as did Bartholomew de Las Casas with his written plea, *The Devastation of the Indies: A Brief Account*, obtaining the establishment of "new laws" in 1542: these stipulated that slavery should be abolished and that Indians should be treated as subjects of the Crown (the laws were never applied). No other colonial power, from the sixteenth and seventeenth centuries and onwards, ever issued such progressive laws. Despite the monstrosities committed during the invasion and their dire consequences, "compared to other colonial regimes, the Spanish distinguished themselves through their efforts towards the natives," writes the renowned American specialist on Peru and its invasion, John Hemming (*The Conquest of the Incas,* 1971).

Much later, methods of colonial conquest were implacably rigorous. The native was considered "the other," in essence an inferior human being. It would be interesting to retrace the origins of the "black legend," which marked the Spanish conquest of America.

The conquest of Peru was quite different, spanning several decades, even though the final blow was given in a single day, during the first encounter. The setting was different as well. The Andes, South America's mountainous backbone, acted simultaneously as barrier, refuge, and reservoir. The Inca capital of Cuzco is at an altitude of 11,600 feet, and Potosi and its silver mines at 14,000 feet. Their winter, our summer, since we are in the Southern Hemisphere, was extremely rigorous, but, hailing from the regions of Estramadur and Castile, the young conquistadors, with the exception of Francisco Pizarro, were accustomed to extremely hot summers and harsh winters. Pizarro was then well into his fifties, which made him quite an old man for those times, and had participated in two unlucky expeditions, the second one leading him to the equatorial coastline. He obtained royal warrants in 1529 to undertake the discovery and conquest of Peru. The conquistadors, especially those chosen to lead expeditions, were not civil servants or Crown officials, they were free entrepreneurs who, with authorization from the Crown, funded expeditions by themselves and took all responsibility for the risks incurred during the discovery and conquest of unknown lands. If they failed, they lost all the capital invested, and more if the expedition led to disaster. If they succeeded, 20 percent of the treasure was given to the Crown—this was called the *royal fifth*. Pizarro financed the expedition with two associates, one of whom decided to embark with him—Diego de Almagro, originating from Castile. During the invasion, the rivalry between the two men accelerated, Pizarro being backed by his three brothers.

The 168 men, of which sixty-two were on horseback, disembarked south of the Equator, ignorant of the lucky fact that they had arrived in the midst of a civil war. Two sons of a deceased emperor were battling over the inheritance: the recently conquered and highly hierarchical territory stretching from the south of Columbia to the north of Chile.

While the Spanish were climbing up the Andes, Atahualpa triumphed over his brother. A few months later, still savoring the victory of capture, Atahualpa learned of the arrival of the Spaniards in the city of Cajamarca, in the north of Peru, not far from where he and his troops had settled. A Spanish emissary on horseback, accompanied by an interpreter, was sent to Atahualpa's campsite to invite him to visit with the Spanish the next day, which he agreed to do. On November 16, 1532, Pizarro tricked the Incas at Cajamarca: the Spaniards had hidden themselves, some with the four small pieces of artillery and the harquebus, others with crossbows. The horsemen were frightening to Atahualpa's troops (and Indians in general), since they were mounted on animals with which they were unfamiliar; the first horse they had ever seen had been the emissary's on the previous day. Loud bells had been attached to the horses' hocks in order to produce a terrifying noise, generating a sonorous, fiercely brutal shock. Pizarro and his companions were determined to take the Inca alive!

It was said that bad omens had predicted the arrival of the Spaniards, but despite these signs, Atahualpa went to meet them as a conqueror, confident in his power. Apparently unarmed, as the different chronicles would have it, the Indians entered a seemingly deserted area. The priest stood before them alone, the Holy Book in his hand, an Indian interpreter by his side. He had this interpreter address the Indians and recite the articles stating the necessity of submitting to the will, the law, and, most importantly, the faith of the Spanish sovereign. Atahualpa, sitting in his palanquin, demanded to see the book, only to open it and then throw it to the ground, prompting Pizarro to give his signal. Gunfire broke out, trumpets rang: the horsemen, screaming "Santiago y ellos!" stormed the crowd of petrified Indians, the bells hanging from their horses' legs clanging noisily. Surprise suddenly gave way to panic, with people fleeing the scene and trampling one another in the process. On foot, Pizarro, followed by a few infantrymen, strode towards the Inca he was to capture. After a brief struggle during which the palanquin fell, the Spaniards managed to take Atahualpa prisoner.

Onsite the slaughter continued while the horsemen pursued those who fled. Despite the absence of their sovereign, no Inca proclaimed himself leader in order to fight the Spaniards. Night fell; the ambush, in which hunter could have become the hunted, had been successful. Without even realizing it, the 168 Spaniards had pulled off one of the most audacious moves in history, suddenly inflicting a mortal blow on the Inca Empire.

To obtain his freedom, Atahualpa offered a significant ransom and, in order to be permanently rid of his rival, had his brother assassinated by his men.

Once both parties had come to an agreement on the conditions of Atahualpa's liberation, the Spanish decided to put him to death. Having executed Atahualpa, and therefore taken revenge for the assassination of the sovereign of Cuzco, they were welcomed as "liberators" there, and placed a new Inca in power, hoping he would remain submissive. Soon however, tired of being systematically humiliated by his new masters, he organized a revolt which weakened Spanish domination for some time. The Spaniards did manage to take back control, but they had internal struggles of their own to deal with, between followers of Pizarro and those of his dissatisfied associate, Almagro. A second rebellion broke out, led by the Inca ruler, at the same time as Pizarro's execution of Almagro; and Pizarro was soon to die by the hand of Almagro's son. Compared to the somewhat classic and linear conquest of Mexico, the invasion of Peru could be easily assimilated with the dark and bloody dramas of the Elizabethan period.

The Spanish Crown sent a Viceroy to the newly conquered terri-
tories of the continent to apply the "new laws"; this was, of course,
necessary, but provoked an insurrection of the conquistadors, led
by one of the Pizarro brothers. The Crown won the battle. By this
time, the Indian revolt had not died down completely, but was limited to certain regions. The Crown decided to put an end to the situation once and for all, and, in 1572, forty years after Cajamarca, the
last Inca was executed in the main square of Cuzco. According to
estimates, the Indian population was reduced to one-third of its initial size as a direct consequence of disease and the Spanish invasion.

Rarely has a defeat been of such magnitude and had such major
consequences in history. Not to be forgotten are the civilizations
that now exist only through memory and whose names punctuate
Antiquity, nor the consequences of certain epidemic diseases, such
as those of the Thirty Year War, which reduced the population of
Germany by half. Disease hit Mexico from the start, but the most
acute phases took place in 1546, 1549, and 1566. Forced labor,
especially that in the mines of Peru, also played a large part, but
perhaps not as large as the collapse of Indian values, which were the
foundation, balance, and basic concept of Indian civilizations. These
destroyed civilizations took refuge in a sort of passive resistance,
while the elite in Mexico and Peru chose to collaborate with their
new masters, sometimes provoking drastic revolts followed by severe repression.

The Spanish had no choice but to impose what they thought to be
the one and only true faith, saving the Indians from the shadows of
idols and sin. Franciscans, Dominicans, and Augustines all aimed to
protect the Indians as much as possible. The Franciscan Bernardino
de Sahagun arrived in Mexico just a few years after the downfall of
the Aztec empire. He learned *Nahuatl*, the native language, and a
few years later, very much in advance on his time, embarked upon a
true work of ethnology, collecting stories and chronicles which composed *The General History of the Things of New Spain,* the most
essential source of knowledge that we have regarding the Aztec civilization. No other colonial power ever carried out this kind of work
until modern times.

The progressive integration of most of Latin America to the Church
and to the Spanish language is the conquistadors' ultimate triumph.
For better or for worse, and without even realizing it, they began the
process of cultural crossbreeding, turning the Hispanic world into

the demographic center of Catholicism and Spanish into the second language of the West.

The narratives in *Mirrors of a Disaster* describe vividly the early stages of the era of conquests, driven by a handful of adventurous men who, for the most part, could only have had a very limited notion of the consequences of their actions.

Gérard Chaliand
July 2004

SELECT BIBLIOGRAPHY

Baudot, Georges, and Tzvetan Todorov. *Récits aztèques de la conquête*. Paris: Seuil, 1983.
Bennassar. *Hernan Cortez*. Paris: Payot, 2001.
Chaunu, Pierre. *Conquête et exploitation des nouveaux mondes (XVIème siècle)*. Paris: PUF, 1961.
Cortez, Hernan. *Lettres de relation*. Paris: La Découverte, 1988.
Diaz del Castillo, Bernal. *La conquête du Mexique* (The Conquest of New Spain). Babel, Actes-Sud, 1998.
Duverger, Christian. *Cortez*. Paris: Fayard, 2001.
Hemming, John. *La conquête du Pérou* (The Conquest of the Incas). Paris: Stock, 1971.
de Jerez, Francisco. *La conquête du Pérou*. Paris: Anne-Marie Métaillié, 1976.
Pizarre, Pedro. *La conquête du Pérou* (Relation of the Discovery and Conquest of the Kingdoms of Peru [tr. 1921]). Paris: Le Félin,1996.
Portilla, Miguel Leon. *L'envers de la conquête*. Paris: Federop, 1972.
The Other Side of the Conquest: Aztec, Mayan and Quechua Narrations about the Conquest (El reverso de la Conquista. Relaciones aztecas, mayas y quechuas de la Conquista), 1964.
Prescott, W. H. *Histoire de la conquête du Mexique* (translated from *History of the Conquest of Mexico*, 1843). Paris: Pygmalion, 2001.
Prescott, W. H. *Histoire de la conquête du Pérou* (translated from *History of the Conquest of Peru*, 1847). Paris: Pygmalion, 2001.
de Sahagun, Bernardino. *Codex florentius: Histoire générale des choses de la Nouvelle-Espagne* (French ed., La Découverte, 1980).
Soustelle, Jacques. *Les quatre soleils*. Terre Humaine, Plon, 1991.
Wachtel, Nathan. *La vision des vaincus, les Indiens du Pérou devant la conquête espagnole, 1531-1570* (The Vision of the Vanquished: The Spanish Conquest of Peru Through Indian Eyes, 1530-1570). Paris: Gallimard, 1971.

PREFACE

There can be no traveler who has not been struck by the sadness of the Indians in the Andes. Compared to the culturally mestizo Indians in the cities, the Indian in the Andean communities is marginalized on every level. There, as in Guatemala and the southernmost states of Mexico, domination has been internalized. Whether one likes it or not, in Spanish America integration works through the imperial language and the patterns of action and behavior of the conqueror. When Alexander von Humboldt visited Spanish America in the 1810s, he estimated that the population was 35 percent mestizo and 50 percent Indian. Today, Indians account for barely 5 percent of the total, measured linguistically. In Mexico, where *indigenismo* as a cultural movement has been powerful this century, the homage rendered to the Indians is one of the world's most sumptuous monuments to the dead: the Museum of Mexico. The new Mexico (largely a postcolonial creation) that emerged in the aftermath of the civil war accepts that it is mestizo. Symbolically, it has agreed to be no longer led by whites, but the only alternatives it can offer the Indians of the southern states are integration or marginalization. The homage paid by the Museum of Mexico is paid in memoriam. It is a past that is grafted on, like adding an Indian forename before a Spanish surname. It is a symbolic fusion like that made by the first great muralists, such as Orozco or Rivera.

Elsewhere, this process, which has begun on the ground, has been only half-accepted in the consciousness of governing groups. The 1952 revolution in Bolivia led to the rise of the mestizos, not the Indians. In Peru, power is still in the hands of the whites of the coast, although the demography of the mestizos and the drift from the rural areas are transforming the face of Lima. In Guatemala, the Indian majority continues to be treated like a dominated minority. Yet everything suggests that the process of integration through cultural mixing is irreversible.

Thus, all that the traveler sees of the Indians is either folklore or the tragic image of the defeated, bleak and passive, that seems to be reflected in the ancient and plaintive melancholy of the music of the Andes. On each of my visits—between 1961 and 1985—I was struck by this marginalization of the Indians. The remote origin of this prostration of the defeated, a prostration punctuated by terrible revolts, must lie in the trauma of a total defeat. It is to that disaster that I wish to go back.

I began on this book five years ago. It attempts to relate the many facets of a conquest. They are the mirrors of a disaster showing through what I feel are the most significant contemporary documents of the Indians' perception of defeat and conquest by the Spaniards and my own telling of a tragedy in which the vanquished could not, ultimately, but be vanquished.

Apart from Alexander's Anabasis, I see three ancient conquests as being, for different reasons, exceptional: the lightning expansion of Islam in the seventh and eighth centuries, from Spain to the borders of China and India; the Mongol conquest of the largest empire ever erected by the organizing will of a nomad of genius; and finally, the conquest of the Americas by a handful of Spaniards. My tastes incline me to prefer the deeds of those out of the ordinary: Genghis and Cortes, neither of them destined, like Alexander or the companions of the Prophet, to be deemed legitimate.

My choice was largely determined by my knowledge of Spanish and of the geographical terrain on which the action unfolded and the physical presence of the descendants of the destroyed cultures.

For Mexico, I have used and translated from Spanish part of the documents originally collected by the Dominican Bernardino de Sahagun and brought together by Miguel Portilla in *Vision de los vencidos*. On the Spanish side, I have chosen from the magnificent story—perhaps, indeed, the finest chronicle in the world—by Bernal Diaz del Castillo, the episodes that throw light on the political and military strategy of Cortes and the Spaniards. Finally, from Cortes, I have taken a few passages from his *Dispatches*. I have not sought to do the work of a historian but to make meaningful the strict chronicle of a conquest through those who lived it, adding a contemporary angle that is informed by the memory of disaster and fellow-feeling with those who, having themselves had their backs to the wall, have been forced to extreme actions.

I would like to thank Gilles Bataillon for his critical reading of several sections of my manuscript.

Paris, 1989

MIRRORS OF A DISASTER

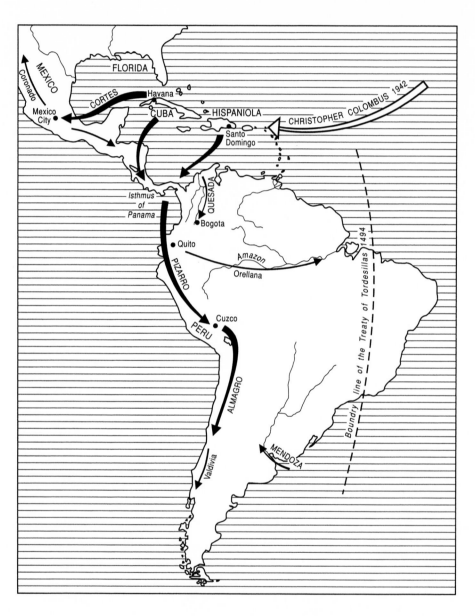

Map 1. Spanish conquests, 1520–1540

PART I

THE CONQUEST OF MEXICO

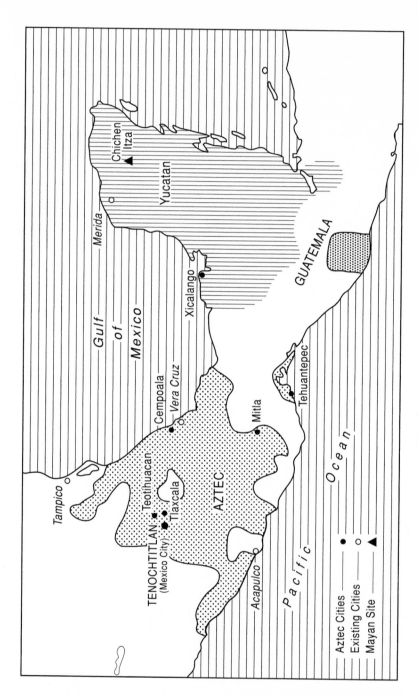

Map 2. *The Aztec empire c. 1500*

Chichen Itza ▲

Yucatan

Merida ○

GUATEMALA

Gulf

of

Mexico

Xicalango ●

Cempoala ●
Vera Cruz

Tehuantepec ●

Mitla ●

Tampico ○

Teotihuacan ■
TENOCHTITLÁN: ■
(Mexico City) ●
Tlaxcala

AZTEC

Acapulco ○

Pacific

Ocean

Aztec Cities ●
Existing Cities ○
Mayan Site ▲

SUMMARY

Cortes left Cuba in February 1519 against the wishes of Governor Velazquez with eleven ships, five hundred soldiers and one hundred sailors, sixteen horses, and fourteen artillery pieces.

After a series of contacts with the Indians, some of them involving considerable casualties, Cortes had the good fortune to acquire interpreters, something his opponents did not have, and succeeded in forming an alliance with peoples opposed to Aztec rule, including the Tlaxcalans.

In November 1519, after overcoming the obstacles put up by Monteczuma, the Aztec ruler, whose people were paralyzed by a mortal dread—the strangers being taken for the gods of the Apocalypse—Cortes peacefully entered Mexico, where he was welcomed as a god. But the Spaniards felt their situation, based on a fragile imposture, was untenable, and they decided to take Monteczuma prisoner, doing so without striking a blow.

After this Cortes had to leave Mexico with some of his men to meet Narvaez, who had been sent by Governor Velazquez with a considerable force to arrest him. Cortes managed, however, to turn the tables.

Meanwhile, the exactions of the Spaniards who had stayed behind in Mexico precipitated an uprising that hastened Cortes's return. Monteczuma died. The Spaniards had no choice but to flee. They withdrew with heavy losses on the night of June 30, 1520. The smallpox epidemic brought by the conquerors decimated the Indians.

Cortes reorganized his forces and, the following year, with the help of a fleet of brigantines and his numerous Indian allies, laid siege to Mexico, which collapsed after three months, in August 1521. The conquest had taken just eighteen months.

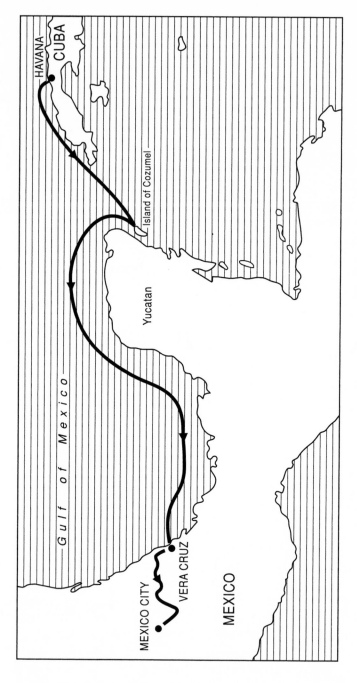

Map 3. Hernando Cortes's route from Havana to Mexico, 1518–1519

1

"MEN FROM DISTANT LANDS"

Cortes set out from Cuba on February 18, 1519, at the head of a fleet of eleven ships. He had with him six hundred men. Among these were Pedro de Alvarado, who would later take part in the conquest of Guatemala; Francisco de Montejo, who would conquer the Yucatan; Cristóbal de Olid, who would be beheaded for rebellion in Honduras; Gonzalo de Sandoval, his favorite among his four lieutenants; and Bernal Diaz, a soldier, who, forty years later, would compile his admirable *True History of the Conquest of New Spain*.

Hernando Cortes took with him sixteen horses, fourteen cannon, a few muskets, thirty-two crossbows, and a quantity of trade goods.

A number of expeditions had already reconnoitered Yucatan between 1516 and 1518, providing a source of information for Cortes. Cortes's forces included many veterans of earlier expeditions.

Aztec rule over almost the whole of central Mexico from the Valley of Mexico-Tenochtitlan was recent and ill-accepted. The tribute demanded was heavy, and, in addition, the Aztecs took boys and girls to be sacrificed to their gods.

From the very beginning, Cortes was lucky in finding two interpreters who gave him an advantage in his meeting with a society that was very different from his own. These were Jerónimo de Aguilar, who had been a captive for three years following a shipwreck and who spoke Maya, and the woman whom the Spaniards called Marina, Malinche, the daughter of a *cacique*. She had been sold as a slave in the province of Tabasco and spoke both Nahuatl and Maya. Aguilar understood Maya and translated it into Spanish. Moreover, Marina quickly learned Spanish.

After a few encounters with the Indians—some of them peaceful, others not—from which Cortes always emerged on top, thanks to his political sense and his determination, the expedition reached the coast at Vera Cruz. They were soon in contact with emissaries of the Aztec ruler Monteczuma. From the beginning, Cortes, with his horses and his firearms, pursued a policy designed to impress.

The Aztecs—making an alliance with the cities of Texcoco and Tlacopan, which they soon outclassed—ruled thirty-eight tributary provinces that retained their own institutions. Within this altogether recent empire, there were pockets of resistance outside Aztec control, such as Tlaxcala. The arrival of Cortes, the interpretation put on his coming, and his skill in playing on political divisions and latent conflicts precipitated the breakup of the Aztec system of rule.

Having ensured his control of the coast (where he left 150 men) and armed with information, Cortes set off with 15 horsemen and 400 foot soldiers. On the way they broke the resistance of the Otomis, while the Indians of Tlaxcala, after an initial clash, rallied to the side of the powerful newcomers, so great was their hatred of the Aztecs.

CORTES, THE GREATEST OF THE CONQUISTADORS

Hernando Cortes, who was the brains and moving force in the conquest of Mexico, was born in Estremadura, at Medellin, in 1485, into a family of hidalgos of modest means. After briefly studying law at the University of Salamanca, he set off for Cuba in 1504. Spain had completed the *reconquista* in 1492, the year Columbus discovered the Americas. Spanish troops were the best army in Christendom. In Italy, Gonzalo de Cordoba, a Spanish General known as *El Gran Capitán*, the Great Captain, had perfected the *tercio*, an innovation combining firepower and close combat weapons for formations that would remain unbeaten until the middle of the next century.

Cortes remained in Cuba for fifteen years. He was very successful; but he wanted more. At the time, Santo Domingo, and above all, Cuba were the jumping-off points for contact with the continent, as Panama would later be for South America. Two half-hearted attempts had already been made to land in Mexico, in which the future chronicler of the conquest of Mexico, Bernal Diaz, had taken part.

When Cortes left Cuba for Mexico, he was effectively a rebel. The governor of Cuba, Diego de Velazquez, who had initially given

Cortes command of an expedition to reconnoiter and take Mexico, wanted to rescind his decision. Cortes was warned and set sail at once. Among his forces were supporters of Velazquez. Soon, hard on his heels came an expedition to arrest him. Cortes thus had no base to fall back on. He left in the port a force of last resort. However, once Cortes's ships had been destroyed, this forestalled any attempt by Velazquez's supporters to go back, and they grumbled. Having agreed to burn their ships, Cortes's men had to create the conditions of success or pay with their lives.

The founding of the city of Vera Cruz in July enabled Cortes to remove himself juridically from the authority of the governor of Cuba by placing himself directly under the king. Whenever it was possible to avoid fighting, Cortes preferred to talk; when conflict was inevitable, the Spaniards invariably won, thanks to their military superiority.

When we reread the fragments of this tragedy left to history, we are struck by how brief it was: it took fewer than eighteen months for a handful of men to bring down a great empire. This is a drama of great intensity that can be set out in a few scenes.

First there is Cortes entering an unknown land—Mexico—with, in the north, its bleak and stony desert; in the south, where he landed, tropical beaches often interspersed with marshy scrub; and in the center, the site of the Aztec empire, where almost the whole of our story unfolds, highlands overlooked by peaks above five thousand meters, such as Popocatepetl and Orizaba. On the Caribbean coast, the sun is leaden, the nights stifling. In the highlands, the heat of the day is followed by cold nights. But for peasants from Castile, Andalusia, and Estremadura, used to torrid summers and harsh mountain winters, these climates were not too unbearable.

From the time of the landing, the preparations lasted six months. The Spaniards' first reliable ally was Cempoala. Cortes formed an alliance with the *cacique*, and in testimony of it received a number of slaves, among them the beautiful Marina. Having thus secured his rear, he set out for Mexico on August 16, 1519. His forces were made up of 450 men and sixteen horses, with a dozen small artillery pieces. So far, all was uncertainty. The nature of the terrain was not yet known, and the military power of the Aztecs, which according to the subject peoples seemed to be considerable, had not yet been tested.

Tlaxcala, the Aztecs' rival, initially hostile to Cortes, accepted his overtures for an alliance (September 1519). Yet Cortes prudently

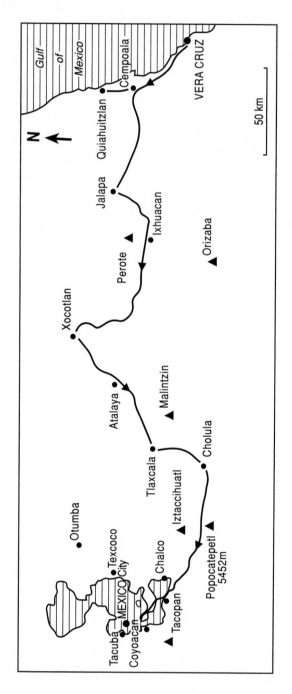

Map 4. Hernando Cortes's march from Vera Cruz to Mexico

stayed in Tlaxcala as though in enemy territory, with guards and sentinels taking turns day and night. He gathered as much information on Mexico and on Aztec power as he could and would henceforth use against Mexico all the alliances made possible by the harshness of Aztec rule.

Cortes was an irregular who needed quick results to justify his conduct. As soon as he found gold, he sent it to the king in order to legitimize his expedition.

The first galleon to return from Mexico arrived in the port of Seville in December 1519. Charles V had the treasures the galleon contained sent to Ghent. Albrecht Dürer, who saw them in Brussels, noted in his diary in August 1520:

> All the days of my life I have seen nothing that rejoiced my heart so much as these things, for I saw amongst them wonderful works of art, and I marveled at the subtle ingenia of men in foreign lands. I saw . . . a sun all of gold a whole fathom broad, and a moon all of silver of the same size.

Cortes wrote to the king to inform him of what was happening, to justify himself, and to dangle before him the fruits of his conquest. Cortes's dispatches were part of a global strategy. They are, moreover, written in a beautiful, restrained, and tight Castilian. In his letter dated October 30, 1519, on the eve of his final departure for Mexico, Cortes suggested that the country he was conquering for the Crown be called "New Spain of the Ocean Sea."

They set out again on the road to Mexico. They had with them not only a few hundred Indians from Cempoala but also several thousand from Tlaxcala.

A trap was set for the Spaniards at Cholula, a vassal of the Aztecs. Forewarned, the Spaniards struck first. In any event, the Cholulans were opponents of the Indians of Tlaxcala, and massacring them cemented the Spaniards' alliance with the others.

On November 1, 1519, they resumed their march toward Mexico. This time, it was the final stage. No obstacles could stand in the way of the Spaniards' ardor and tenacity. On November 8, 1519, in the suburbs of Tenochtitlan, the unique meeting took place between the Aztec ruler, Monteczuma, and the Spanish captain. It was in no sense a dialogue: two voices spoke with radically differing visions of the world. The conquest of Mexico was indeed the first colonial adventure in the sense the term acquired in the last century.

Cortes saw Monteczuma. He heard what Marina translated for

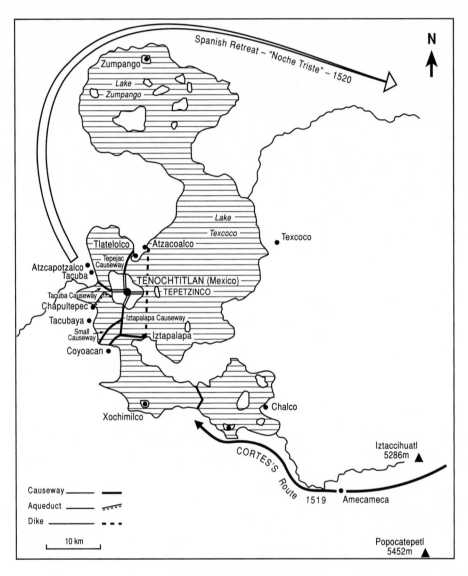

N

Spanish Retreat – "Noche Triste" – 1520

Zumpango

Lake
Zumpango

Lake
Texcoco

Texcoco

Tlatelolco

Atzacoalco

Tepejac
Causeway

Atzcapotzalco
Tacuba

TENOCHTITLAN (Mexico)

Tacuba Causeway

TEPETZINCO

Chapultepec

Tacubaya

Iztapalapa Causeway

Small
Causeway

Iztapalapa

Coyoacan

Xochimilco

Chalco

Iztaccihuatl
5286m

CORTES'S Route

1519

Amecameca

Causeway

Aqueduct

Dike

10 km

Popocatepetl
5452m

Map 5. The conquest of Mexico

him. He doubtless glimpsed that he and his companions seemed to have a status very different from their actual condition. Perhaps he questioned Marina to learn more. Was the Aztec ruler playing tricks? Did he really believe that the strangers were gods who had returned to take possession of what was rightly theirs? The invasion of Mexico was a gamble. While the Spaniards triumphantly crossed the causeways in close order and discovered Tenochtitlan, the lake city, and all its splendor, there was anguish in their souls. But they were at the heart of the citadel.

While carrying out an armed invasion, accompanied by opponents of the Aztecs, the Spaniards were endowed with a divine aura. Yet, this was fragile, since Cortes, their leader, knew their divinity was an imposture, and they might at any moment find themselves in a trap. They soon found the Aztecs' hidden gold: the fever was at its peak. They had reached their goal, but how could they leave with the treasure?

It was now that Cortes and his colleagues—the men he trusted who accepted his decisions—resolved to seize Monteczuma. An audience was sought. There were six Spaniards. They would try a swift knockout blow, a commando operation. They were few so as not to raise any alarm, but their numbers were insufficient if the ruler should resist, and they would be at the mercy of the enemy if he called his guards for help.

These men thus entered the Aztec ruler's apartments with a heavy heart. Would he give himself up without making too much of a fuss, or would he resist? Cortes's calculation rested on his perception of Monteczuma: he felt intuitively that the ruler was weak. Everything in Monteczuma's behavior since their first meeting indicated an absence of arrogance toward the Spaniards, an inward submission. They must act while it was still possible to subdue him. However, the sovereign protested; he wanted to retain his autonomy. Abdicating his power symbolically was something about which he had no choice, but agreeing to lose all his freedom was something he could not do without a protest. Monteczuma refused to admit what he had already accepted—that he was no longer master. He argued. It was at that point that he was threatened. One of the Spaniards raised his voice and moved his hand to his sword. Monteczuma did not call for help. He suffered the ascendancy of the strangers and went with them. He reassured his own men that all was well. He did not seek confrontation. He bowed his back before fate. He was resigned. He handed himself over, submissive, to the goodwill of those who had imposed their rule in his house.

All was now lost for Monteczuma. The men from distant lands who had come by sea, who rode strange beasts of great power, who spat fire that broke rocks and trees, who wore thick beards and swords that did not lose their sharpness, whose dogs were fierce—these men had now come. Nothing had been able to stop them, neither incantations nor sacrifices, neither tricks nor obstacles, neither presents nor bribes. They had come, bringing with them the Aztecs' opponents, those who had been conquered and reduced to subjection, those who were still resisting but fearfully. And now here they were protected by the men from distant lands, confidently disporting themselves in Mexico. The hour of catastrophe was approaching. It was impossible to hide, impossible to flee. Perhaps it might be possible to move the newcomers by docility, or perhaps there was nothing to be done but to accept defeat.

In the beginning, Monteczuma was left his serving women and other servants. The imprisoned ruler still enjoyed the shadow of his power. He could reassure his subjects and keep them quiet for the benefit of the men from distant lands. He could retain his ceremonies and his habits. That much tranquillity was left him by Cortes. A thread bound Monteczuma to Mexico: the people of his household and the messengers that both Monteczuma and Cortes needed for reassurance.

The days went by, full of uncertainty. There were stupor and doubtless anger among the Aztecs, whose ruler was held by strangers. Those who, before the Spaniards' intrusion into the city, had suggested opposing their entry felt they had been right. But what could be done without the ruler's agreement? It was a precarious armistice for the Spaniards that would last only as long as Monteczuma cooperated. Now he was indeed a prisoner. To rule out any possibility of flight, he had been put in chains. He had been guarded day and night from the moment of his capture. How long could such a situation last? Tenochtitlan was a trap with the three causeways leading out of the city so easy to block.

Suddenly, this tension erupted into a crisis for the Spaniards. Men sent by the governor of Cuba had landed. They had emerged victorious from a minor clash with the few troops that Cortes had left with the ships at Vera Cruz, and they were coming to arrest the conquistador.

Cortes had no time to lose. The expedition had to be stopped or neutralized before it reached Mexico. There could be no question of sharing the city's loot—and even less of abandoning it—or of fighting each other in front of the Aztecs. Cortes gained his ends both by cunning—suborning his opponent Narvaez's men—and by force, operating by night, using surprise. He thus rid himself of a rival and returned with more than twice the number of men.

But during his absence his lieutenant Pedro de Alvarado had sought to take the initiative. Alvarado had thoughtlessly broken the tacit armistice that the two sides had been observing. Taking advantage of a meeting of caciques and other leading figures, he had opened fire. His aim had been to liquidate the Aztec aristocracy and thus terrorize the city. It was typical of him. Earlier, landing on the island of Cozumel at the beginning of the expedition, he had terrorized the people, and Cortes had later had great difficulty in reassuring them. Pedro de Alvarado was a man of great courage and was aggressive by nature. He was an excellent lieutenant as long as he was controlled and did not have to make political decisions.

The second entry into Tenochtitlan was quite unlike the first. This time, the hostilities were open. Fortunately, the Spaniards still held a trump card in the person of Monteczuma. At the Spaniards' suggestion, he tried to intervene between the belligerents. He was hit by a stone thrown from the Aztec side and died—much to the regret of the Spaniards, who were now left to fend for themselves. The Aztecs chose a new ruler. War resumed with the besieged Spaniards.

It was a peculiar moment in history, with the Spaniards at the very heart of the citadel of an empire, with the royal treasure in their possession. They had reached their goal but were in a trap, and escaping from it was bound to cost them dearly. For escape they must. Their position was untenable. There were too many Aztec warriors and not enough room to maneuver. The conquistadors were caught in a crazy military situation by the force of circumstance, the accident of misunderstanding, and Alvarado's mistake.

A movable bridge was cobbled together to cross the ditches and an attempt was made to flee by night. There was no hope of getting away unseen. At the least there must have been three or four thousand Spaniards and their Indian allies, not to mention the baggage.

Cortes's advice was to carry as little as possible. The sensible ones among them agreed. To flee, one needs to travel light. The rest, mostly Narvaez's men, could not bring themselves to leave the gold behind. The weight of it contributed to their fate.

That night, June 30, 1520, there was a fine drizzle, depressing and tepidly warm, typical of that time of year in Mexico. The Spaniards had opted for the shortest road out to the west (toward Tlacopan or

Tacuba). Before setting out, they all commended themselves to God. Their only comforts were that they were among their own and they had some hope of getting out alive. The predictable alarm was sounded. The Spaniards had to fight their way out. Then the unexpected happened: the portable bridge that was intended to be used several times collapsed under the press of men going over it and was of no further use. The organized flight was transformed into a rout. Estimates of Spanish losses range from one-quarter to two-thirds of their total numbers. This was the *Noche triste.*

With great difficulty, the Spaniards managed to force their way out of Tenochtitlan. Meanwhile, among the Aztecs, a smallpox epidemic was already cutting swaths through the population, striking down even Monteczuma's successor. The Spaniards were not pursued immediately, perhaps because it took some time to organize the warriors' departure. They should not have been given that respite. Whatever the reason, the Spaniards had enough time to get themselves together a bit, tend their wounds, and count how many of them were left, for they still had to fight.

At Otumba, on July 7, 1520, the most important and most difficult battle that Cortes ever had to fight took place. It was a battle fought with the energy of despair by a retreating force that had suffered heavy losses. Barely half the original number of Spaniards were fit.

With considerable foresight, Cortes had not wanted to tire the horses by using them to transport the wounded. He knew that the enemy had every incentive to press the advantage and transform what was a major setback into an absolute catastrophe. The horses had been kept fresh, for they were Cortes's striking force, the shock element in the battle.

And so the Aztec troops appeared, very close, with their yelling, their drum rolls, the ever more deafening noise of war to impress the enemy, strike fear into them and make them too afraid to move. But the battle-hardened troops knew how to resist the shock of the noise of battle; discipline and organization were the foundations of the cohesion that made them stand fast. But this time, after the nightmare of escaping from Tenochtitlan, in full retreat and with all the wounded, with no expectation of reinforcements or help from any quarter, absolutely alone and so few, so tired, the Spaniards must have felt the shadow of death passing over them.

Cortes spoke. He exhorted. He conjured up past victories and the valor of his men. It was victory or nothing. With the help of God and the Virgin Mary. And striking first.

However desperate their situation, throughout the conquest of Mexico, and indeed of Peru, the Spaniards always chose to attack first. Not only did hitting the enemy first show that they were not afraid of them and expected to defeat them, but it was solely in attack or in pursuit that full use could be made of the horsemen.

Once again, the horsemen were decisive. The Spaniards were in serious danger of being overrun despite the fact that Cortes had sacrificed depth for breadth, but they managed to turn the situation around. In ancient warfare, the death of the commander-in-chief— ruler or general—led to a rout. So it was with the Aztecs. With a handful of horsemen, Cortes succeeded in making a breakthrough right up to the Aztec commander with his sumptuous attire. His death gave more than the day to the Spaniards. It saved their lives and sealed the fate of the Aztec empire. Safe now, the Spaniards would return.

In Tenochtitlan, the smallpox epidemic raged. What was the source of this curse? What god could help? What charm would work? Sacrifices were stepped up. The priests brought obscure replies; people were dying in droves. Everyone was terrified. How did the illness spread? What amulet could give protection?

The strangers had left, driven out, but they had left their curse behind. But at least they would not return. Two centuries earlier, the Mongols had been seeking annihilation. The Aztecs were living in another world, and they would pay the price.

The Spaniards' losses were considerable. As always, the sources differ on the figures. The most likely estimate is that the Spaniards lost between 25 and 45 percent of their men. But the most valorous of Cortes's companions, except for Alonso de Avila, had survived— even Alvarado, who led the rearguard.

And then Marina, Cortes's companion and interpreter, was the intermediary of fate who gave a glimpse of the opponent' universe.

Marina stands out as a special figure. Rejected by her own people, she had thrown in her lot with the strangers. Cortes loved her, and she almost certainly loved him and served his plan to the very end. She moved about and passed on information; she taught and explained.

In 1523, three years after her first meeting with Cortes, she would have a son, Martin, whom Cortes acknowledged. What must she have felt in the way, not of love or attachment, but of strangeness in this meeting of worlds with such divergent beliefs? What part of her understood the way the Spaniards behaved? What gap was there between understanding the language and grasping its signifiers? If she can be seen—in an age when nativist movements and nationalisms are à la mode—as the Malinche, the traitor (why more so than the Tlaxcalans who thought that in Cortes they had found a heaven-sent ally against the Aztecs?), she can also and perhaps above all be seen as a figure of destiny based on language as power (did she not share in that of the gods?) and a lover living out all the consequences of her choice, as do all tragic lovers.

The Aztecs thought that the strangers had gone forever. On September 7, 1520, a day dedicated in their calendar to death, they enthroned a new ruler, Cuitlahuac. The smallpox epidemic was gradually diminishing. Seven months went by in peace.

* * *

Four worlds had preceded that in which the Aztecs lived. Each of them had been destroyed by a cataclysm, the last by a flood. The Aztecs believed that the fifth world, like the previous ones, was doomed to disappear at a date set from the very beginning. The West had experienced the fear of the year 1000. A dread of the end of the world, an anguish of the Apocalypse had long prevailed. Even today dread is appearing anew in the most modern societies.

The sun created by the gods owed its existence and its movement to the original sacrifice of the gods and their blood. (Does not *sacer facere* mean to make sacred?) In order for the sun to continue its course each day, people, like the gods, must offer blood in sacrifice. Blood nourishes the sun, and the death of victims is necessary for the survival of the human species. The gods approve the sacrifice, such as that of Iphigenia among the Greeks. The French anthropologist Jacques Soustelle says, "Human sacrifice is a transmutation by which life is fashioned out of death."[1]

To the Spaniards, however, cutting out the heart of a victim offered in sacrifice was a sign of extreme cruelty. How could the Spaniards see as belonging to the same species people guilty in their eyes of idolatry, sodomy, and cannibalism (*pecado de sodomia, y de idolatria y de comer hombres*)? How could they have imagined that the Aztecs thought they were consuming the very flesh of god?

For their part, and in their own way, the Spaniards indulged in terrible cruelties, as Diego de Landa and Las Casas recorded.

---

1. Jacques Soustelle, *La vie qutidienne au temps de l'empire Azteque*, Paris: Hachette, 1954.

Originally, the Aztecs were a relatively small tribe that had come from the northwest and settled in the Valley of Mexico in the thirteenth century. In 1325 they founded their city, Tenochtitlan, on Lake Texcoco, and a century later they emerged as a major power and formed a triple alliance with the neighboring cities of Texcoco and Tlacopan (Tacuba). Under the leadership of the Aztecs, this alliance established its rule over the neighboring tribes, which paid it tribute while retaining their own autonomy. Disagreement broke out among the allies, and the Aztecs imposed themselves as undisputed masters and established their rule over virtually the whole of central Mexico in the last quarter of the fifteenth century. Tenochtitlan became, fewer than fifty years before the arrival of the Spaniards, the capital of the empire. The population of the city was estimated to be some 300,000 (at this time, Paris had a population of 65,000).

The Aztecs' conception of war largely explains their defeat. They waged war for religious and economic motives: to honor the god Huitzilopochtli (Huichilobos) with victims and to collect tribute.

Military operations were codified by propitiatory preparations and embassies, the adversary being duly warned of what was coming. Attacks by night were carried out only when there was a full moon. The use of surprise was beyond the Aztecs' military conception.

The Aztecs did not have a regular professional army except for their corps of elite warriors, which by definition was very small. However, all young men received military training from the age of fifteen, which made it possible to mobilize considerable numbers of men. A young man had to take a prisoner in order to become a warrior, and he needed four to be considered an elite warrior. Most returned to their homes after a period of training and resumed their work in the fields.

The elite corps, with their distinctive clothes, who made up the sovereign's bodyguard, were the jaguar warriors and the eagle warriors. The small units had about twenty men each, the large ones varied between two hundred and eight hundred men. Warriors painted their faces red, white, and black. The leading men were immediately recognizable by their sumptuous dress, and they were naturally sought as prisoners. Warriors were protected with jackets made of tightly packed cotton four or five centimeters thick, which the Spaniards were quick to adopt when they realized how much the climate militated against the wearing of chain mail or armor. The warriors' shields were made of leather.

Before battle, drums, conchs, and whistles were sounded. The warriors' weapons included bows with obsidian-tipped arrows or with fire-hardened wooden tips that were not very effective, the short obsidian-tipped javelin, and above all the sling, which the Aztecs handled with skill. In hand-to-hand fighting, the Aztecs used three weapons: the obsidian-tipped lance, two to two and a half meters long; the *macana*, a round-headed, heavy wooden mace; and the *maquahuitl*, a wooden mace with obsidian-tipped spikes all over it. These last two could be very dangerous, obsidian being sharper than steel but much more fragile.

Tactics were primitive: to impress the enemy with noise, unleash missiles, and then engage in hand-to-hand fighting. When necessary, reserves would replace the front lines. Feinting consisted of pretending to flee. Victory in these ritualized wars resulted from seizing the leader of the opposing army—or even better—burning his temple and taking captives for sacrifice. Battles were short and violent and involved few casualties, the aim being not to kill but to capture. It is significant that traditionally defeated enemies were not pursued in order to annihilate them. The road network was good, but the Aztecs had no draft animals, and everything had to be transported on men's backs, which meant that lengthy campaigns were few and far between.

For the Spaniards, warfare in the Americas was quite different. It was not ritualized like that of the *condottieri* or the knights of the Middle Ages, who also sought to take aristocrats prisoner for ransom. The conquistadors aimed at permanent subjugation and occupation by means of total war.

The conquistadors, or at least the vast majority of them, were not professional soldiers or veterans of the wars in Italy; but many of Cortes's companions had taken part in the two expeditions on the North American continent in 1516–1518 that had preceded this one. We would like to emphasize this point: they were men with experience—above all young peasants from Castile, Estremadura, and Andalusia—sober, used to the very harsh winters and very hot summers of the mountains of their provinces. They were sustained by a seamless faith over which the priest who accompanied them watched, legitimized by the Crown, and carried forward by the desire to get rich and cover themselves in glory.

All those taking part in this expedition knew what they were risking. For them, the nature of this war was total. It was even different from the war waged just a little earlier against the Muslims. This time they were dealing not with a different faith but with a *radically different species.* The enemy had to be subjugated and its military strength annihilated; there could be no compromise. The Spaniards had a duty to impose what they saw as the true faith and the authority of the emperor.

Like revolutionaries, the Spaniards sought neither to change nor to adjust to a particular state of affairs. They wanted to bring down their opponent's order and replace it with a new one. It was a war to the death.

The conquistadors' weaponry far outclassed that of the Indians. Firearms, missiles, cannon, muskets, and crossbows had infinitely superior power. However, firearms played a relatively limited and mainly psychological role. Before the siege of Mexico, during the first march on the city, Cortes had only five hundred kilograms of powder. Muskets required very dry powders and a match had to be struck to fire it; crossbows, although effective, took time to be properly stretched, and humidity affected the string.

Never perhaps since Hannibal's elephants or the Mongols' horses had animals played such a major role as the horse, an unknown animal, played in the conquest of the Americas. This role was at once psychological and physical.

Not only did the horse give mobility; its shock power was considerable. Initially there were only sixteen horses in Cortes's expedition. While in Europe, with the introduction of the pike by the Swiss squares and the musket, the cavalry was beginning to lose its previous virtually absolute superiority, in the Americas, against the Indians it was master. With the lance and the sword, the lightly mounted Spanish cavalry was highly effective. After the cavalry, the infantry, with its cohesion, its long, two-edged rapiers made of steel, and its attacking qualities, was the Spaniards' trump card.

Both Cortes and Pizarro were able to play on internal dissension in the indigenous societies. Rapidly formed alliances turned all malcontents against the existing government, whose yoke was heavy. The conquest unfolded in four main zones—Mexico and Peru, where two centralized empires held sway, and Colombia and La Plata and the Argentine hinterland—and in two secondary areas; Chile and Central America.

The societies lacking a properly constituted state resisted penetration best and longest: the Araucans in Chile, the Indians of the Argentine pampa, and the Chichimecs of northern Mexico. Once the head had been stricken, highly hierarchical societies like those of the Aztecs or the Incas were fatally shaken and collapsed in disarray.

Meanwhile, Cortes had prepared a second expedition. He wanted
to conquer Mexico. He saw the *Noche triste* as an unfortunate
episode, but not as the end of the war. Cortes was a great man, certainly the greatest Spaniard of the generation of the conquest when
outstanding men were not lacking. He proved himself also to be a
statesman, setting up the structures that governed Mexico. He was a
man of action, a war leader with political nose. In his last dispatch to
Charles V, when he was rebuilding Mexico, he wrote:

> In the five months that we have been rebuilding the city, it is
> already most beautiful, and I assure you that . . . just as before it
> was capital and center of all these provinces so it shall be
> henceforth. And it is being so built that the Spaniards will be
> strong and secure and well in charge of the natives, who will be
> unable to harm them in any way.

Cortes very quickly became the undisputed leader of the expedition. He opposed nobody but exerted his authority. He took part in
the fighting, often in the front line—in this respect he takes on the
aura of a heroic leader—and along with his companions he carried
out everyday manual tasks. Bernal Diaz, who railed against the
hagiography written in Spain by Gomara, saw considerable qualities
in Cortes: "He could draw on inexhaustible inner resources . . . he
had the heart and mind that are vital in this sort of business."

This time, Cortes knew the ground. The Mexico-Tenochtitlan system of defense was based on the fact that the city was built on a
lake. Its causeways were easy to block. Cortes developed a master-
piece of strategy and grand tactics: a combined land and water operation. The taking of Mexico was perhaps above all a naval operation. Cortes organized a blockade by the fleet, and the combined
land and water operations brought impregnable Mexico to its knees.

In March 1521, nine months after the *Noche triste,* Cortes again
took the road to Mexico from his base at Tlaxcala. The route lay
eighty kilometers through the mountains that stretch as far as Texcoco. Through these mountains a long line of Indian porters accompanied by three hundred Spaniards and several thousand Tlaxcalans
transported the equipment necessary for the construction of a small
fleet of thirteen boats.

The Spaniards built the brigantines and, during the month and a
half it took to build them, the Indians dug a canal two kilometers
long to link Texcoco to the lake. A reservoir was built upstream
from the channel. On April 28, everything was ready. Mass was

said, the boats were blessed, and the Spaniards took communion. The reservoir was opened and, while the water gradually floated the thirteen brigantines, the artillery sent off a few salvos. Cortes reviewed his troops. With the new recruits from the islands and from Spain, there were a total of 925 men, including 96 horsemen and 118 crossbow men and musketeers. There were also three large cannon, fifteen small pieces, and ten quintals of powder.

By the end of May everything was in position for the siege.

Each brigantine had twelve oarsmen, twelve fighters including six crossbow men and musketeers. Cortes took command of the fleet, which shows how important it was: it had 325 men. He divided the land forces into three companies. One headed by Sandoval, now his closest lieutenant, included 24 horsemen, 4 musketeers, 13 crossbow men, 150 foot soldiers, and several thousand Indian allies (maybe as many as thirty thousand). This force was to set up camp near Iztapalapa. Pedro de Alvarado's company was made up of 30 horsemen, 18 crossbow men and musketeers, 150 foot soldiers, and several thousand Indian allies (perhaps as many as twenty-five thousand). This force was based at Tacuba. Cristóbal de Olid's company was made up of 32 horsemen, 18 crossbow men and musketeers, 160 foot soldiers, and several thousand allies (perhaps twenty thousand).

Assuming that Mexico had a population at the time of some 300,000, it probably had 75,000 able-bodied men.

The siege began dramatically with an operation carried out by Olid and Alvarado: to destroy the Chapultepec aqueduct that supplied the city with drinking water. The aqueduct was destroyed on May 26, 1521. This was a disaster for the Mexicans. The very next day, the Spaniards sent messengers to offer peace after surrender. This proposal was rejected.

By May 31, Sandoval was in full control of Iztapalapa, which the Mexicans had abandoned. Cortes came out of Texcoco with three brigantines to back him up. The city was destroyed and Sandoval's forces advanced along the main road as far as Mexico, where they met Olid's forces, which had been moving forward from Coyoacan. The blockade was rapidly made total except for a single exit that Cortes had deliberately left open toward Tepeyal. The Aztecs' only choice was to fight or surrender. Their new ruler, Guatemoc, was an energetic leader. Against the advice of the moderates, he wanted not to negotiate or to flee but to fight.

On May 31, the brigantines' first attacks, against the Tepopolco rock, made a strong impression on the Aztecs. These two victories on the same day encouraged Cortes to undertake a third operation: with about thirty men he landed at Xoloc, the fort where the Coyoacan and Iztapalapa causeways met. After a fierce fight, he managed to land three small-caliber cannon and took up position.

This first phase of the siege culminated on June 9 with a combined attack by Alvarado's and Sandoval's forces, which the Mexicans withstood.

But as June went by, the blockade began to bear fruit. The brigantines gave relentless and effective chase to the light vessels of the Mexicans, who were seeking food supplies for the city. Brackish water had replaced the water from the aqueduct. Before long, many of the non-Aztec inhabitants of the lagoon surrendered and paid allegiance. Cortes took advantage of this respite to reorganize the fleet. Swords were too short for fighting on the water and had to be replaced by pikes.

With his customary brashness, Alvarado attempted to seize the market-place by force. His retreat was soon cut off by the Aztecs, and only with great difficulty was he able to fight his way out, leaving five prisoners behind. They were beheaded, and their heads, stuck on stakes, were displayed prominently so the Spaniards could see the fate that awaited them. Bernal Diaz was a member of this group and barely escaped with his life.

During the siege, Cortes also had to deal with a plot aimed at assassinating him and his lieutenants to the benefit of Diego de Velazquez. Having unmasked the plot, Cortes cunningly pretended not to know the identity of the other conspirators, who were only too happy to get away so lightly.

For a time the outcome of the struggle seemed uncertain. The Indian allies abandoned the struggle en masse. Cortes just missed falling into the hands of the Aztecs, thanks to a soldier who saved his life at the cost of his own. The Aztecs took more than ten Spaniards prisoner in just a few days. They put rumors about. They threw six heads in front of Sandoval's forces, one of which was allegedly Cortes's. For a whole week the Aztecs seemed to be regaining the initiative. But in fact they were at the end of their tether.

Cortes moved his headquarters to Tlatelolco and made peace overtures several times, all of which were rejected.

Among the besieged, despair was spreading. The lake water was brackish, and food had long since been no more than roots, plants, and decoctions. Domestic animals had been eaten, then rats and other rodents. Typhoid fever, typhus, cholera were all present. The wounded died for lack of care; every wound, especially in what was the rainy season, quickly festered. People were hungry, and they were always thirsty. There was no rain and there would be none before October.

What was to be done? Every day prayers rose to the gods; Spanish captives were sacrificed in the hope of turning the flow of events in favor of the besieged. Bodies were no longer buried. Warriors who had fought every day for almost three months were exhausted by the lack of food. Small children had died already; women no longer had anything to succor them. All day and all night could be heard drums beating to sound both the call to war and further sacrifices. The Aztecs' allies had surrendered. The Spaniards' allies, especially those from Tlaxcala, were extremely cruel. Old accounts were settled as ancient hatreds were stoked with tales passed from mouth to mouth, and death followed death, retold by a survivor so that others might in turn take up the sword of vengeance.

The ecstasy induced by killing those who lord it over one is well known; people are mutilated for their past arrogance. Pinned down, there is no end to the unloading of one's hatred and fear. Nothing escapes; everything can be tormented. Later there would be time enough for laws and codes. For the present, a thousand times experienced from the dawn of history right down to the present day, nothing exists except the law of the victor, and how heavy that is depends on how deep the hatred is. People commit horrors that they have formerly denounced but that are now deemed acceptable because they are inflicted on the enemy.

On August 13, 1521, the final attack was launched. Alvarado attacked from Tacuba, Cortes from Iztapalapa, Sandoval on the water. The Aztec defenses collapsed. They fled. A soldier saw a richly decorated canoe and seized it. In it was Guatemoc, the Aztec ruler. He was soon taken before Cortes. Cortes embraced him.

The chronicle relates that the Aztec ruler asked Cortes to kill him after saying, "I did all I could to defend myself and mine before coming to this. Do with me as you will."

Cortes spoke kindly to him and bade him take a seat at his table. Later, at the insistence of his men, he agreed to let him be tortured to make him tell where Mexico's gold was hidden.

Silence reigned. The drums were no longer heard. The victors entered the city. The stench was terrible. As always, they looked for

booty and women. They had free rein. In some armies, the troops
were entitled to three days' and three nights' pillaging.

For the Spaniards, the conquest was in the nature of a crusade:
they were bringing the light of the faith to creatures who had hitherto lived in abject darkness. What they were doing in the name of
their ruler was conquering a new empire, covering themselves with
glory, and becoming rich. Bernal Diaz sums it up with his usual tal-
ent: "To serve God and His Majesty, to carry the light to those who
live in darkness and to become rich, as all men desire."

For the Aztecs, at least in the first stage, the newcomers were
gods whose return had been foretold. Some societies are more mortal than others, and this fragility is always a matter of the spirit.

Once the struggle was joined, the Aztec gods proved ineffective.
Despite their courage and their desperate defense, the Aztecs were
abandoned by their gods; their temple came under attack. On the
Spanish side, every morning, the Ave Maria was said at the foot of
the cross. Their enterprise was sustained by faith, and evangelization
justified the conquest for the greater glory of God and the Spanish
king. What was hardest to bear, apart from the almost permanent
insecurity, the extreme tension, the exhaustion, and sometimes the
hunger, were the diseases. They killed more surely than did the Indians; wounds frequently led to gangrene.

WHY DID THE SPANIARDS WIN?

Of the many explanations that have been given of the amazing conquest of the Americas by such a small force there are two key ones.

The general level of civilization of the Amerindian peoples was
infinitely lower than that of the Spaniards. When the Spaniards met
with the Muslims (whether the Almoravids or the Ottomans) or
other European societies such as during the wars in Italy, the match
was much more equal, even if the Spanish army—the best in the
Western world at the time—almost always won. The civilization of
the Amerindians was above all organized around an economy of
expenditure. It was ill equipped to confront the technically skilled
and conquering Spaniards of the time. That did not prevent pre-
Columbian art and culture from producing absolute masterpieces
(have there ever been any greater than those of Lascaux?). Cortes's
genius and luck did the rest: political alliances, the presence of interpreters, his initiative, and tenacity, and being able to make the best

of situations. In Mexico, as in Peru, the Spaniards took the initiative against opponents who were momentarily paralyzed by mortal dread to strike at the head and sow disarray.

The second explanation lies in the terrible smallpox epidemic that struck Mexico in 1519 and then affected the Americas as a whole, reaching the Incas by 1525–1526. The Inca himself died of smallpox while he was waging a campaign in the north of his empire, along what are now the southern borders of Colombia. That was just after the arrival of Pizarro. In Mexico, as in Peru, the epidemic affected the Indians greatly and the whites only slightly, because of their immunity to this microbe. The Indians inevitably saw in this seeming protection of the strangers one more sign unfavorable for them. The same phenomenon has been observed much more recently, for example, in the first contacts between the aborigines and missionaries in Amazonia.

In his work *Plagues and People in History*, William McNeill writes:

> Until the First World War—except perhaps during the American Civil War and the Franco-Prussian War—disease and epidemics killed more soldiers than battles. . . . In the Crimean War (1854–1856), ten times more British soldiers died of dysentery than from all the Russian weapons put together and half a century later, in the Boer War (1899–1902), British deaths from disease and infections recorded were five times as great as those from enemy action.

Estimates of the number of inhabitants of the Americas have varied greatly over the last fifty years, ranging from ten to eighty million. This latter estimate, made by the Berkeley school from extrapolations, is currently believed to be likely (although it is difficult to see how, especially in the Andes, it could have been possible to find subsistence for twenty or twenty-five million people—the population of Mexico being estimated at twenty-five or thirty million—or why the Indians of the time should have had a population comparable to that of China with its rivers with fertile silt and exceptionally resourceful peasantry).

One thing is certain. Following the epidemic the continent experienced a demographic collapse. By 1568, less than half a century after the Spaniards landed, the population of Mexico was estimated at 3 million; by 1620, it had fallen to 1.6 million.

The Spaniards also contributed to this fall. The collapse of empires and the values that they represented and the resulting trauma, exactions, and forced labor all played their part. But at no time did the Spaniards have either the human means—certainly not the numbers necessary—or the *intent* to eliminate those who provided their manpower. What hit the Americas in the sixteenth century must be compared to the great plague that devastated Europe in the fourteenth century, removing 30 or 50 percent of the population of some areas in just twenty or thirty years.

The Spanish invasion totally destroyed the traditional universe: god, institutions, language were all imposed by a victor who had a different conception of the universe, arms to impose it, and even the keys to the kingdom of heaven, while offering the vanquished the consolation of a better world beyond. For the Aztecs as for the Incas, the foundations of all they held certain had been undermined. All the Indian peoples were defeated—including those who, without fully realizing the consequences, made a tactical alliance with the Spaniards to shake off the yoke of the Aztecs or the Incas. The greatest gap between the Spaniards and the Indians was not in numbers but in level of civilization.

As victors, the Spaniards could not but cause the world of their idolatrous opponents to disappear from the map. Spiritual power had to be based on Christianity and the Holy Church. Only at that price could souls be saved. The history of the colonization of the Americas is that of a dispossession achieved by force and persuasion. It was the fate of the Indians to forget the past until, only in recent years, *indigenismo* attempted to regraft onto it a past from which it is hardly possible to fashion a future. The triumph of colonization was the transformation of the Indians into Christians and, in their overwhelming majority, Spanish-speakers.

2

THE AZTEC OMENS

And all of this happened to us
we saw it
we watched it
we are overwhelmed
by a sad and lamentable fate.
Broken spears lie in the roads;
we have torn our hair in grief.
Now the houses are roofless, and their walls
are red with blood
Worms are swarming in the streets and plazas,
and the walls are splattered with gore.
The water has turned red, as if it were dyed,
and when we drink it,
it has the taste of brine.

We have pounded our hands in despair
against the adobe walls
for our inheritance, our city, is lost and dead.
The shields of our warriors were its defense,
but they could not save it.

So spoke the Aztec chroniclers as they told of the last days of Mexico.

The landing of the Spaniards was preceded in Mexico by a succession of bad omens.

An evil omen appeared in the sky, ten years before the Spaniards first arrived here. It was like a flaming ear of corn, a fiery signal, or the blaze of daybreak; like a wound in the sky, it seemed to bleed fire, drop by drop.

. . .[The Omen] appeared to us for a full year, beginning in the year 12-House.

As its first appeared, there was a great outcry and confusion. The people beat their hands against their mouths; they were bewildered and frightened, and wondered what it could mean.

Another bad omen:

Huitzilopochtli's temple burst into flames. People felt that no one had set it afire, that it burned down of its own accord.

. . . And now it is burning, its wooden columns are burning! The flames, the tongues of fire shoot out, the bursts of fire flare up into the sky!

The blaze destroyed all the woodwork of the temple rapidly. . . . But when [people] threw water on the blaze, it only flamed higher. They could not put the fire out, and the temple burned to the ground.

Another omen:

Fire streamed through the sky while the sun was still shining. It was divided into three parts. It flashed out from where the sun sets and raced straight through to where the sun rises, showering sparks like a red-hot coal. When the people saw its long train streaming across the heavens, there was a great outcry and confusion like the ringing of a thousand little bells.

Another bad omen appeared on Lake Texcoco:

The wind lashed the water until it boiled. It was as if [the water] were boiling with rage, as if it were shattering itself in its frenzy. [The waves] began from far off, rose high in the air, and dashed against the walls of the houses. The houses that were flooded collapsed into the water. This was in the nearby lake.

Another omen:

People heard a woman weeping night after night. She passed by in the middle of the night, moaning and crying out loud: "My children, we must flee far away from this city!" At other times she cried: "My children, where shall I take you?" (Portilla and Garibay)

In all there were eight bad omens in Mexico; others appeared shortly before the Spaniards' arrival in the province of Tlaxcala.

Even before news of the Spaniards' arrival, Monteczuma, a ruler whose behavior and actions reveal a rather unenergetic person. Worried by the increasing number of bad omens, he sent a messenger to the magicians, saying:

> Tell the magicians to state what they believe: whether sickness is going to strike, or hunger, or locusts, or storms on the lake, or droughts; and whether it will rain or not. If war is threatening Mexico, or if there will be sudden deaths, . . . they are not to hide it from me. They must also tell me whether they have heard the voice of *Cihuacoatl*, for when something is going to happen, she is the first to predict it, long before it occurs.

The magicians replied:

> What can we say? The future has already been determined and proclaimed in heaven . . . and since it must surely take place, we can only wait for it.

When the ruler's messenger returned to tell him that what was to come would come swiftly, Monteczuma said:

> Ask them whether it will come from the sky or the earth, and from what direction or place and when it will come.

The messenger could no longer find the magicians; they had disappeared as if by magic. Yet guards had been put at the doors. The messenger said:

> I believe that they flew away, for they know how to become invisible, which they do every night, and can fly to the ends of the world. That is what they must have done.

Monteczuma said to his chiefs:

> "Go to the villages where the magicians live . . . [and] kill their wives and all their children, and . . . destroy their houses." He [Monteczuma] also ordered many servants to go with them to ransack the houses. When the chiefs arrived, they killed the women by hanging them with ropes, and the children by dashing them to pieces against the walls. Then they tore down the houses and even rooted out the foundations. (Portilla and Garibay)

3

RECONNAISSANCE

Cortes's lieutenant, Pedro de Alvarado, was the first to land on the island of Cozumel. Young and impatient, he came upon a village from which the Indians fled on learning of the landing. He took three prisoners and seized jewels and ornaments belonging to the local gods as well as some fowls.

Cortes arrived with his fleet, just as we returned. The first thing he did after settling was to have the pilot, Camacho, put in irons for failing to obey orders and wait for him at sea. When he saw the town empty of its inhabitants and learned that Pedro de Alvarado had been to the other place and had taken fowls and hangings and other objects of small value from the idols, as well as some half-copper gold, he was as angry with our captain as he had been with the pilot. [Cortes] reprimanded him severely, telling him that he would never pacify the country by robbing the natives of their possessions. He sent for the two Indians and the woman we had captured, and spoke to them through Melchior, the Indian, who knew their language well, and whom we had brought from Cape Catoche. . . telling them to summon the *caciques* and Indians of their town, and not to be afraid. He had the gold, hangings, and everything else restored to the natives; and in return for the fowls, which had already been eaten, he ordered that they be given some beads and little bells. In addition, he gave each Indian a Spanish shirt. They set off to summon the Chief of the town, and the next day [the chief] came with all his people. Men, women, and children, they went about among us as if they had been friendly with us all their lives, and Cortes ordered us not to harm them in any way. (Diaz)

The fleet reached the coast of Yucatan and learned of the existence of two shipwrecked Spaniards who had been on the peninsula for eight years. One of them, Jerónimo de Aguilar, a priest, joined them and later became a vital figure as an interpreter, for he spoke Maya. The other Spaniard, named Guerrero, had become so well integrated into Indian society that he refused to join those who had been his own people.

> He [Aguilar] said, when questioned about Gonzalo Guerrero, that he was married and had three children. He was tattooed, and his ears and lower lip were pierced, and he was a seaman and a native of Palos. The Indians considered him very brave. Aguilar also told that a little more than a year ago, when a captain and three ships arrived at Cape Catoche—it must have been Francisco Hernandez de Cordoba's expedition—it had been at Guerrero's recommendation that the Indians had attacked them, and that he himself had been in the company of [the] *cacique* of a great town. When Cortes heard this he said: "I wish I could get my hands on him. Since it will never do to leave him here." (Diaz)

They landed at Tabasco, where the Indians sought to prevent the Spaniards from entering their village. Despite brave resistance by the Indians, the Spaniards succeeded in penetrating one of their strongholds while others took the Indians from behind.

The Indians withdrew, taking their gods with them. Cortes ordered that they not be pursued.

They spent the night in the village protected by sentinels. The next day, Cortes ordered Pedro de Alvarado and Francisco de Lugo to go and reconnoiter. Then it was noticed that the Indian interpreter, Melchior, who had been taken on at Cape Cotoche (where Jerónimo de Aguilar had been) had disappeared. "Cortes was much annoyed by his escape, and feared that he might tell his fellow Indians things that would be damaging to us" (Diaz.)

Francisco de Lugo's column, a hundred soldiers, had not gone far when they were attacked by vastly more numerous forces.

> When they realized it, they began retreating toward the camp in good order, sending a Cuban Indian, a swift and daring runner, ahead to beg Cortes for help. Meanwhile, by careful handling of his crossbow men and musketeers—some loading while the others fired—and by occasional charges, Francisco de Lugo was able to hold off the squadrons attacking him. (Diaz)

The Spaniards captured three prisoners.

> Through our interpreter, Aguilar, we asked the prisoners why they had attacked us, and warned them that they would be killed if they did so again. Then, as an overture of peace, Cortes sent back one of them carrying some beads for the *caciques*. This messenger told us that the Indian Melchior whom we had brought from Cape Catoche, and who had fled to them the night before, had advised them that if they attacked us by day and night we would be beaten, because we were fewer in number. So it turned out that we had brought an enemy with us instead of a friend.
>
> The Indian messenger never returned, but from our two other prisoners Aguilar learned that by next day all the *caciques* of the neighboring towns of that province would come together fully armed to make war on us. They intended to surround our camp, as Melchior had advised. (Diaz)

When Cortes learned that the Spaniards were about to be attacked the next day, he ordered all the horses to be landed so that they could regain their ability to move. He enjoined the horsemen to attach little bells to the horses' breastplates and not to waste time on each enemy but to move on and aim their lances at the faces of the enemy.

The next morning, after hearing mass, the Spanish foot soldiers got into formation. They soon fell in with a force of Indians on a plain, on the way to the Spaniards' camp. Cortes made a detour with the horsemen to take the enemy from behind.

> Men wore great feather crests; they carried drums and trumpets; and their faces were painted black and white. They were armed with large bows and arrows, spears and shields, swords like our two-handed swords, slings and stones, and fire-toughened darts, and all wore quilted armor. . . . They . . . surrounded us, discharging such a rain of arrows, darts, and stones upon us that more than seventy of our men were wounded in the first attack. Then, in hand-to-hand fighting, they damaged us with their spears. . . . With our muskets and crossbows and good swordplay we put up a stout fight . . . they came to feel the edge of our swords. . . . But with all the hurts and wounds we dealt them, we could not drive them off . . . for there were three hundred Indians to every one of us. . . .
>
> At that very moment we caught sight of our horsemen. The great host of Indians, however, was so crazed by their attack

that they did not notice them approaching behind their backs. As the plain was bare and the horsemen were good riders, and some of the horses were very swift and nimble, they came quickly upon the Indians and speared them as they chose. As soon as we saw the horsemen, we fell on the enemy so vigorously that, caught between the horsemen and us, they soon turned tail. Since they had never seen a horse before, the Indians thought that the horse and rider were one creature.

This was the first battle that we fought under Cortes in New Spain. (Diaz)

They bandaged their wounds with cotton cloths. Both men and horses had their wounds sealed with fat.

As I have said, in this battle, we captured five Indians of whom two were captains. These two were interrogated by Aguilar, the interpreter, who discovered from their answers that they would be suitable as messengers. Therefore, he advised Cortes to free them, so that they could return and talk to the *caciques* of the town and any others they might see. They were given green and blue beads, and Aguilar addressed them in a flattering speech, telling them that they had nothing to fear, since we meant to treat them like brothers, and that the recent battle was entirely their own fault. He told them to call together the *caciques* of all the towns, as we wished to talk to them. . . .

The next day, thirty important men, dressed in fine cloaks and bearing fowls, fish, fruit, and maize-cakes, came. They asked Cortes to allow them to burn and bury the bodies of those killed in the recent battle. . . . Cortes, who was very shrewd in all matters, said with a laugh to those of us who happened to be standing with him: "Do you know, gentlemen, I believe it is the horses that the Indians are most frightened of. They probably think that it is the horses and the cannon that they have been fighting against, and I've thought of a way to confirm their belief. Let us bring Juan Sedeno's mare, which foaled on board ship the other day, and tie her up where I am standing. Ortiz the Musician's stallion is very randy, and we can let him get a sniff of her. Then, we will have both of them led off in different directions, and make sure that the chiefs who are coming do not hear them neighing, or see them, until they are standing and talking to me. . . ." But this was not all. Cortes ordered that the biggest cannon we had be loaded with a large ball and plenty of powder.

By this time it was midday. Forty Indians arrived, all *caciques* of fine appearance, dressed in their customary rich cloaks. . . . They asked our pardon for their past conduct. . . .

Cortes answered them somewhat sternly through our interpreter. Appearing angry, he reminded them how often he had requested them to maintain the peace, and said that they had committed a crime, and together with all the inhabitants of their towns they deserved to be put to death. He then pointed out that we were vassals of a great king and lord called the Emperor Charles, who had sent us to these parts with orders to help and favor those who would enter his royal service . . . but if they were not [well disposed], something would jump out of those *tepuzques—tepuzque* is their native name for iron—which would kill them, for some of the *tepuzques* were still angry with them for having attacked us. At this time, he secretly ordered for the cannon to be fired, and it went off with the requisite thunderous report, the ball whistling away over the hills. It was midday and very still; the *caciques* were thoroughly terrified. Never having witnessed anything like this before, they believed Cortes's story to be true. He told them through Aguilar, however, that they need not be afraid, because he had ordered that no harm should come to them.

At that time, they brought the horse that had scented the mare, and tied him up close to where Cortes was talking to the *caciques*. As the mare had been tethered at that actual spot, the horse began to paw the ground, neigh, and create an uproar, looking toward the Indians where the scent of the mare came from. But the *caciques* thought the horse was roaring at them and were terrified once more. When Cortes saw their fear he rose from his seat, went over to the horse, and ordered two orderlies to lead him away. He then told the Indians that he had asked the beast not to be angry, because they [the *caciques*] were friendly and had come to make peace. (Diaz)

At Tabasco the Spaniards were given twenty Indians as slaves as a sign of peace. One of them, Malinche, was from a good Aztec family and had been sold to the Mayas. As we have seen, she subsequently played an important role in the conquest. She spoke Maya and Nahuatl, the language of the Aztecs. Thanks to the simultaneous presence of Jerónimo de Aguilar and the woman whom the Spaniards called Doña Marina, for she was baptized almost at once, Cortes could communicate with the Aztecs. He spoke in Spanish with Aguilar, who translated into Maya for Marina, who spoke to messengers from the Aztec ruler Monteczuma from the very first meetings.

Thus, from the beginning, the Spaniards had the advantage of understanding their opponent and the possibility of seeing through his weaknesses.

> Many *caciques* and important persons from Tabasco and the neighboring towns came to pay us great respect, early next morning, March 15, 1519. They brought gold presents, consisting of four diadems, some ornaments shaped like lizards, two shaped like little dogs, and five like ducks, also some earrings, two Indian face masks, two gold soles for sandals, and some other objects of small value. . . .
>
> These gifts were nothing, however, compared to the twenty women whom they gave us. Among them was a most excellent person, who took the name of Doña Marina, when she became a Christian. I will say no more about them, but speak of the pleasure with which Cortes received these overtures. He pulled aside the *caciques* and Aguilar the interpreter, to converse with them and to tell them how grateful he was for what they had brought. But there was one thing he must ask of them, he said, that they should bring back all their men, women, and children to the town, which he wished to see settled again within two days. This he would recognize as a true sign of peace. The *caciques* summoned all the inhabitants immediately, and they, their wives, and their children resettled the town in the given time. . . .
>
> Cortes asked [the *caciques*] why after we had requested them to make peace three times they had attacked us. They replied that they had already asked and received pardon for this. The chief said that it was his brother, the chief of Champoton, who had advised him, and that he feared the accusation of cowardice. He also said that the Indian we had brought as interpreter and who had fled in the night, had also advised them to attack us by day and night.
>
> Cortes ordered them to bring this man before him at once. They replied that when he saw the battle going against them, he had fled. Search had been made for him, but they did not know where he was. We discovered, however, that they had offered him as a sacrifice, because his advice had cost them dearly. Cortes then asked them where they procured their gold and jew-

els, and they answered from the direction of the sunset, saying
"*Culua*" and "*Mexico*". But as we did not know what these
words meant, we did not note them. (Diaz)

A few days later, a common man who lived at the place known as
the "Forest of the Region of the Dead," not far from the coast at
Vera Cruz, asked for an audience with the Aztec ruler.

As I went near the shores of the great sea, there was a mountain range or a small mountain floating in the midst of the water,
moving here and there without touching the shore. My lord,
although we guard the coast and are always on watch, we have
never seen anything like this. (Portilla and Garibay)

Monteczuma decided to send someone to investigate.

We arrived at the port of San Juan de Ulua, with all the fleet,
on Holy Thursday 1519. . . . The royal standards and pennants
were raised on the flagship, and within half an hour of our
anchoring two large canoes or pirogues full of Mexican Indians
came to us. Seeing the large ship with its standards flying, they
knew that it was there they must go to speak with the Captain.
So they went straight to the flagship, went aboard and asked for
the *Tatuan*, which in their language means the master. Doña
Marina, who understood them, pointed him out; and the Indians
paid Cortes great respect in their fashion. They said that their
lord, a servant of the great Monteczuma, had sent them to find
out what kind of men we were and what we were seeking, also
to say that if we required anything for ourselves or our ships,
we were to tell them and they would supply it.

Through our interpreters, Cortes thanked them and ordered
food, wine, and some blue beads be given to them. After they
had drunk the wine, he told them that he had come to visit and
trade with them, and that they should think of our coming to
their country as fortunate rather than troublesome. The messengers went ashore contented, and the next day, which was Good
Friday, we disembarked with our horses and guns. . . .

On Easter Eve, Saturday, many Indians arrived who had
been sent by a *cacique* . . . one of Monteczuma's governors. . .
. They brought fowls, maize-cakes, and plums, which were in
season. . . .

On Easter Sunday, the governor they had spoken of arrived
along with him [another *cacique*]. They were followed by many
Indians carrying presents of fowls and vegetables. . . . Cortes

took these two and our two interpreters aside and explained to
them that we were Christians, and vassals of the Emperor Don
Carlos . . . and that it was at his orders that we had come to their
country, since for many years he had heard rumors of it and of
the great prince who ruled it. Cortes said that he wished to be
friends with this prince. . . . Moreover, he wished to trade with
their prince and his Indians in a friendly way, and to know the
place the prince would appoint for their meeting.

To this [the *cacique*] replied proudly: "You have only just
arrived, and already you ask to speak with our prince. First
accept the present that we give you in your master's name and
later tell me whatever you wish."

From some sort of a chest, he took out many golden objects,
beautifully and richly worked. . . . There were other things too
that I do not remember. . . . Cortes received all this graciously,
and in return gave them some beads of twisted glass and other
little beads from Spain, asking them to send to their towns and
summon the people to trade with us, since he had plenty of
these beads to exchange for gold.

Cortes ordered our gunners to load the lombards with a big
charge of powder, so that when fired, they would make a loud
noise; and told Pedro de Alvarado to have all his horsemen
ready with little bells tied to their breastplates, to gallop in front
of Monteczuma's servants. He too mounted his horse. "It would
be a good thing," he said, "if we could gallop on these dunes.
However, they will see that we get stuck in the sand even on
foot. Let us go down and gallop on the beach when the tide is
low." And he put all the horsemen under the command of Pedro
de Alvarado, whose sorrel mare was a great runner and very
quick on the rein.

The show was carried out in the presence of two ambassadors, and in order to have them see the shot leave the gun,
Cortes pretended that he wished to speak to them and some
other *caciques* again, just before the cannon was fired. As it was
quite still at that moment, the balls resounded with a great din
as they went over the forest. The two governors and the rest of
the Indians were frightened by this strange happening, and
ordered their painters to paint it, so that Monteczuma could see.
Apparently, one of our soldiers had a helmet that was half-gilt
but somewhat rusty. Tendile noticed this, and being of a more
inquiring nature than his fellow *cacique*, he asked if he might
see it. It was like one that had been left them by their ancestors

of the race from which they sprang and was placed on the head of their god Huichilobos [Huitzilopochtli]. He said that Monteczuma, his master, would like to see this helmet, and it was given to him. Cortes said, however, that as he wished to know whether the gold of their country was the same as the gold found in our rivers, they might send it back filled with grains of gold, as a present for our great Emperor. After his departure, we discovered that Tendile was not only an important man of affairs but the most active of Monteczuma's servants. (Diaz)

Then Monteczuma decided to send emissaries to the coast to find out what was happening.

> . . . It is true that strange people have come to the shores of the great sea. . . . They have very light skin, much lighter than ours. They have long beards and their hair comes only to their ears. (Portilla and Garibay)

Monteczuma ordered two goldsmiths to make some gold jewelry inserted with emeralds to be offered as gifts to the creatures who had come miraculously out of the ocean.

In the magical context in which the Aztecs saw the appearance of the Spaniards, hanging over everything was that holy fear that ate away at the spirit of Monteczuma and his counselors. Was this the return of the god Quetzalcoatl that had been foretold?

Monteczuma's emissaries, loaded with gifts, arrived where the Spaniards were anchored. They were hauled on board. There were five of them, and one by one they kissed the ground in the presence of Cortes.

They communicated through Jerónimo de Aguilar and the Malinche. The emissaries spoke: "If the god will deign to hear us, your deputy Monteczuma has sent us to render you homage. He says: 'The god is weary'" (Portilla and Garibay).

The emissaries dressed Cortes in the turquoise mask and the quetzal feather pendant and other insignia of divinity. To impress the emissaries, Cortes ordered the cannon to be fired. As Portilla records: "The great cannon was fired off. The messengers lost their senses and fainted away. They fell down side by side and lay where they had fallen."

Cortes proposed a tournament to them for the next day, but the emissaries declined. They had been entrusted with one mission only: they had come to greet the gods, not to measure themselves with them. But they had with them painters who quickly made sketches on cloth of the conquistadors, their horses, and their equipment in order to inform Monteczuma. Cortes organized mock fights and demonstrations of strength for them.

The emissaries returned to Mexico. They reported what they had seen and heard to Monteczuma.

> He was also horrified to learn how the cannon roared, how its noise resounded, how it caused people to faint and deafened them. The messengers told him: "Something like a ball of stone comes out of its entrails: it shoots sparks and rains fire. The smoke that comes out with it has a noxious odor. . . . The odor penetrates even to the brain and causes the greatest discomfort. If the cannon is aimed at a mountain, the mountain splits and cracks open. If it is aimed at a tree, it shatters the tree into splinters. This is a most unnatural sight, as if the tree exploded from within. . . . Their trappings and arms are all made of iron. . . . They dress in iron and wear iron helmets on their heads. Their swords . . . their shields are iron. Their deer carry them on their backs wherever they want to go. These deer, our lord, are as tall as the roof of a house.
>
> The strangers' bodies are completely covered, so that only their faces are seen. Their skin is white, as if made of lime. They have yellow hair, though some have black. Their beards are long and yellow. . . ." (Portilla and Garibay)

"Spies were sent to the province that we wished to conquer so that they could observe the conditions in the country. . . . They came back bringing the king a painting of all these things so that he could have a clear picture of conditions in the country," writes Bernardino de Sahagun in his *General History of the Affairs of New Spain.*

> With flat ears and long, dangling tongues, their dogs are enormous. Their eyes are a burning yellow color; their eyes flash fire and shoot off sparks. . . .
>
> As Monteczuma heard this report, he was filled with dread. It was as if his heart had fainted, as if it had shriveled. It was as if he were overcome by despair.
>
> Worrying, Monteczuma could neither sleep nor eat. No one spoke to him anymore. . . . He sighed all the time. He was demoralized and prostrated. And he murmured to himself all the time: "What will be left of us? What indeed will be left standing?" (Portilla and Garibay)

Like their monarch, the people of Mexico were terror stricken too.

Monteczuma sought to avert the coming of the gods. The return
of Quetzalcoatl would herald the final catastrophe, the Apocalypse.

It was then that Monteczuma sent out a delegation. He sent
as many of his most gifted men, his prophets and wizards, as he
could gather. He also sent his noblest and bravest warriors.
They had to carry provisions with them on the journey: live
hens, eggs, and tortillas. They also took with them what the
strangers might request, or what might please them.

Monteczuma also sent captives to be sacrificed, for the
strangers might wish to drink their blood. The captives were sacrificed in the presence of the strangers, but when the white men
saw this, they were disgusted. They spat on the ground, wiped
away their tears, or closed their eyes and shook their heads in
loathing. They refused to eat the food that was sprinkled with
blood, because it reeked of [blood]; it made them sick. . . .

Monteczuma ordered the sacrifice because he thought the
Spaniards were gods; he believed in them and worshiped them
as deities. (Portilla and Garibay)

Six or seven days went by this way. One morning [the
cacique] returned with more than a hundred Indian porters
accompanied by a great Mexican chief, who in face and body
looked much like our Captain. The great Monteczuma had chosen him on purpose. . . .

. . . Upon arrival before our Captain, these people kissed the
earth and perfumed him and the soldiers around him with
incense that they had brought in earthenware braziers. Cortes
received them kindly and seated them beside him. . . .

The prince . . . ordered them to bring forward the gifts. The
various objects were placed on mats. . . . The first was a disk in
the shape of the sun, as big as a cartwheel and made of fine
gold. It was a marvelous object, engraved with many figures. . .
. There was a larger disk of brightly shining silver in the shape
of the moon, with other figures on it. . . . [He] also brought back
the helmet full of small grains of gold, just as they come from
the mines, worth three thousand pesos. . . . The gold in the helmet was worth much more to us, because it proved that there
were good gold mines in the country. . . .

. . . the ambassadors told him that they wished to repeat
[Monteczuma's] message. First, that he was pleased such
valiant men, as he had heard we were, should come to his coun-

try—for he knew what we had done at Tabasco—and that he would much like to see our great Emperor, who was such a mighty prince that his fame had reached him even from the distant lands from where we came. Secondly, that he would send a present of precious stones to the Emperor, and serve us in any way he could during our stay in that port. But as for a meeting, he said not to think of it, because it was not necessary; and he listed many objections.

Cortes thanked them . . . [and] gave each governor two holland shirts, some blue glass beads, and other things. He begged them to return to Mexico as his ambassadors and inform their lord, the great Monteczuma, that since we had crossed so many seas and journeyed from distant lands solely to see him and speak with him in person, we would not be well received by our king and lord, if we were to return without seeing Monteczuma. Wherever their king might be, said Cortes, we should like to go and visit him and carry out his commands.

The governors said that they would return with this message, but that they considered the request unnecessary. . . .

We awoke one morning to find not a single Indian in any of the huts, neither those who brought us our food, nor those who came to trade with us; . . . they had all fled without a word. The reason for this, as we learned afterward, was that Monteczuma had sent orders to break off all communication with Cortes. . . .

We thought they meant war and put ourselves on the alert, when we heard the news. One day, posted on some sand dunes, I and another soldier were keeping a lookout when we saw five Indians coming from the beach. . . . When they came to Cortes, they bowed to him; . . . they were quite different in dress and speech from the Mexicans, who had been staying with us. Doña Marina asked in Mexican if there were any *Nahuatlatos*—meaning, interpreters of the Mexican language—among them. Two of the five said that they understood it, and welcomed us, saying that their chief had sent them to inquire who we were, and to tell us that he would be glad to be of service to such valiant men. Apparently, they knew of our deeds at Tabasco and Champoton. They added that they would have come to see us earlier, had it not been for their fear of the people of Culua who had been with us. . . . As this conversation went on, Cortes learned with great delight, that Monteczuma had opponents and enemies. . . . (Diaz)

Provisions were running low. This was the moment the partisans of Governor Diego de Velazquez chose to call for a return to Cuba. They owned Indian slaves in Cuba, unlike Cortes's followers, who did not. They had joined the expedition to settle and make their fortunes. Cortes made a pretense of needing to be begged, but he agreed to adopt the line that had in fact always been the one he preferred: move forward. But he made it a condition that he be named captain and chief justice and, in addition, be given one-fifth of the gold remaining once the royal fifth had been deducted. The order was given to found and settle a city that the Spaniards named Villa Rica de Vera Cruz.

> When Diego de Velazquez's party realized that we had elected Cortes Captain and Chief Justice, and founded the town and appointed our officers, they were so furious that they began to stir up factions and call meetings and to revile Cortes and those of us who had elected him. . . .
>
> Cortes replied that he would not detain anyone by force. . . .
>
> Therefore, Cortes decided to arrest them with our assistance. We kept these men prisoners in chains and under guard for several days, making sure that the rest create no disturbance.
>
> After the arrests Pedro de Alvarado was sent inland to visit some nearby towns . . . and to bring back maize and other provisions.
>
> On the very day of his arrival, Pedro de Alvarado found these places well provisioned and all deserted. Indeed, we could not find more than two Indians to carry maize, and each soldier had to carry and vegetables. Although he had plenty of opportunity, Alvarado returned to camp without doing any more damage, because Cortes had given orders not to repeat the events at Cozumel. In the camp, we were pleased enough with the very little food they had brought us, for evils and hardships vanish when there is enough to eat.
>
> Cortes, always capable of taking great pains, succeeded in making friends with Velazquez's party and bringing them round, some with presents of gold, which breaks down all opposition, and others with promises. He then released all the prisoners except Juan Velazquez de Leon and Diego de Ordaz, whom he kept in irons aboard ship. But a few days later he released them too, and with gold, the great peacemaker, he made good and loyal friends of them, as will be seen hereafter. (Diaz)

The Spaniards reached Cempoala. They were well received. Cortes ordered that no soldier should cause any trouble and that no one should leave the area. The *cacique* of Cempoala welcomed them with gifts.

> Cortes replied through our interpreters that he would repay this gift in services, and that if the *cacique* would tell him what he wanted to learn, it would be done for him, since we were vassals of the Emperor Charles, a great prince who ruled over many kingdoms and countries, and who had sent us to redress grievances, to punish evildoers, and to order that all human sacrifices cease.
>
> He explained many things concerning our holy religion. After listening to all this, the fat *cacique* heaved a deep sigh and started bitter complaints against the great Monteczuma and his governors, saying that the Mexican prince had recently subjected him, taken away all his golden jewelry, and so grievously oppressed him and his people that they could do nothing but obey him, since he was the ruler of many cities and countries, and ruled over countless vassals and armies of warriors.
>
> Since Cortes knew that he could not attend to their complaint at that point, he replied that he would see their wrongs set right. . . .
>
> Next morning we left Cempoala with over four hundred Indian porters. . . . Each could march fifteen miles carrying fifty pounds on his back. We rejoiced at the sight of so many porters. (Diaz)

The Spaniards were peacefully welcomed in the village of Quiahuitzlan.

> When we got to the square on top of the fortress, where temples and great idol-houses stood, we found fifteen Indians, all dressed in fine cloaks and each bearing a clay brazier full of incense, waiting. They came up to Cortes, and perfumed him and all the soldiers near him. Then, with deep bows they apologized for not having come out to meet us, assured us that we were welcome, and invited us to rest. They said that they had kept away out of fear, until they saw what sort of creatures we were, for they had been afraid of us and our horses. They promised to recall all the inhabitants of the city that night. . . .
>
> As we were talking, someone came to tell Cortes that the fat *cacique* had arrived in a litter borne on the shoulders of many

Indian dignitaries. Upon his arrival he joined the *cacique* and
the principal men of that town in their complaints against Monteczuma. Speaking of his great strength, they were in tears and
sighed so that Cortes and the rest of us were moved to pity. . . .

During this conversation five Indians came rushing from the
town to inform the *caciques* who were talking to Cortes that
five of Monteczuma's Mexican tax-gatherers had just arrived.
The *caciques* turned pale at the news. Trembling with fear, they
left Cortes and went off to receive the Mexicans. They quickly
decorated a room with flowers, cooked them some food, and
made them quantities of chocolate, which is their best drink.

When the five Mexicans entered the town, they . . . passed us
by with cocksure pride, speaking not a word to Cortes or anyone else they saw. . . . Each was smelling the roses he carried,
and each had a crooked staff in his hand. Their Indian servants
carried fly whisks. . . .

The tax-gatherers sent for the fat *cacique* and the other
chiefs, as soon as they had dined. [They] scolded them for having entertained us in their villages, for now they would have to
meet and deal with us, which would not please their lord Monteczuma. Without his permission and instructions, they should
neither have received us nor given us golden jewels. They continued to reproach the fat *cacique* and his nobles for their
actions, and ordered them to provide twenty Indians, male and
female, as a peace offering to their gods for the wrong that had
been done. . . .

When Cortes understood what the *caciques* were saying, he
reminded them that, as he had explained earlier, our lord the
King had sent him to chastise evildoers and prevent sacrifices
and robbery. Therefore, he ordered them to arrest the tax-gatherers for having made such a demand and to hold them prisoners until Monteczuma, their lord, was informed of the reason for
this arrest, namely that they had come to rob the Totonacs, to
enslave their wives and children and commit other violence.

When the *caciques* heard this, they were appalled at his daring to order them to manhandle Monteczuma's messengers!
They were too frightened and did not dare to do it. But Cortes
insisted that they be arrested at once; and they obeyed him. . . .
Furthermore, Cortes ordered all the *caciques* to stop paying
tribute and obedience to Monteczuma, and to proclaim their
refusal in all the towns of their friends and allies. Also [he

ordered them] to announce that he must be informed if tax-gatherers came to any other towns, and he would send for them. So
the news spread throughout the province, because the fat
cacique sent messengers out immediately. . . .

The act they had witnessed was so astonishing and of such
importance to them that they said no human beings would dare
do such a thing, and so it must be the work of *Teules*. Therefore,
from that moment on they called us *Teules*, meaning gods or
demons.

Returning to the prisoners, all the *caciques* believed that they
should be sacrificed, so that none could return to Mexico to tell
the tale. But Cortes said that they should not be killed, and that
he would take charge of them. He set a guard over them, and at
midnight summoned the soldiers of this guard to instruct them:
"Choose the two most intelligent prisoners and set them loose.
Then, bring them to my quarters. But do not let any of the village Indians see what you are doing." When the prisoners were
brought before him, as if he knew nothing of the matter, he
asked them through our interpreters why they were imprisoned
and from what country they came. They answered that the
caciques of Cempoala had arrested them, with the aid of their
followers and ours, and had held them prisoner. Cortes told
them that he knew nothing about this and was very sorry. He
ordered food to be brought them and talked to them in a
friendly way. He then told them to return to their lord Montezuma at once and tell him that we were all his good friends
and entirely at his service. They were to explain also that he had
quarreled with the *caciques* who had arrested them and had
released them because he feared that they would be harmed.
Furthermore, he would do all he could to help them, and would
see to it that their three companions were also released and protected. He then told them to go off quickly and not return,
because they would be captured and killed.

The two prisoners thanked him for his kindness, but said they
were still afraid of falling into the enemy hands, since they had
to pass through their country. So Cortes ordered six sailors to
take them in a boat at night and put them ashore on friendly territory outside the boundaries of Cempoala some twelve miles
away. When next morning the fat *cacique* and the village chiefs
saw that two prisoners were missing, they were even more anxious to sacrifice the remaining three. But Cortes got these three

out of their clutches. Pretending to be furious at the escape of
the other two, he had a chain brought from the ships and bound
them with it. Then he transported them aboard, saying that since
such a bad watch had been kept over the others, he would look
after them himself. Once they were aboard, he had their chains
taken off and told them in a very friendly way that they would
soon be sent back to Monteczuma.

After these events the *caciques* of this village and of Cempoala, and all the Totonac dignitaries who had assembled, asked
Cortes what was to be done, for all the forces of Mexico and of
the great Monteczuma would descend upon them, and they
could not possibly escape death and destruction.

With a most cheerful smile, Cortes replied that he and his
brothers who were with him would defend them and kill anyone
who tried to harm them; and the *caciques* and their villagers one
and all promised to stand by us, to obey our orders, and to join
their forces with ours against Monteczuma and all his allies. . . .

Meanwhile in Mexico, the great Monteczuma received news
of the arrest of his tax-collectors, the rebellion of the Totonac
towns, and their withdrawal of allegiance. This enraged him
against Cortes and our people. . . .

At this point, the two Indian prisoners whom Cortes had set
free arrived; and when Monteczuma learned who had released
and sent them back to Mexico, and when he heard the messages
and promises that Cortes had entrusted to them, thanks be to
God his anger subsided, and he decided to find out something
about us. For this purpose, he sent two of his nephews along
with four old men, *caciques* of high rank, and a present of gold
and cloth; and he told these messengers to thank Cortes for free-
ing his servants.

He also registered several complaints, saying that if it were
not for our protection, the rebels would never have had the
courage to commit the great treason of refusing him tribute and
renouncing their allegiance to him. Moreover, since he was now
certain that we were the ones whose coming had been foretold
by his ancestors, and therefore [we] must be of his own race, he
failed to understand why we were living in the houses of the traitors. Still, he would not send to destroy them immediately. . . .

Cortes embraced the envoys, telling them that we were all
very good friends of their lord, and that it was as Monteczuma's
servants that we had kept guard over the three tax-collectors. He

then had them brought from the ships, where they had been well treated, and delivered them over dressed in fine clothing.

Then Cortes complained bitterly to Monteczuma regarding the secret nocturnal departure of Governor Pitalpitoque from our camp. He said that this was a mean action which he believed had been committed without lord Monteczuma's instructions, and that it was because of this that we had come to these towns where we were staying, and where we had been well received by the inhabitants. And he begged Monteczuma to pardon these people for their disrespect. But as for the prince's protest regarding their refusal of tribute, he observed that they could not serve two masters, and that they had sworn allegiance to us in the name of our lord and King for the duration of our stay with them. But as he, Cortes, and all his brothers were now on their way to visit Monteczuma to place themselves at his service, all his commands would soon be attended to.

After this and several other conversations, Cortes ordered blue and green beads to be given to the two young *caciques*, and to the four old men who were in charge of them and were men of importance. He paid them every sign of honor and, he ordered Pedro de Alvarado, on his fine and well-trained sorrel mare, and some other horsemen to gallop and skirmish in front of them in the near by fields . . . .

Here, I must note that since these allies of ours from the hill towns and from Cempoala had been much afraid of the Mexicans before, and expected the great Monteczuma to send his large armies to destroy them, the sight of his relatives coming to Cortes with presents and declaring themselves his servants was a great surprise to them. Their chiefs said among themselves that we must indeed be *Teules*, because Monteczuma was afraid of us and had sent us presents of gold. So if we already had a reputation for valor, from this point on it was greatly increased. (Diaz)

Monteczuma had sent the magicians to learn what sort of people the strangers were, but they were also supposed to find out whether they could work some charm against them or create some mischief. They might be able to direct a harmful wind against them, or cause them to break out in sores, or injure them in some way. Or they might be able to repeat an enchanted word, over and over, that would cause [the strangers] to fall sick, or die, or return to their own land.

In carrying out their mission against the Spaniards, the magicians failed completely. They could not harm them in any way whatever.

Therefore they hurried back to the city to tell Monteczuma what the strangers were like and how invulnerable they were. They said to him: "Our lord, we are no match for them: we are mere nothings!" . . .

Distraught and bewildered, Monteczuma was filled with terror, not knowing what would happen to the city. The people were also terrified, discussing the news among themselves. There were meetings and arguments and gossip in the street; there was weeping and lamenting. The people were depressed: they went about with their heads bowed down greeting each other with tears. . . .

Also at this time, the Spaniards asked many questions about Monteczuma. . . . "Is he a young man, or mature, or in his old age? Is he still vigorous, or does he feel to be growing old?" . . .

When Monteczuma learned of their inquiries about his person, and that the "gods" wished to see him face to face, his heart shrank, and he was filled with anguish. He wanted to run away and hide; he thought of escaping to hide in a cave to evade the "gods." . . .

But he could not do it. He could not run away or go into hiding. He had lost his strength and his spirit, and he could do nothing. The magicians' words had overwhelmed his heart; they had vanquished his heart and confused him, so that now he was too weak and listless and too uncertain to make a decision.

Hence, he did nothing but wait. He did nothing but resign himself waiting for [the Spaniards] to come. At last, he overcame his heart and waited for whatever was to happen. (Portilla and Garibay)

Shortly after dusk, the next day, we arrived at some farms near Cingapacinga. The town's inhabitants had heard of our approach. As we were climbing toward the houses and the fortress, on the great, craggy cliffs, eight Indian chieftains and *papas* came to meet us in peace, and to ask Cortes why, in view of our reputation for doing good to all and avenging robberies, and after our arrest of Monteczuma's tax-collectors, we now wanted to kill people who had done nothing to deserve this. They said that the Cempoalan Indians, who accompanied us, were their enemies because of old feuds concerning lands and boundaries and that now, under our protection, they had come to rob and kill them. . . .

As soon as our interpreters had explained to Cortes what they had said, he ordered Captain Pedro de Alvarado, Cristóbal de Olid the quartermaster, and the rest of us to prevent the Cempoalans from advancing any further, which we did. Although we acted quickly, they had already begun to loot the farms. Then in a fury, Cortes sent for the commanders of the Cempoalans and ordered them with angry threats to bring him the Indians, the cloth, and the poultry they had stolen from the farms. He also forbade any Cempoalan to enter the town. . . .

Observing the justice in our behavior and hearing Cortes's kind words through our interpreters, the *caciques* and *papas* of Cingapacinga became well disposed toward us . . . called together the people of the neighboring towns. These people then swore obedience to His Majesty, and began making the same grievous complaints against Monteczuma that the Cempoalans had made when we were at Quiahuitzlan.

The next morning, Cortes sent for the Cempoalan captains, who were waiting in the fields for our orders. . . . When they appeared before him, he made them make friends with the people of that town. . . .

We then took another road to Cempoala . . . and rested, for the sun was fierce and the weight of our arms made us tired. . . . Cortes happened to notice de Mora, a soldier from Ciudad Rodrigo, take two fowls from an Indian's house. Enraged that any soldier should do such a thing in a friendly town and before his very eyes, he immediately ordered to throw a halter around his neck; and de Mora would have been hanged, if Pedro de Alvarado, who was standing beside Cortes, had not cut the halter with his sword. . . .

We left these towns in peace and resumed our march to Cempoala, where we found the fat *cacique* and other dignitaries awaiting us at some huts with food. . . .

. . . They told Cortes that as we were their friends now, they would like to have us for brothers and to give us their daughters to bear us children. So, to cement our friendship, they brought eight Indian girls—all the daughters of chiefs—and gave one . . . to Cortes. . . . Cortes received them with a gracious smile, and thanked the chiefs for their gift. He said, however, that before we could become their brothers and accept the ladies, they

would have to abandon their idols which they mistakenly worshiped, and not sacrifice any more souls to them; and that when
he saw those cursed things thrown down and the sacrifices
stopped, the bonds of our brotherhood would be much firmer.
The girls, he added, must become Christians before we could
receive them. . . .

The *caciques, papas,* and all the dignitaries said that it would
be wrong for them to give up their idols and sacrifices, because
their gods brought them health and good harvests and all that
they needed. . . .

This disrespectful response was more than Cortes or any of
us who had seen all their cruelties and indecencies could stand.
Reminding us of the doctrines of our holy faith, Cortes asked
us: "If we do not pay God so much honor as to stop them from
making sacrifices to their idols, how can we ever accomplish
anything worth doing?" He told us to throw down the idols that
same day and be completely prepared to fight if they tried to
stop us. . . . Cortes told the *caciques* that the idols must come
down at once. Thereupon, the fat *cacique* and his captains
ordered their warriors to assemble and defend them. And when
they saw us preparing to ascend the numerous steps—I do not
remember how many there were—of their *cue* or temple, which
was very high, the fat *cacique* and the rest shouted to Cortes in
anger, inquiring why he wanted to destroy their gods, since if
we desecrated and overthrew them their whole people would
perish, and we with them. In a fierce voice Cortes replied that
he had already told them to stop sacrifices to these evil images
and that we were going to destroy them in order to save them
from their false beliefs. He warned them that if they themselves
did not remove their idols at once, we would send them rolling
down the steps. He said that we could no longer consider them
our friends, rather our mortal enemies, since they would not
trust the good advice we had given them. . . .

When the Indians heard these threats—and Doña Marina was
not only quite capable of interpreting in their language, but also
threatened them with the power of Monteczuma, who might fall
on them any day—they replied in fear that they were unworthy
of approaching their gods, and that if we were to overthrow
them it would be without their consent, but that we could throw
them down or do whatever else we liked.

As soon as the words came out of their mouths, fifty of us

soldiers clambered up and overturned the idols, which rolled down the steps and were smashed to pieces. . . .

The *caciques* and the *papas* who were with them wept and covered their eyes, when they saw their idols shattered; and they prayed to their gods for forgiveness in the Totonac language, saying that they had been overborne and were not to blame, that it was these *Teules* who had overthrown them, and that they dared not attack us for fear of the Mexicans. (Diaz)

Velazquez's friends and dependents began to plot against Cortes again and decided to sail secretly for Cuba. But Cortes was warned. He hurriedly had the sails and rudder removed from the ship and ordered the arrest of anyone advocating a return to Cuba. They were questioned and admitted the truth. Two of the plotters were sentenced to be hanged and the pilot to have his feet cut off.

Bernal Diaz del Castillo writes: "I remember that, as Cortes signed the sentence, he exclaimed with a deep and sorrowful sigh: 'It would be better not to know how to write. Then one would not have to sign death sentences.' " And he adds, to show that he is not fooled: "I think this observation is very common among judges who have to sentence men to death."

> We assembled at Cempoala and discussed our military dispositions and the journey ahead with Cortes. And as the conversation continued from one point to another, we who were his friends advised him . . . not to leave a single ship in port, but to destroy them all immediately, in order not to leave any cause of trouble behind. For like the last time we had marched inland, others of our people might rebel. Besides, our forces would be greatly reinforced by their captains, pilots, and sailors, who numbered nearly a hundred and would be better employed fighting and keeping watch than lying in port.
>
> As far as I can judge, our plan for destroying the ships had already been decided on by Cortes. But he wanted it carried out by us, so that if afterward we were asked to pay for the ships he could say that he had acted on our advice. . . .
>
> The ships were destroyed with our full knowledge and not, as the historian Gomara alleges, in secret. Then after mass one morning, during a general discussion on military matters, begging for our attention Cortes spoke to the effect that we now understood what work lay ahead, and with the help of our lord, Jesus Christ, we must succeed in all battles and engagements.

We must be properly prepared, he said, for each one of them, because God forbid, if we were ever defeated, we would not be able to raise our heads again, being so few. He added that we could look for no help or assistance except from God, for now we had no ships in which to return to Cuba. Therefore, we must rely on our own good swords and stout hearts.

Cortes went on drawing comparisons with the heroic deeds of the Romans, and we all stated that we would obey his orders and that the die was cast for good fortune, as Caesar had said at the Rubicon, for we were all ready to serve God and His Majesty. After this very fine speech, which was more honeyed and eloquent than I have indicated, Cortes sent for the fat *cacique* at once and . . . told him . . . that he needed two hundred Indian carriers to transport his artillery. He also asked for fifty of the *cacique's* best warriors to accompany us. (Diaz)

4

THE MARCH ON MEXICO

After fully discussing our departure for Mexico, we asked the *caciques* of Cempoala which road we should take. They all agreed that the best and easiest way was through the province of Tlaxcala, because the Tlaxcalans were their friends and the deadly enemies of the Mexicans.

Forty chieftains, all fighting men, were now ready to accompany us; and they gave us valuable assistance on our march. The Cempoalans also provided us with the two hundred porters we needed to carry our artillery. But we, the poor soldiers, did not need any help; all we had to carry at the time was our arms—lances, crossbows, muskets, shields, and alike—with which we both marched and slept. As for footwear, we wore hempen shoes, and, as I have often said, we were always prepared for battle.

Marching in good order, with scouts and some of our swiftest soldiers in advance, we left Cempoala in mid August 1519; and the first day's march took us to a town called Jalapa, from which we went to Socochima, a fortified place with a difficult approach. . . .

Francisco de Lugo had a very large greyhound, which barked a great deal at night, and it seems that the *caciques* of this town asked our Cempoala friends whether it was a tiger or a lion or an animal we used for killing the Indians. And they answered, "They have brought it to kill anyone who annoys them."

They also acquired how we used the guns we carried with us, and the Cempoalans answered that with some stones we placed inside them we could kill whomever we liked, and that the horses ran like deer and could catch anyone we told them to chase. [Their leader] and all the chiefs exclaimed: "Surely they must be *Teules*!" And our friends replied: "Now that you have learned this, make sure that you don't annoy them, for they'll know immediately. They know what is in your thoughts. These are the *Teules* who captured your great Monteczuma's tax-gatherers, and ordered that no tribute be paid anywhere in the hills or in our town of Cempoala. These are the *Teules* who threw our *Teules* out of our temples and put their own instead. They have conquered the people of Tabasco and Cingapacinga. . . . Moreover, you've seen how the great Monteczuma, powerful as he is, sends them gold and cloths. Now they have come to your town, and we see don't see you giving them anything. . . ."

It seems that we had brought good persuaders. For the townspeople quickly brought us four pendants, three necklaces, and some lizards, all of gold although of poor quality; and they gave us four women to grind maize for our bread, and a load of cloth. Cortes gladly received these presents and expressed many thanks. . . .

We decided to set out for Tlaxcala, which according to our friends was not far. In fact, they said, the boundary, marked by a number of stones, was quite close. So we asked the chief which was the best and most level road to Mexico. He said that it passed through the large town of Cholula. But the Cempoalans told Cortes: "Don't go that way. The Cholulans are very treacherous, and Monteczuma always keeps a large garrison in their town." They recommended going through Tlaxcala, which was friendly to them and hostile to the Mexicans. So we decided to take their advice, for God always guided us well.

Cortes then asked for twenty of the *cacique*'s best warriors to go with us, and he complied at once. Then next morning, we took the road to Tlaxcala. . . .

Hence, we set out . . . and started our march, with our scouts always ahead and on the alert constantly, our musketeers and crossbow men in regular order, and our horsemen placed even better. Each man carried his own arms, as was our custom. But enough of this. It is a waste of words, for we were so alert all the time, night and day, that if the alarm had been given ten times we would have been found ready on each occasion. . . .

Today one might ask why were all these preparations necessary when there was no enemy in sight to attack us? I reply in Cortes' words: "Comrades, since we are few, we must always be as ready and on the alert as if we already see our enemy coming to attack us. And we must not only act as if we see them approaching, but as if we are already fighting them." (Diaz)

As they neared Tlaxcala, the Spaniards were attacked and four were wounded, but they managed to drive the Tlaxcalans off. On September 2 and 5, the Spaniards again fought two victorious battles against the Tlaxcalan warriors. Cortes offered them peace. Bernal Diaz del Castillo notes that ever since Villa Rica de la Vera Cruz:

> Cortes had taken the path of peace and left friendly villages behind us. . . .
> While talking to Monteczuma's ambassadors, Cortes received a message that Captain Xicotenga was arriving with many other *caciques* and captains. . . . Xicotenga said that he had come on behalf of his father and all the *caciques* and the commonwealth of Tlaxcala to pray Cortes to accept them as our friends, and to ask forgiveness for having taken up arms against us. He said that they had done so only because they did not know who we were, and had been quite certain that we had come in their enemy Monteczuma's interests.. . . .
> The Mexican ambassadors, who were present during all these discussions and heard all the offers that were made, were terribly depressed by the conclusion of the peace; they realized that no good would come of it for them. Therefore, when Xicotenga had left Monteczuma' ambassadors asked Cortes half laughingly whether he believed any of the promises made on behalf of Tlaxcala, for they were the promises of traitors and liars, which deserved no credence. . . .
> However, to return to our new friends the *caciques* of Tlaxcala: when they realized that we were not going to their city, they came to our camp with fowls and prickly pears, which were in season . . . [and they were] always asking Cortes to accompany them to their city soon. But since we had promised the Mexicans to wait six days for their return, he put them off with fair speeches. At the end of the agreed time, six chieftains, all men of importance bearing a rich present from the great Monteczuma, came from Mexico. . . .
> He begged Cortes most earnestly neither to accompany the people of Tlaxcala to their town, nor to trust them. For they wanted to take him there in order to rob him. (Diaz)

After hesitating for several days, Cortes and his men entered Tlaxcala as the *caciques* of the town had insistently asked them to

Quitlauhtique

Tlaxcalan envoys bring gifts to Cortes and offer him virgins and hostages.

do. It was September 23, 1519. Seeing that the Spaniards were constantly vigilant, the *caciques* of Tlaxcala suggested to Cortes that he take any hostages he wished. Cortes refused. "As to our being on the alert," he said, "this was our usual custom. . . . "Shortly afterward, the *caciques* of Tlaxcala offered to give their daughters to the noble Spaniards as wives.

Relations had become so friendly that one day Cortes took the *caciques* aside and asked them very detailed questions about Mexico.

> Finally they came. Finally they began marching toward us. . . .
>
> They found Tecoac, in the land of the Tlaxcalans, inhabited by Otomis. The Otomis came out to meet them in battle array; they greeted the strangers with their shields. But the strangers conquered and utterly destroyed the Otomis of Tecoac. They divided their ranks, fired the cannons and attacked them with their swords, and shot them with their crossbows. Not just a few, but all of them, perished in battle.
>
> Soon after Tecoac had been defeated, the Tlaxcalans heard the news of what had happened there. They felt premonitions of death: terror overwhelmed them, and they were filled with foreboding.
>
> The chiefs assembled; the captains met in a council. They . . . said: "What shall we do? Shall we go out to meet them? The Otomi is a brave warrior, but he was helpless against them: they scorned him as a mere nothing. . . . We should go over to their side; we should make friends with them and become their allies. Otherwise, they will destroy us as well. . . ."
>
> Therefore [they] went to meet them. They said to the strangers: "Our lords, you are weary."
>
> The strangers asked: "Where are you from?"
>
> They said: "We are from Tlaxcala. You have come here; you have entered our land. We are from Tlaxcala; our city is the City of the Eagle, Tlaxcala."
>
> . . . They paid them great honors, attended to their every desire, joined with them as allies, and even gave their daughters to them.
>
> The Spaniards inquired: "Where is the City of Mexico? Is it far from here?"
>
> They said: "No, it is not far; it is only a three-day march. And it is a great city. The Aztecs are very brave. They are great warriors and conquerors and have defeated all their neighbors."

(Portilla and Garibay)

The Tlaxcalans had long been at war with the Cholulans. They said: "Cholula is our enemy. It is an evil city. The people are as brave as the Aztecs and they are the Aztecs' friends." (Portilla and Garibay)

Cortes learned that Cholula, a town a day's march away, was an ally of Mexico and an enemy of Tlaxcala. But he wanted to know more about Mexico. The *caciques* described their opponents.

> [The *caciques*] brought us pictures painted on large sisal cloths of their battles against the Mexicans, and their way of fighting. . . .
>
> These *caciques* also told us of a tradition they had heard from their ancestors, that one of the idols which they particularly worshipped had predicted that men from distant lands in the direction of the sunrise would come and conquer them and rule them. If we were these men, said the *caciques*, they rejoiced, since we were so brave and good. They went on to say that, hey had remembered their idol's prophecy after they had made peace with us, and so they gave us their daughters in order to have kinsmen to defend them against the Mexicans. When they had concluded their speech we wondered in amazement whether what they had just said could be true. (Diaz)

The Spaniards moved toward Mexico. They reached the foot of the Popocatepetl volcano. Some Spaniards decided to go and see it despite the contrary advice of the Indians, who refused to go with them beyond the foot of the volcano. The Spaniards climbed up. When they were halfway up, the volcano began to throw out great tongues of flame and half-burnt stones of no great weight and a great deal of ash. They stopped, afraid to go on. But after an hour, when things had calmed down, they went on up. From the summit they could see the City of Mexico.

For Cortes, armed confrontation was a last resort; he acted more as a diplomat, a supremely adept politician. The march to Mexico was a model of ingenuity, even if his religious zeal was excessive. In his second dispatch to Emperor Charles, dated October 30, 1520, he wrote:

> While I was back in my camp fighting against all the forces of that province, six lords who were among the principal subjects of Monteczuma, visited me with an entourage of over two hundred men. They told me that their master had sent them to tell me how much he wished to be my friend and the vassal of Your Highness. . . .

They stayed with me throughout the fighting; they saw the end of it and understood what the Spaniards were capable of. They witnessed the submission of the province, the offers of service from the *caciques* to Your Sacred Majesty, which displeased Monteczuma's envoys a great deal, because they did all they could to cause trouble between me and my new allies: saying that they were deceiving me; that the friendship they had sworn to was false; that it was intended to lull me into a false sense of security; and to prepare for some treachery. For their part, the people of the province told me that I should be wary of Monteczuma's envoys; that they were all deceptive; that it was through lies and treachery that they had subdued the entire land, and that they were telling me this as my friends and as they had long familiarity with them. Seeing the contradictions between them, I was greatly pleased, because they seemed to be so keen on their alliance with me that it would be easier for me to subjugate them; and I recalled that saying in the Gospel that the house divided against itself cannot stand: *Omne regnum in scipsum divisum desolabitur.* Therefore, I negotiated with both of them, secretly thanking each for the advice and assuring them both of my friendship. (Cortes)

Monteczuma's ambassadors suggested that the best way to Mexico lay through Cholula, saying that the inhabitants were vassals of their emperor. Consequently, the Spaniards could be sure of being well treated there. The Tlaxcalan *caciques* tried to dissuade the Spaniards from taking that route; in their view, Cholula was a trap.

While Cortes was . . . talking to us and the Tlaxcalan *caciques* about our departure and matters of war, news was brought to him that four ambassadors, all men of importance bearing presents from Monteczuma, had arrived. . . .

The ambassadors then said on behalf of their lord Monteczuma that he was quite surprised that we had stayed for so long among such poor and ill-bred people, who were so wicked and treacherous, and such thieves that they were not even fit to be slaves. . . . He then urged us to come to his city at once. (Diaz)

When the *caciques* saw that the Spaniards were going to go by way of Cholula, they offered Cortes warriors to accompany him. Two thousand warriors from Tlaxcala joined them.

As the Spaniards neared Cholula, some dignitaries came out to meet Cortes and asked that he be told that they did not want their enemies, the Tlaxcalans, to enter their city armed. Cortes agreed to leave his allies outside the town and entered to take up his quarters in Cholula.

> On the same day, these ambassadors were joined by others from Monteczuma, who told Cortes quite shamelessly that their prince had sent them to say we must not go to his city, for he had no food to give us, and that they wished to return immediately with our reply.
>
> When Cortes realized the unfriendliness of their message, he replied most blandly. (Diaz)

Cortes felt that this message boded nothing good.

On the third day, they stopped bringing the Spaniards anything to eat, and the *caciques* stopped coming. Cortes called his officers together, and it was decided to call on the *caciques* to deliver what the Spaniards needed to enable them to leave the next day. He learned that Monteczuma had ordered that the Spaniards be given no more food and that they not be allowed to proceed any farther. So, at least, Bernal Diaz del Castillo reports.

> While this conversation was going on, three of our Cempoalan friends came in and secretly told Cortes that in the streets near our lodgings, they had noticed some holes dug and covered over with wood and earth so that they could not be seen without close examination. They had removed the earth from above one of these holes and had found it to be full of sharp stakes to kill the horses as they charged. They also said that the roofs had breastworks of dried clay and were piled with stones, and this could not be for a friendly purpose, since they had also found barricades of stout timbers in another street. (Diaz)

They discussed what to do. Some argued for returning to Tlaxcala. Others suggested making a detour. But the majority felt differently. They felt that to leave such treachery unpunished and simply retreat would invite all kinds of trouble. Since there was no shortage of provisions, they should combine with the Tlaxcalans to attack the enemy in the town itself. This was the plan agreed on.

Since it had been announced that the Spaniards were leaving the next day, they made a show of preparing to do so. This would enable them to take the Indians unaware.

> As for Monteczuma's ambassadors, [Cortes believed that] we

should conceal our feelings from them, telling them that the wicked Cholulans had planned a treacherous attack and intended to throw the blame on their lord Monteczuma and his ambassadors, but that we did not believe Monteczuma had given such orders, and therefore, urged them to stay in their apartments and not to communicate with the people of that city, so that we would have no reason to think that they had any part in this treachery. We would then ask them to guide us to Mexico.

As it turned out, the ambassadors responded that neither they nor their lord Monteczuma knew anything about what we were telling them and, although they did not like it, we put a guard on them so that they would not get away without our permission and that Monteczuma would not find out that we knew it was he who ordered the whole matter.

That night we were on the alert and armed, with our horses saddled and bridled. Although it was customary to keep a good watch, we had more guards and patrols than usual, for we were sure that all the companies, Mexican and Cholulan, would attack us that night. (Diaz)

At dawn, the Cholulans gathered in the great square. The Spaniards, armed and helmeted, stayed where they were. At the agreed signal, the Spaniards fell on the Cholulans. Shortly after, the Tlaxcalans arrived for the kill. They went about their work so zealously that Cortes intervened to stop them doing any more harm.

Some of the *caciques* who lived in the suburbs begged Cortes to put an end to the carnage. Cortes agreed, seeing that they were subjects of Monteczuma, for whom he had "the greatest respect."

At Cholula, Cortes had to deal with a real crisis and, nipping a real or imagined plot in the bud, retained the initiative.

I met several envoys of Monteczuma there, who had come to confer with the townspeople; they told me that they had come solely to find out and inform their master about the agreement between the chiefs of this city and myself. Then after talking, they all went away, taking along even the leader of the embassy who had hitherto stayed with me.

Over the first three days, the inhabitants supplied us with fewer and fewer provisions and my meetings with the leaders of the town grew less and less frequent. I was getting quite anxious, when a Cholulan woman came to confide in my interpreter, an Indian woman [Marina]—who was given to me at

Potunchan, the great river about which I wrote to you in my first dispatch—that large numbers of Monteczuma's people were gathering nearby, that the inhabitants of the town had sent their wives and children away, that they had hidden their valuables, and that they were going to attack us and massacre us. She wanted her to escape with her, and she would be responsible for her. The Indian woman kept me informed of this conspiracy, through Jerónimo de Aguilar, whom I had brought from Yucatan. I had brought to me a native who was passing by and took him to my apartment without anyone seeing; I questioned him, and he confirmed everything that the Indian woman and the Tlaxcalans had said.

Prompt action was needed. I assembled some of the town notables saying that I wished to speak with them; as they came I locked them in a room. I warned my men to be alert and at the signal, the sound of a blunderbuss, to attack the crowd of Indians filling the square and the surrounding areas. My men obeyed. I tied the men up in the room and gave the signal. We mounted our horses and fell on the host of Indians, killing three thousand of them in two hours. Your Majesty should know that everything had been so well prepared that even before we appeared from our house, the streets were barricaded and the Indians at their posts; if we took them by surprise a little and if they were so quickly overcome, it is because they lacked leaders, whom I had imprisoned. . . . [These latter] begged me to pardon them. They swore that in future they would not be deceived again, and that they would be my friends and faithful and loyal subjects of Your Majesty. After reprimanding them for their treachery, I freed two of them. The next day the town was full of people again, including women and children, as if nothing unusual had happened. I immediately released all the other prisoners, who promised their loyalty to Your Majesty. (Cortes)

The massacre at Cholula, as seen from the Aztec side shortly after the collapse of the empire and the destruction of Mexico, looked quite different.

. . . When they had all assembled, the entrances were closed, so that there was no way of escaping.

Suddenly the slaughter began: knife strokes, sword strokes, and death. The people of Cholula had not anticipated this, they had not suspected it. They faced the Spaniards without weapons, without their swords or their shields. They died blindly, without knowing why. . . .

News of the event was brought to Monteczuma. The messengers came and departed. . . . The ordinary people were terrified by the news; they . . . trembled with fear. It was as if the earth trembled beneath them, or as if the world were spinning before their eyes. . . .

When the massacre at Cholula was over, the strangers set out toward the City of Mexico once again. They came in battle array, as conquerors, and the dust rose in whirlwinds on the roads. Their spears glittered in the sun, and their pennons flapped like bats. They made a loud clamor as they marched, because their coats of mail and weapons clashed and rattled. Some of them were dressed in glistening iron from head to foot; they terrified everyone who saw them.

Their dogs ran ahead of the column. They raised their muzzles high. . . . They raced on ahead with saliva dripping from their jaws. . . .

Monteczuma sent various chiefs. . . . They went out to meet the Spaniards in the vicinity of Popocatepetl . . . in the Eagle Pass.

They presented the "gods" with . . . golden necklaces. And when they were given these presents, the Spaniards burst into smiles; their eyes shone with pleasure; they were delighted by [the gifts.] They picked up the gold and fingered it like monkeys; they seemed to be carried away by joy, as if their hearts were illuminated. . . .

In fact they longed and lusted for gold. Their bodies swelled with greed and voracious hunger; they hungered like pigs for that gold. . . . (Portilla and Garibay)

Monteczuma tried a trick. He attempted to pass one of his dignitaries off as the monarch. But the Spaniards were not duped.

Then there was another group of envoys: magicians, wizards, and priests. They also left the city and went to meet the strangers, but they were totally helpless: they could not blind [the Spaniards'] eyes or overcome them in any way. On the way, the envoys were terrified by an apparition.

"Why have you come here? It is hopeless. Mexico will be destroyed! Mexico will be left in ruins!" He said: "Go back, go back! Turn your eyes toward the city. What was destined has already happened!"

Then they looked toward Tenochtitlan. The temples were burning in flames, and so were the communal halls . . . and all the houses. It was as if a great battle were raging in the city. The envoys did not go forward to meet the Spaniards; they did not speak with them. The priests and magicians returned to report to Monteczuma.

As they arrived in the city, the envoys told Monteczuma what had happened and what they had seen. Monteczuma listened to their report and bowed his head without speaking a word. For a long time he remained that way, with his head bent down. And finally, when he spoke, he only said: "What help is left there now, my friends? Is there a mountain we can climb? Should we run away? But there is no help. What can we do? Is there nothing left to do? We will be judged and punished. And however and whenever it may be, we can do nothing but wait." (Portilla and Garibay)

Three and a half thousand years before the Indian stories of the conquest, the stele known as the stele of Naram-Sin (2254–2218 B.C.), the grandson of Sargon the Assyrian, described the terrible arrival of strangers flooding over Mesopotamia for the first time. They were without pity and unbeatable, and they were getting closer. Then Naram-Sin summoned one of his officers and said to him:

Use the spear and the rapier against them,
strike [them] with the spear and pierce with the rapier,
if blood flows, then they are men like us,
if their blood does not flow, they are spirits, angels of death,
demons and devils conjured up by Enlil!

There was one final discussion, in which, against the advice of his own brother, Cuitlahuac, Monteczuma decided to welcome the Spaniards peacefully. His brother said: "I pray our gods that you will not let the strangers into your house. They will cast you out of it and overthrow your rule, and when you try to recover your loss, it will be too late." (Portilla and Garibay)

The Spaniards headed straight for Mexico. They approached the capital from the south. It was November 8, 1519.

Preparing to go out to meet them, Monteczuma dressed himself in his finery. The other great princes also adorned themselves, as did the nobles and their chieftains and knights. They all went out together to meet the strangers. . . .

Thus Monteczuma went out to meet them, there in Huitzillan.

He presented many gifts to the Captain and his commanders. . . .

Cortes asked him: "Are you Monteczuma? Are you the king? Is it true that you are the king Monteczuma?"

And the king said: "Yes, I am Monteczuma."

[He continued:] "Our lord, you are weary; the journey has tired you. You have come to your city, to Mexico. You have come here to take your throne, to rest under its canopy.

"Your representatives, the kings who have gone before, guarded it and preserved it for your coming. The kings Itzcoatl, Monteczuma the Elder, Axayacatl, Tizoc, and Ahuitzol[2] ruled the City of Mexico for you. They protected the people by their swords and sheltered them by their shields. Do the kings know the destiny of those they left behind, of their posterity? If only they are watching! If only they can see what I see!

"No, this is not a dream. I am not sleepwalking. I am not dreaming of you. . . . I have seen you at last! I have met you face to face! I was in agony for five days, for ten days, with my eyes fixed on the Region of the Mystery. And now you have come out of the clouds and mists to sit on your throne again.

"This was predicted by the kings who governed your city, and now it has come true. You have come down from the sky. Rest now, and take possession of your royal houses. Welcome to your land, my lords!"

Speaking first to La Malinche, Cortes responded: "Tell Monteczuma that we are his friends. There is nothing to fear. We have wished to see him for a long time, and now we have seen his face and heard his words. Tell him that we love him and that our hearts are gratified. . . . We have come to your house as friends. There is nothing to fear." (Portilla and Garibay)

This key meeting, which established the nature of relations between the Aztec ruler and the Spanish captain, is reported as follows by Cortes. In his dispatch to Charles V, Cortes states that Monteczuma spoke to him as follows:

Long ago, by tradition, we learned from our ancestors that neither I nor any of those who live in this land are natives of it; we are strangers and we came from distant lands. We also know that it was a great ruler who brought us to this land, where we were all his vassals; he went back to his own country, from

2. Fourth, fifth, sixth, seventh, and eighth Aztec rulers, who reigned between 1428 and 1503.

Meeting of Aztec ruler Monteczuma and Cortes in Tenochtitlan, 1519. Doña Marina, Cortes's translator, is standing behind him. In the foreground are gifts from Monteczuma to Cortes. The chairs are the artist's invention.

which he returned only long afterward, so long afterward that
he found those he had left behind him had married women from
the new land and were living in families in the many villages
that they had founded. He wanted to take them away with him,
but they refused and did not even wish to acknowledge him as
their lord. So he went away. Since then, we have always
believed that his descendants would come back one day to conquer our country and make us their subjects. From the part of
the world from which you say you come, which is in the direction where the sun rises, and the things you tell me about the
great king who has sent you, we are convinced that he is our
true lord, especially as you tell me, he has long been aware of
our affairs. Rest assured, then, that we shall obey you and
acknowledge you as master acting for the great king of whom
you speak, and that there would be no doubt about that whatsoever. . . . (Cortes)

On November 8, 1519, St. John's Day, the Spaniards arrived
within sight of Tenochtitlan. The city was built on water. To enter
and leave, it was necessary, in order to follow the causeways leading there, to cross narrow bridges. For a small group of men to enter
the city meant running a considerable risk. Looking back at it,
Bernal Diaz writes: "What men in all the world have shown such
daring?"

We left Iztapalapa early the next day . . . and followed the
causeway, which is eight yards wide and goes straight to the
city of Mexico without curving. Although it was wide, it was so
crowded with people that there was hardly room for all of them.
Some were going to and others coming from Mexico, besides
those who had come out to see us; and we could hardly get
through the crowds that were there. For the towers and the
[temples] were full and they came in canoes from all parts of
the lake. . . .
The lake was crowded with canoes. Along the causeway, at
intervals, there were a number of bridges, and before us was the
great city of Mexico. As for us, we were scarcely four hundred
strong and could well remember the words and warnings of [our
allies] . . . to beware of entering the city of Mexico, because
they would kill us as soon as they had us inside. . . .
When Cortes saw, heard, and was told that the great Monteczuma was approaching, he dismounted from his horse, and

> when he came closer to Monteczuma they bowed deeply to each other. . . .
>
> [Cortes also] attempted to embrace him. But the great princes who stood around Monteczuma grasped Cortes's arm to prevent him, for they considered this an indignity. (Diaz)

Monteczuma spoke. Bernal Diaz *saw* the scene. He did not hear it. However, he does record the key passage: the Aztec monarch took the Spaniards to be gods, saying: "Now that he had us with him he was not only at our service but would share all his possessions with us. He ended by saying that we must truly be the men who, according to his ancestors' prophesy long ago, would come from the direction of the sunrise to rule over these lands."

The Spaniards were lodged all together in buildings that had belonged to Monteczuma's father. He had set up great shrines for his gods. Bernal Diaz says: "Perhaps their reason for lodging us here was that, since they called us *Teules*, and considered us such, they wished to have us near their idols."

For four days after their arrival, the Spaniards did not leave their apartments except to wander through the palace and the gardens. Cortes decided to go and see the great square and the temple of Huitzilopochtli. Monteczuma agreed to allow the Spaniards to visit the temple.

At the bottom of the temple's 114 steps, some dignitaries wanted to take Cortes by the arm to help him climb up as they did for their lord. But Cortes would not allow it. When they reached the summit, the Spaniards were greeted by Monteczuma, who welcomed them and asked if they were tired after climbing all those steps. Cortes replied that none of them was ever exhausted by anything.

From the top of the temple, the Spaniards—who saw the whole of the city—were amazed. Some who had traveled and seen the cities of Italy and Rome and Constantinople said they had never seen a marketplace that was so large, so beautiful, and so full of people. Cortes spoke:

> "Lord Monteczuma, I cannot imagine how a prince as powerful and wise as your Majesty has failed to realize that your idols are not gods but evil things, the proper name for which is devils. In order to prove this to you and to make it clear to all your papas, grant me one favor. Allow us to erect a cross here on the top of this tower, . . . and then you will see, by the fear that your idols have of her, how grievously they have deceived you."

Monteczuma, however, replied with aggravation . . . : "Lord Malinche, had I known that you were going to utter these insults, I would not have shown you my gods. We believe them to be very good. They give us health, rain, crops, and weather, and all the victories we desire. . . ."

Hearing this reply and seeing Monteczuma's fury, our Captain said no more on the subject but observed cheerfully: "It is time for your Majesty and ourselves to depart." Monteczuma agreed but said that he had to pray and offer certain sacrifices because of the great . . . sin which he had committed by allowing us to climb his great temple. . . . (Diaz)

A few days later, two Spaniards, one of whom was a carpenter, noticed some marks on the wall of one of the rooms where they were lodged that showed that there was a door hidden under a layer of paint. Cortes was informed, and the door was opened. Cortes went in with some of the captains: the room was full of gold. Monteczuma's treasure was there, before the Spaniards' very eyes.

But this discovery did not prevent the Spaniards from feeling anxiously that they were prisoners of a situation that could easily turn against them. Any time that Monteczuma and his men felt like it, the Spaniards could be rendered helpless: food supplies could be cut off and bridges could be raised, cutting off any avenue of retreat.

All things carefully considered, it looked as if there were no alternative but to seize the very person of Monteczuma and hold him at their mercy. This seemed all the more urgent, for some Tlaxcalan Indians told the Spaniards that the Mexicans seemed to be less well disposed toward them than they had been recently.

It was just then that two Tlaxcalan Indians arrived with a letter from the Spaniards who had been left at Vera Cruz with the news that seven of them had been killed in an attack by the Mexicans.

Whereas until now our men had been respected as *Teules*, after this misfortune Mexicans and Totonacs alike were behaving like wild beasts. . . . It was our first defeat in New Spain. . . .

To have seen ourselves making a triumphal entry into the capital and being solemnly received, and swimming in wealth thanks to Monteczuma's magnificent gifts daily; to have glimpsed the large room full of gold that I have mentioned; to have been taken for *Teules*, i.e., for creatures equal to gods; to have been victorious in every battle fought thus far . . . and now to be struck by this disaster which would inevitably diminish

our respect and reputation among our enemies, and show us as
men who could be defeated . . . it was agreed that very day that
we would seize Monteczuma by any means possible or die in
the attempt. (Diaz)

They spent the night in prayer. In the morning, Cortes, accompanied by five of his captains—Pedro de Alvarado, Gonzalo de Sandoval, Juan Velazquez de Leon, Francisco de Lugo, and Alonso de
Avila—and Marina, his interpreter, went to visit Monteczuma.

Cortes complained that two Spaniards had been killed by captains
who were Monteczuma's vassals, who must have been following the
monarch's orders. They would have to be punished. And in any
case, until this matter was cleared up, it would be best if Monteczuma came with them.

Monteczuma was dumbfounded and did not move. He said that he
had not ordered his people to take up arms against the Spaniards and
that if his captains were guilty they would be punished. But he
refused to leave his palace. They discussed the issue inconclusively.
Running out of patience, one of the captains raised his voice and
said that they should take him by force or kill him on the spot.

The impressionable Monteczuma asked Marina what they were
saying. She advised him to accompany the Spaniards immediately to
their quarters to avoid a far worse fate.

Monteczuma offered his son and two daughters as hostages, but
the proposal was rejected. In despair, Monteczuma agreed under
threat to leave his palace with the Spaniards. He was carried in a litter to the Spaniards' quarters.

> The prince was still apprehensive, despite all our leader told
> him. . . . In addition, without further discussion, Cortes sen-
> tenced the captains [guilty of killing the Spaniards] to be burned
> to death before the royal palace. The sentence was carried out
> immediately and, to prevent any interference, Cortes had Mon-
> teczuma put in chains during the burning. The prince roared
> with anger at this indignity, and became even more alarmed
> than before. After the burning, Cortes went to Monteczuma's
> apartments along with five of his captains, and removed the
> chains himself; and spoke to the prince with such affection that
> his anger soon passed away. For Cortes told him that he looked
> on him as more than a brother and . . . that if he wished to go to
> his palace he would allow him to do so. He talked through inter-
> preters, and while he was speaking tears were seen to spring to

Monteczuma's eyes. The prince replied most courteously that he was grateful for the kindness, but he knew well that Cortes's speech was mere words, and that for the present it would be better for him to remain a prisoner. . . .

From what we gathered, however, there was little doubt that, on Cortes's instructions, Aguilar had told Monteczuma privately that though Malinche might order his release the rest of us captains and soldiers would never agree to it.

On hearing this reply, Cortes threw his arms round the prince and embraced him, saying: "How right I am, Lord Monteczuma, to love you as dearly as I love myself." (Diaz)

Bernal Diaz reflected on their action: what soldiers in the world, numbering only 450, would have dared to enter a city as strong as Mexico?

. . . first, in destroying our ships; then in daring to enter that strong city despite many warnings that we would be killed once they had us inside; then in having the boldness to seize the great Monteczuma, king of that country, in his own city and inside his very palace, and to chain him while carrying out the execution. . . .

The governor of Cuba, Diego de Velazquez, sent a force to seize Cortes: eighty horsemen and eight hundred infantrymen, including eighty musketeers and eighty crossbow men. Cortes left Mexico to meet his opponents.

He left Pedro de Alvarado in command of Mexico. Through the use of guile and skillful military maneuvering, Cortes defeated the force, which was commanded by a certain Narvaez, and incorporated the defeated soldiers into his own forces. At the same time, some men were instructed to proceed to Cempoala and disable the vessels of Narvaez's expedition so that no one could go to Cuba and warn Governor Diego de Velazquez.

Cortes ordered that Narvaez's men be given back their weapons and horses, which caused some resentment among his own men. To which Cortes replied that he had no choice but to win over Narvaez's men by gifts and promises, since they needed these men.

Narvaez was a much more redoubtable opponent than the Aztecs. He came with twice the men and equipment that Cortes had, and thus, given the garrison that had been left in Mexico, had a superiority of one to five. Cortes reports:

Shortly after midnight, on Whitsunday, I set out for Cem-

poala; soon, I met Narvaez's two guards; I seized one of them,
who gave me information; the other escaped. I made forced
marches so that he would not get there before me and announce
my coming, but he arrived half an hour earlier. When I
approached Narvaez's camp, I found the whole force in arms,
the horsemen mounted and two hundred men watching each
quarter. But we advanced so quietly that, when they saw us and
gave the alarm, I had already entered the temple courtyard,
where the bulk of the troops were assembled; they occupied
three or four towers and other fortified points.

Narvaez had set up his headquarters in one of these temples,
where he had placed nineteen artillery pieces on the steps of the
pyramids; we attacked this pyramid so forcefully that the
artillery men had time to fire only a single shot, which, thanks
be to God, harmed nobody. Once we had climbed the pyramid,
we entered the room where Narvaez and fifty of his men were
entrenched and who fought with Sandoval, my first *alguazil*; he
called on him several times to surrender, but he refused and the
struggle continued; he surrendered. While Gonzalo de Sandoval
captured Narvaez, my men and I were defending the approaches
to the pyramid against those rushing to help their captain. I had
used all the artillery to fortify the pyramid, which was unap-
proachable; so that with no loss of men, except for two who
were killed by a cannonball, we had taken all those who were
important; all the weapons had been handed to us and all the
soldiers had sworn allegiance to Your Majesty. They told me
that Narvaez had deceived them until then, telling them that he
had powers from Your Highness, that I was nothing but a rebel,
a traitor to Your Majesty, and other such slander. When they
learned the truth about the evil plans of Velazquez and Narvaez
and how badly they had acted, they were all very happy that
God had decided otherwise.

I can assure Your Majesty that, if God had not acted mysteriously in this matter, and if Narvaez had emerged victorious, it
would have been the greatest disaster that Spain has suffered for
a long time; for he would have obeyed Velazquez's instructions
who had ordered him to arrest me and most of my companions
so that there would be no one to protest against what was happening. Moreover, I knew that the Indians understood perfectly
that, if Narvaez had taken me as he had sworn to do, it would
not have been done without heavy losses on both sides. Taking
advantage of the circumstance, they would have massacred all

those I had left behind in the city; then they would have come together to attack the survivors so that their country would be freed from the presence of the Spaniards for ever. Your Highness may be certain that, if this plot had succeeded, it would have taken twenty years to reconquer and pacify this country, which was already conquered and pacified.

While Cortes was dealing with Narvaez's forces, in Mexico Pedro de Alvarado took the initiative of massacring Mexican dignitaries who were gathered to celebrate the festival of Huitzilopochtli.

At this point during the fiesta, when the dance was loveliest and when one song was linked to the next, the Spaniards were seized with an urge to kill the celebrants. They all ran forward, armed as if for battle. They closed the entrances and passageways, all the gates of the patio: the Eagle Gate, . . . the Gate of the Canestalk, and the Gate of the Serpent of Mirrors. They posted guards so that no one could escape, and then rushed into the Sacred Patio to slaughter the celebrants. . . .

They rushed in among the dancers, forcing their way to where the drums were played. They attacked the drummer and cut off his arms. Then they cut off his head, and it rolled across the floor.

They attacked all the celebrants, stabbing them, striking them with their swords. They attacked some from behind, and these fell to the ground instantly with their entrails hanging out. Others they beheaded: they cut off their heads, or split their heads in pieces. . . .

Some attempted to run away, but their intestines dragged as they ran; their feet became entangled in their own entrails. No matter how they tried to save themselves, they could not escape.

Some attempted to force their way out, but the Spaniards killed them at the gates. Others climbed the walls, but they could not save themselves. . . . Others lay down among the victims and pretended to be dead. But when they stood up again, the Spaniards saw them and killed them. The blood of the warriors flowed like water. . . .

When they heard the news of this massacre outside the Sacred Patio, a great cry went up. . . . This cry was answered with a roar of grief and anger: the people shouted and wailed and beat their palms against their mouths. The captains assembled at once, as if the time had been predetermined. They all carried their spears and shields.

Then the battle began . . . and the cloud of missiles spread out over the Spaniards.

Immediately, the Spaniards took refuge in the palace. They began to shoot their iron arrows and fire their cannons and guns at the Mexicans. And they shackled Monteczuma in chains.

The Mexicans who had died in the massacre were taken out of the patio one by one, and inquiries were made about their names. The fathers and mothers of the dead wept and lamented. (Portilla and Garibay)

THE SETBACK

It was after Cortes had incorporated Narvaez's men that news of the uprising in Mexico reached him.

Perdo de Alvarado was besieged in his quarters. He sent to ask for immediate assistance.

> Cortes, concerned that Narvaez's followers would not will-ingly assist us in the relief of Alvarado's garrison, implored them to forget their hostility, and promised to make them rich and give them commands. He told them that since they had come in search of a livelihood and were in a country where they could serve God and His Majesty and enrich themselves, now was their chance. He was so persuasive, in fact, that all of them offered to come with us. Had they known the Mexicans' strength, not one of them would have volunteered. (Diaz)

Cortes reviewed his troops: he had 1,300 soldiers, 96 horses, 80 crossbow men, and as many musketeers. In addition there were 2,000 Tlaxcalan warriors. So they set out for Mexico. They arrived there on June 24, 1520, St. John's Day. Bernal Diaz tells us that Monteczuma came out to speak to Cortes, but Cortes refused to listen.

Fighting soon started in Mexico. The Spaniards who tried to get out of their quarters were attacked in the narrow streets and shot at with arrows from the roofs and had to pull back.

> If at times we gained a little ground or cleared part of a street, they would pretend to retreat in order to lure us into following them. Thus attacking at less risk, they believed they would pre-vent us from fighting back alive, for they did us most damage when we were retiring.
>
> Then, as for going out to burn their houses, I have already

described the drawbridges between them, which they now raised so that we could get across only through deep water. Then we could not stand up to the rocks and stones they hurled down from the roofs in such numbers that many of our men were hurt or wounded.

. . . At night too, they went on yelling and whistling in the same way and showering us with darts, stones, and arrows. . . .

At the break of dawn, we commended ourselves to God and sallied forth with our towers. The cannon, muskets, and cross-bows went ahead, and the horsemen charged. But, as I have said, it was no use. Although we killed many of them, we could not drive them back. Bravely though they fought on the two previous days, they were much more vigorous on this occasion and brought up even greater forces. However, we were deter-mined, even at the cost of our lives, to advance with our towers to the great temple of Huichilobos.

I will not describe the fighting in one fortified house, or talk about how they wounded our horses, which were useless to us. For although they charged the enemy bands, they received so many arrows, darts, and stones that, no matter how well-armored they were, they could not break the enemy's ranks. If they caught up with any Mexicans, these warriors would quickly jump into the canals or the lakes for safety, beside which they had raised new walls against the horsemen. There many other Indians were stationed with very long lances to fin-ish them off. Our horses were useless. . . .

The Spaniards decided to attack the great temple:

. . . So we made for the great temple. Suddenly more than four thousand warriors ascended it, to reinforce the bands already posted there with long lances and stones and darts. . . .

The towers were already destroyed, so we did not take them. But in the end we reached the top.

Here Cortes showed how brave a man he was! The battle was fierce and the fighting intense. . . . We set fire to their idols; a large part of the hall in which Huichilobos and Tezcatlipoca stood was burnt down. We received considerable help from the Tlaxcalans in all this. (Diaz)

From the top of the temple, the Indians launched a counteroffen-sive and tumbled the Spaniards down the steps of the great stairway. After losing fifty dead they resolved to withdraw.

The Spaniards are besieged in the palace of Axayacatl.

The situation became increasingly unfavorable to the Spaniards. Already Narvaez's men were hurling abuse at Cortes. He resolved to invite Monteczuma to speak to the assailants from the roof and call on them to halt their attacks. Under duress, Monteczuma appeared before his people and began to speak. A hail of stones and darts fell on the roof. Monteczuma was hit on the head, the arm, and the leg, and Bernal Diaz writes: "Then quite unexpectedly we were told that he was dead."

THE NIGHT OF SADNESS

On June 20, 1520, Cortes decided to leave Mexico.

> Our forces diminished every day, and the Mexicans increased in numbers. Many of our men had died, and the rest were wounded. Although we fought most valiantly, we could not drive back the many bands which attacked us by night and day, or force them to a standstill. First, we were short of powder, and then food and water. We had sent to ask them for a truce, but because of Monteczuma's death they would not leave us in peace. In fact we stared death in the face, and the bridges had been raised. Therefore, Cortes and all of us captains and soldiers decided to depart during the night, choosing the moment when their warriors were most careless. (Diaz)

A portable bridge was built to enable the artillery and horses to cross the canals. Sandoval and de Lugo would be in the van, with a hundred soldiers; Cortes in the center, with the bulk of the troops, the baggage, and the prisoners; and Pedro de Alvarado in the rear, with a hundred soldiers and almost all of Narvaez's men.

Before leaving, the horses were loaded with ingots from Monteczuma's treasure, and Cortes said everyone was free to carry whatever he wanted, although he advised them to keep light. Some, especially Narvaez's men, loaded themselves with treasure.

It was a dark night with some mist and drizzle. They set off before midnight. The bridge was put in place, and they crossed in the planned order. But the alarm was soon raised.

> Suddenly, many bands of warriors descended on us, and the whole lake filled with canoes and we could not defend ourselves, since many of our men had already crossed the bridge.

Meanwhile, a great crowd of Mexicans charged down on us to remove the bridge and kill and wound our men, who could not help one another. And since misfortune is cruel at such times, one disaster followed another. Because of the rain two of the horses slipped and fell in the lake. Just as we saw this, I and some others of Cortes's detachment struggled to the other side of the bridge, but we were attacked by so many warriors that, no matter how hard we fought, no further use could be made of it. The channel, or water-gap, was soon filled up with dead horses, Indians of both sexes, servants, bundles, and boxes. . . .

For although Cortes and the captains and soldiers who rode first hurried along the causeway and succeeded in reaching dry land and saving their lives, . . . I declare that if the horsemen had waited for the soldiers at each bridge, it would have been the end of us all: not one of us would have survived. Because as we passed along the causeway, charging the Mexican bands, the water was on one side of us and flat roofs on the other, and the lake was full of canoes. There was nothing we could do. In addition, all the muskets and crossbows were left behind at the bridge, and it was night. What more could we have attempted than we did, which was to charge and deal sword thrusts at those who tried to seize us, and push ahead till we were off the causeway?

Things would have been even worse had it been daytime. . . . It must be terrifying to merely read of the hosts of warriors who descended on us that night, and the canoes that attacked our soldiers. . . .

However, [Cortes himself, Cristóbal de Olid, Alonso de Avila, and Gonzalo de Sandoval] turned back, with the horsemen and those soldiers who had not been wounded. But they could not get far, for Pedro de Alvarado soon met them, badly wounded, on foot —since they had killed his sorrel mare—and with a spear in his hand. He brought with him four soldiers as badly wounded as himself and eight Tlaxcalans, blood pouring from their wounds. . . . Cortes asked where the others were and he was told that they were all dead. (Diaz)

At midnight the Spaniards and Tlaxcalans came out in closed ranks, the Spaniards going first and the Tlaxcalans following. The allies kept very close behind, as if they were crowding up against a wall. The sky was overcast and rain fell in the darkness all night. It was a gentle rain, more like a drizzle or a heavy dew.

For crossing the canals, the Spaniards carried portable wooden bridges. They set them in place, crossed over, and raised them again. They passed over the first three canals—the Tecpantzinco, the Tzapotlan, and the Atenchicalco—without being seen. But when they reached the fourth, the Mixcoatechiattitlan, they were discovered.

A woman who was drawing water at the bank of the canal raised the first alarm. She cried: "Mexicanos, come running! They are crossing the canal! Our enemies are escaping!"

When they heard this cry, the warriors leaped into boats and set out in pursuit. . . . These boats . . . were protected by the shields of the warriors. The boatmen paddled with all their strength. . . .

Other warriors set out on foot, . . . to cut off the retreat.

From both sides of the causeway the boats converged on the Spaniards, and the warriors released a storm of arrows at the fleeing army. The Spaniards also turned to shoot at the Aztecs with their crossbows and guns. The Spaniards and Tlaxcalans suffered many casualties, but many of the Aztec warriors were also killed or wounded.

When the Spaniards reached the Canal of the Toltecs, in Tlaltecayohuacan, they threw themselves headlong into the water, as if leaping from a cliff, . . . all came to the brink and plunged over it.

Soon the canal was choked with the bodies of men and horses; they filled the gap in the causeway with their drowned bodies. Those who followed crossed to the other side by walking on the corpses.

Then they marched on to Popotla.

At the break of dawn they entered the village. Their hearts were cheered by the brightening of the new day: . . . But suddenly they heard war cries, and the Aztecs swarmed through the streets and surrounded them. They had come to capture Tlaxcalans for their sacrifices. They also wanted to take revenge against the Spaniards.

The Aztecs pushed the army all the way to Tlacopan. . . .

As soon as daylight broke, the Aztecs cleared the dead Spaniards and Tlaxcalans from the canals and stripped them of their cloths. They loaded the bodies of the Tlaxcalans into canoes and took them out to where the rushes grow; they threw them among the rushes without burying them, without as much as giving them another glance.

8

They also threw out the corpses of the women killed in the retreat. The naked bodies of these women were the color of ripe corn, because they had painted themselves with yellow paint.

They laid out the corpses of the Spaniards apart from the others; they lined them up in rows in a separate place. Their [the Spaniard's] bodies were as white as the new buds of the cane stalk, as white as the buds of the maguey. . . .

Then they collected everything the Spaniards had abandoned in their panic. . . . all the weapons that had been left behind or fallen into the canal—the cannons, guns, swords, spears, bows and arrows. . . . They recovered the gold ingots, the gold disks, the tubes of gold dust, and the jade collars with their gold pendants. . . . (Portilla and Garibay)

The Spaniards managed to get out of the town but were still pursued. Of Narvaez's soldiers, says Bernal Diaz, "the majority fell at the bridge, weighed down with gold." Marina escaped. Almost everyone was wounded, and only twenty-three horses survived; the artillery was all lost. There remained a few crossbows for which fresh arrows were made. They decided to set off again in the pitch dark. The Tlaxcalans went in front as guides. In the middle went the wounded, the very ill on the croups of horses unfit for fighting. In front and on the flanks, the horsemen acted as protection. They went on until daylight. They halted in a village, where they drove off an attack with the loss of a few men and one horse. On July 7, 1520, the Spaniards fought the battle of Otumba with cold steel.

. . . we resumed our march early next morning, sending half the horsemen ahead. When we reached a plain about three miles farther on and were beginning to think we could march on in safety, we were informed by our scouts riding back from the land they had reconnoitered, that the fields were full of Mexican warriors who were lying in wait for us. Although we were alarmed by this news, we were not dismayed. Ready to meet them and fight them to the death, we halted for a short time, while orders were given to the cavalry to charge and return rapidly, aiming at the enemies' faces. . . .

I would like to describe the actions of Cortes, Cristóbal de Olid [and] Gonzalo de Sandoval . . . who rode from one part of the field to the other breaking the enemy's ranks, although they were themselves badly wounded, and to record Cortes's instructions to those of us who were in the thick of the enemy to aim our cuts and thrusts at distinguished chieftains, who wore great golden plumes and rich armor and devices. . . .

Here, by God's grace, Cortes and his accompanying captains came to where the commander-in-chief of the Mexicans marched with his banner displayed, in rich golden armor and high silver plumes. . . . Then, commending themselves to God, our horsemen charged, and, riding straight for the Mexican commander, Cortes made him drop his banner, while the other captains broke the large bands of Indians who followed him. Cortes's charge had not thrown the Mexicans down, but Juan de Salamanca, . . . dealt him a lance thrust and snatched his rich plume. . . . When the Mexican commander and a number of chiefs had been killed, it pleased the Lord that their attack should slacken. . . .

One of Narvaez's followers, a black man, was suffering from smallpox; and a severe epidemic spread among the Indians, who were unfamiliar with this disease. (Diaz)

When the Spaniards left Tenochtitlan, the Aztecs thought they had left for good and would never return. Hence, they repaired and decorated the temple of their god, sweeping it clean and throwing out all the dirt and wreckage. . . . They adorned the impersonators of the gods, . . . arraying them with necklaces and turquoise masks and dressing them in sacred clothing. This clothing was made of quetzal feathers. . . .

While the Spaniards were in Tlaxcala, a great plague broke out here in Tenochtitlan. It started to spread during the thirteenth month[3] and continued for seventy days, striking everywhere in the city and killing a large number of our people. Sores erupted on our faces, our breasts, our bellies; we were covered with agonizing sores from head to toe.

This illness was so dreadful that no one could walk or move. The sick were utterly helpless. Unable to move their limbs or even their heads, they could only lie on their beds like corpses. They could not lie face down or roll from side to side. When they moved their bodies, they screamed with pain.

A great many died from this plague, and many more of hunger. They could not get up to find food, and everyone else was too sick to care for them, so they starved to death in their beds.

3. The Nahuatl calendar was divided into eighteen months of twenty days.

Some people came down with a milder form of the disease. .
. . But they could not escape completely. They looked ravaged,
for wherever a sore broke out, it left an ugly pockmark in the
skin. And a few of the survivors were completely blinded. (Portilla and Garibay)

5

THE SIEGE AND FALL OF MEXICO

Ten months later, strengthened by fresh troops and after methodi-
cally preparing the ground and securing control of all the Aztec villages, Cortes once again attacked Mexico to reduce it once and for
all.

His trump card, apart from fresh troops, was the use of a flotilla
of brigantines. These were built in separate parts and carried on
men's backs before they were assembled and launched in the water
on the canals of Mexico. The siege and fall of Mexico were decided
as much on water as on land.

There were numerous Indian allies; they hoped both to use the
Spaniards to free themselves from the Aztec yoke and to take part in
the sack of the city.

On Whit Monday 1521, Cortes reviewed his troops in the great
square of Texcoco. There were 80 horsemen, 650 foot soldiers
armed with swords and lances, and 194 crossbow men. The fleet of
thirteen brigantines employed 300 men: for each brigantine there
were 12 oarsmen, 12 crossbow men, and a captain. Each brigantine
was also armed with boat guns. The rules for the campaign were
also announced:

First, there should be no ill treatment of the Indian allies; nothing
whatever must be taken from them.

Second, there must be no blasphemy, under heavy penalties.

Third, no soldier should leave the camp for any reason whatever.

Fourth, all soldiers should have the necessary equipment.

Fifth, there should be no gambling for horses or arms.

Sixth, everyone should sleep in complete armor and with his sandals on, in case of a surprise attack.

Forces of Cortes and his allies converged upon
Tenochtitlan from all directions.

The troops set off with their equipment and the parts for the fleet. The route was essentially the same as on the first expedition.

Monteczuma's successor, Cuitlahuac, had died of smallpox. The Aztecs were now ruled by Guatehemoc, who proved himself a redoubtable opponent.

Cortes divided his forces into three companies. He commanded the first; the other two were under the command of Pedro de Alvarado and Gonzalo de Sandoval.

The Aztecs had placed concealed stakes in the water, which greatly impeded the brigantines' movements. The Spaniards decided to advance along three routes toward the center of the city, gradually gaining control of the suburbs as they went.

> The Spaniards came back again. They . . . set up their head-quarters in Tlacopan and then divided their forces. . . .
>
> The first battle began outside Tlatelolco, either at the ash pits or at a place called the Point of the Alders. . . .
>
> At last a dozen ships came from Texcoco. . . .
>
> One of the canals . . . was so twisted and narrow that only two of the smaller ships were able to pass through it.
>
> The Spaniards now decided to attack. . . .
>
> As the ships approached the Zoquiapan quarter, the people were terrified at the sight. They put their children into the canoes and fled hastily across the lake. . . .
>
> Two of the brigantines, with cannons mounted in their bows, attacked a flotilla of our shielded canoes. The cannons were fired into the crowd of the flotilla, where the canoes were close together. Many of our warriors were killed outright; others drowned because they were too crippled by their wounds to swim away.
>
> . . . Those who were hit by the steel arrows were also doomed; they died instantly and sank to the bottom of the lake.
>
> Once the Aztecs discovered that the shots from the guns and cannons always flew in a straight line, they stopped running away in the line of fire. They ran to the right or left or in zigzags, not in front of the guns. . . .
>
> The brigantines approached and anchored nearby. They had been pursuing our war canoes in the open lake, but after almost running them down, they suddenly turned and sailed toward the causeway. As soon as the cannons were reloaded, the soldiers aimed and fired them at the new wall.
>
> The first shot cracked the wall in a dozen places, but it

remained standing. They fired again; this time it cracked from one end to the other and crumbled to the ground. . . .

The warriors all fled when they saw the wall collapsing. . . .

Then the Spaniards disembarked and filled in the canal. Working swiftly, they threw in the stones from the shattered wall, the roof beams and adobe bricks from the nearest houses— anything they could find—until the surface of the fill was level with the causeway. Then a squad of about ten horsemen crossed over it. They galloped to and fro, scouting both sides of the road. . . . Soon they were joined by another squad that rode up to support them. . . .

A group of Tlatelolcas . . . met the Spanish cavalry unexpectedly. The lead horseman stabbed one of the Tlatelolcas, but the wounded man was able to clutch the lance and cling to it. His friends ran to his aid and twisted [the lance] from the Spaniard's hands. They knocked the horseman down from his saddle, beat and kicked him as he lay on his back on the ground, and then cut off his head. . . .

Then the Spaniards brought up the largest cannon and set it on the sacrificial stone. Immediately, from the top of the pyramid, the priests of Huitzilopochtli began to beat their ritual drums. . . . But two of the Spanish soldiers climbed the stairway to the temple platform, killed the priests with their swords, and threw them headlong over the brink.

The great captains and warriors who had been fighting from their canoes now returned and landed. . . . As soon as they landed, they ran through the streets, hunting the enemy. . . .

Seeing that an attack was imminent, the Spaniards tightened their ranks and clutched the hilts of their swords. The next moment, all was noise and confusion. . . .

The battle was so fierce that both sides had to withdraw . . . the Spaniards retreated to their camp in Acachinanco, abandoning the cannon they had set up on the sacrificial stone. Later the warriors dragged this cannon to the edge and toppled it in the canal. (Portilla and Garibay)

At the beginning of the siege, Cortes was unwise enough to move too far forward with his men, while the Aztecs feigned a retreat. When the Spaniards entered a narrow causeway that was covered by water in some places, the Aztecs returned in force and pressed down on them. The retreat was disorganized; they were caught up in the mud. Cortes was wounded in the leg and was grabbed by several of the enemy, but he managed to free himself, thanks to the timely intervention of two of his soldiers. More than sixty Spaniards had been killed.

The Aztecs had established a cordon of warriors to cut off the roads that enabled the three companies of Spaniards to communicate, and they let Cortes believe that his two captains were dead. Cortes sent four horsemen, who managed to get through the opposing lines in order to confirm the news.

The two companies of Spanish forces under the command of Alvarado and Sandoval continued, in fact, to fight under their respective leaders. Cortes's emissaries, reports Bernal Diaz, after describing what happened, "did not care to tell us how many had been killed. They gave the number as about twenty-five. . . ."

In Alvarado's camp (where Bernal Diaz was), a brigantine had grounded on underwater obstacles. There was a hard-fought struggle between the Spaniards and the Aztecs to seize the ship. The Spaniards managed to win and withdrew, separated from the enemy by a deep, wide ditch. They could breathe. The captains discussed the events of a heavy day.

> . . . the dismal drum of Huitzilopochtli sounded again, accompanied by conchs, horns, and trumpetlike instruments. It was a horrifying sound, and when we looked at the tall temple from which the sound was coming, we saw our comrades who had been captured in Cortes's defeat being dragged up the steps to be sacrificed. When they were dragged to a small platform in front of the shrine where they kept their damnable idols, we saw them put plumes on their heads and make them dance in front of Huitzilopochtli with a sort of fan. After they had danced, the *papas* laid them down on their backs on some narrow stones of sacrifice and, cutting open their chests, drew out their palpitating hearts, which they offered to the idols before them. Then they kicked the bodies down the steps, and the Indian butchers waiting down below cut off their arms and legs and stripped their skin off their faces, which they afterward prepared like glove leather. . . . Then they ate their flesh with a sauce of peppers and tomatoes. They sacrificed all our men in this way, eating their legs and arms, offering their hearts and blood to their idols. . . .
>
> After his victory, Guatemoc did more. He sent the hands and feet of our soldiers, the skin of their faces, and the heads of the horses that had been killed, to all the towns of our allies and friends and their relations, with the message that since more

than half of us were dead and he intended to finish off the rest
soon, they had better break their alliance with us and come to
Mexico. Otherwise, if they did not desert us quickly, he would
come and destroy them. (Diaz)

As the siege dragged on, every day the Aztecs made their sacrifices in the principal temple of Tlatelolco. They beat the drum there
continuously, accompanied by trumpets, conchs and yelling. Every
night they lit big fires and sometimes, by the light of the flames, the
Spaniards could see some of their companions being dragged off to
be sacrificed.

Seeing that the Spaniards were bogged down and could not win,
most of the allies, the Tlaxcalans and Texcocans, deserted. In
Cortes's camp there remained some forty Indians, including the ruler
of Texcoco's brother. In Sandoval's camp, about fifty Indians
remained, while in Alvarado's camp, eighty Tlaxcalans remained.

> When we found ourselves abandoned by our allies, Cortes
> and Sandoval asked those who remained in their respective
> camps why the rest had gone. They responded that they had
> witnessed the Mexicans consulting their idols during the night,
> and the idols had promised that we and they would all be killed.
> Our allies had believed this to be true and had departed in fear.
> What made this prophecy seem more credible to them was the
> fact that many of us had indeed been killed and all the rest
> wounded, and that they themselves had lost more than twelve
> hundred men. (Diaz)

Despite the psychological blow of the departure of many of their
allies, the Spaniards continued to be optimistic and kept up the
siege. Thanks to the fact that they controlled the water, they retained
a certain advantage, while the artillery caused considerable losses
among the enemy.

> It was of great help to us, that our launches now had the
> courage to break the stakes placed in the lake to impale them.
> They did it by rowing with all their strength, and giving their
> spurt greater impetus by starting it some distance back, and get-
> ting the wind into their sails as well. So they became masters of
> the lake, and of a good many isolated groups of houses. . . .
> For their part, the enemy battalions kept attacking us relent-
> lessly; fired by their recent victory, they advanced on us, all but
> mingling with our own ranks, and sometimes they relayed each
> other to force us to face fresh new troops. . . .

Due to the protection offered by the brigantines, which no longer feared the stakes, we gradually moved forward into the city. We would fight so until the approach of dusk told us that it was time to retrace our tracks. . . . This had to be carried out in perfect order, because meanwhile, the Mexicans devoted all their attention to cutting off our retreat on the causeway and at difficult points. . . . The fact that these efforts had already won them one victory over us made them even more eager to try them again. . . . They had succeeded in breaking through our ranks in three places. . . . At the cost of having a large number of wounded ourselves, we managed to recover by killing a lot of their men and taking many prisoners. Moreover, we no longer had any allies whom we could instruct to clear the causeway. In this, our horsemen were of great help to us; two of their horses were injured during the fighting. We returned to our quarters covered with wounds; we treated our wounds with oil and covered them with cotton cloth. Our meals consisted of tortillas with pepper and a little green stuff and prickly pears. Once all that was done, we resumed watch. . . .

The Mexicans would beat their drums at the top of their temples every night. . . . The Mexicans would light a big fire and resume their yelling; this was when they would sacrifice our unfortunate comrades. These bloody ceremonies went on for ten days. (Diaz)

The warriors advanced to the sound of flutes. They shouted their war cries and beat their shields like drums. They pursued the Spaniards, harried and terrified them, and at last took fifteen of them prisoners. The rest of the Spaniards retreated to their ships and sailed out into the middle of the lake.

The prisoners were sacrificed in the place called the House of the Arsenal. Their captors quickly plundered them, seizing their weapons, their cotton armor and everything else, until they stood naked. Then they were sacrificed to the god, while their comrades on the lake watched them being put to death.

As soon as the sacrifices were finished, the Aztecs ranged the Spaniards' heads in rows on pikes. They also lined up their horses' heads. They placed the horses' heads at the bottom and the heads of the Spaniards above, and arranged them all so that the faces were toward the sun. However, they did not display any of the allies' heads. All told, fifty-three Spaniards and four horses were sacrificed there.

teçiquauhtitlã

The assault on Tenochtitlan. The Spaniards and their allies, Tlaxcalans,
fight their way down the causeway supported by boats on the lake.

It was during these sacrifices that Huitzilopochtli, speaking to our enemies, promised them victory and assured them that we would perish by their hand within eight days, on the condition that they keep up the pressure, regardless of the losses they incurred. . . .

The general wrote to us repeatedly telling us how to fight and what to do, recommending particularly that we keep a proper guard, always leaving half of our horsemen at Tacuba to protect the baggage and the Indian women who made our bread, and to be on the alert all the time in case the enemy break through our lines at night. . . . We had hard battles every day, but we continued to capture bridges and barricades and to control the channels; and the brigantines were of great assistance, since they could go wherever they wished on the lake and were not afraid of the stakes. The ones that Cortes had available in his camp gave chase to canoes carrying water and provisions for the city. . . .

Thirteen days had now passed since Cortes's defeat, and Don Carlos, the brother of Don Fernando, king of Texcoco, saw that we were recovering our strength. Realizing that the Mexicans had been wrong in saying that they would kill us all within ten days, which was promised them by their idols, he sent to advise the king—his brother—to send Cortes all the warriors he could get from Texcoco, and two days after this message, more than two thousand warriors arrived.

Cortes was delighted to see this reinforcement, and he spoke most flatteringly to them. At the same time, many Tlaxcalans returned with their captains. . . . Many Indians also came from Huexotzingo and a very few from Cholula.

When Cortes heard the news, he ordered all our allies to come to his camp . . . so that he could speak to them. . . . If he had ordered them to join us in destroying the Mexicans when we reached the city, it had been his intention, he said, to benefit them and send them home rich, and to give them vengeance on their enemies. Our purpose in capturing this great city was not merely to benefit him. (Diaz)

The siege continued. It rained every afternoon, and the Spaniards rejoiced when it started raining early since then the enemy troops fought with less ardor. On the Spanish side, where there were no reserves, the men were fighting every day and fatigue, accentuated by wounds of greater or lesser gravity, was intense.

Thanks to the water blockade, however, the city was no longer receiving any supplies, either of food or of drinking water, and was experiencing increasing difficulties. Famine was beginning to cause more deaths than the fighting. The siege was in its third month.

The Spaniards were moving forward systematically. The common objective of the three columns was the great square of Tlatelolco. Meanwhile, in a small square taken by assault, the Spaniards saw a number of posts from which were hanging the heads of several of their companions killed in recent fighting.

> After some days had passed and Cortes saw that they were not appealing for peace and had no intention of doing so, he consulted all our captains and decided that we must lay some ambushes. . . . We gathered about thirty horsemen and a hundred soldiers, the most active and pugnacious that Cortes could find, and he summoned a thousand Tlaxcalans from all three camps. We took up position in some large houses that had belonged to a Mexican lord. This we did early in the morning; then Cortes advanced along the streets and causeways with the rest of his horsemen, soldiers, crossbow men, and musketeers, fighting in the usual way and pretending to be filling in the bridge over a certain channel. The Mexican bands detailed for the task were already fighting him. . . . On seeing the enemy's great numbers, Cortes pretended to retreat, and ordered the allies to got off the causeway, so that the Mexicans would think that he was retiring. They came and followed him, at first slowly, but when they noticed him act as if he were really in flight, all the troops on the causeway came after him and attacked him. As soon as he knew that they had advanced just beyond the houses in which the ambush was placed, he ordered two shots to be fired close together, as a signal for us to emerge from our hiding place. The horsemen came out first, followed by all of us soldiers, and we fell on the enemy without resistance. Cortes then quickly faced his men about, and our allies, the Tlaxcalans, did great damage to the enemy. Thus, many of them were killed and wounded, and afterward they did not follow us when we retired. Another ambush was laid for them in Alvarado's camp, but it resulted in nothing. (Diaz)

They waited for three days. This time was, in fact, used by the Aztecs to mend bridges; make openings in the causeways; prepare arrows, javelins, and stones; and build barricades. Then, breaking the truce, the Aztecs launched a surprise attack. But the Spanish counterattack was immediate.

In fact, those inside the besieged city were exhausted. The fighting ceased, and for several days attempts were made to parley, but without much success. Then, by night, driven by hunger, a large number of Indians came out of their quarters and crossed over to the Spanish lines.

> The people suffered from hunger, and many starved to death. There was no fresh water to drink, only stagnant water and the brine of the lake, and many died of dysentery.
>
> The only food was lizards, swallows, corncobs, and the lake's salt grasses. The people also ate water lilies and colorin seeds and chewed on deerhides and pieces of leather. They . . . ate the bitterest weeds and even dirt.
>
> Nothing can compare with the horrors of that siege and the agonies of the starving. We were so weakened by hunger that, little by little, the enemy forced us to retreat. Little by little they pushed us against the wall. . . .
>
> At this same time the Spaniards set fire to the temple and burned it to the ground. The blaze and smoke leaped high into the air with a terrifying roar. The people wept when they saw their temple on fire; they wept and cried out, fearing the eventual plunder. . . .
>
> Guatemoc consulted with a group of his captains and then called in Opochtzin, a great captain. . . . They dressed him in the finery of the Quetzal-Owl, which had belonged to King Ahuitzol. Then Guatemoc said to him: "This regalia belonged to my father, the great warrior Ahuitzol. Terrify our enemies with it. Annihilate them with it. Let them behold it and tremble."
>
> . . . The Quetzal-Owl departed with the four captains, and the quetzal feathers seemed to open out, making him appear even greater and more fearful. When our enemies saw his advance, they trembled as if they thought a mountain was about to fall on them. They trembled with dread, as if they knew the finery could work magic. . . .
>
> At nightfall it began to rain, but it was more like heavy dew than rain. Suddenly, blazing like a great bonfire in the sky, the omen appeared. Like a whirlwind, it wheeled in enormous spirals showering sparks and red-hot coals, some great and some small. It also made loud noises, rumbling and hissing like a metal tube put on a fire. It circled the wall nearest the lake shore

The assault on Tenochtitlan. The Spaniards and their allies break into the city of Tenochtitlan.

and then . . . moved out into the middle of the lake, where it suddenly disappeared. . . . (Portilla and Garibay)

At this point, Cortes decided to cease hostilities and wait for a capitulation. But days went by and nothing happened. Sandoval was ordered to take the twelve operational brigantines and invade the area of the city in which Guatemoc was living. As a matter of fact, the palace and the adjacent dwellings could be approached only from the water.

Cortes instructed that the buildings on the lake be destroyed but that the people be spared, unless they attacked.

The Aztec monarch had prepared fifty pirogues for just this eventuality, and when he saw that he was being surrounded, he fled. The lake seemed to be full of canoes, and Sandoval ordered that they be followed. The king was recognized from his appearance and was taken prisoner. Cortes promised him his life would be safe but subsequently, at the insistence of the majority of his troops, had him tortured to get him to say where his treasure was hidden.

After ninety-three days, with the surrender of Guatemoc on August 13, 1521, the siege of Mexico came to an end. Bernal Diaz records: "All the shouting and other noises stopped." Throughout the whole siege, they had had to hear the drums and trumpets and kettledrums. Suddenly, after the capture of Guatemoc, "All we soldiers became as deaf as if all the bells in a belfry had been ringing and had then suddenly stopped."

> Guatemoc asked Cortes to allow all the remaining Mexican forces to go out to the neighboring towns, and they were promptly told to do so. For three whole days and nights they streamed out, and all three causeways were crowded with men, women, and children so thin, sallow, dirty, and stinking that it was pitiful to see them. Once the city was free of them, Cortes went out to inspect it. We found the houses full of corpses, and some poor Mexicans who could not move still in them. Their excretions were the sort of filth passed by thin swine that have been fed nothing but grass. The city looked as if it had been ploughed up. The roots of all edible greenery had been dug out, boiled, and eaten; they had even cooked the bark of some of the trees. There was no fresh water to be found; all of it was brackish. (Diaz)

The flight from the city began, and with it the war came to an end. The people cried: "We have suffered enough! Let us leave the city! Let us go live on weeds!" Some fled across the lake, others along the causeways, and even then there were many killings. The Spaniards were angry because our warriors still carried their shields and macanas. . . .

Those who owned canoes left during the day, but others, the majority, fled by night. In their haste, they almost crashed into each other as they paddled away from the city.

The Spanish soldiers were positioned on the roads to search the fleeing inhabitants. They were looking only for gold and ignored jade, turquoise, or quetzal feathers. The women carried their gold under their skirts, and the men carried it in their mouths or under their loincloths. Some women, aware of the fact that they would be searched if they looked prosperous, covered their faces with mud and dressed in rags. They put on rags for skirts and blouses; everything they wore was in tatters. . . .

A few men were separated from the others. They were the bravest and strongest warriors with manly hearts. The youths who carried them were also made to stand apart. The Spaniards branded them on the cheek or the lips with hot irons.

The day on which we laid down our shields and admitted defeat was the day 1-Serpent in the year 3-House. (Portilla and Garibay)

Cortes wished to throw a banquet to celebrate the victory. He got plenty of wine and pork. He invited all of his captains and a few soldiers from the three columns.

But when we came to the banquet there were not enough seats or tables for even a third of the invited guests. Consequently, there was much disorder. Indeed, so many discreditable things occurred that it would have been better if the banquet had never been held. . . . (Diaz)

This bizarre banquet marked the end of the siege of Mexico and the fall of the Aztec empire, defeated forever.

A few years after the fall of Mexico the following sad song about the conquest was collected:

> Our cries of grief rise up
> and our tears rain down,
> for Tlatelolco is lost.
> The Aztecs are fleeing across the lake;
> running away like women.
> My people, how can we save our homes?

The Aztecs are abandoning the city:
the city is in flames, and
darkness and destruction everywhere. . .
Weep, my people:
beware that with these disasters
we have lost the Mexican nation.

PART II

THE CONQUEST OF GUATEMALA & YUCATAN

1

THE CONQUEST OF GUATEMALA

The conquest of what is now Guatemala lasted only from 1523 to 1525. That of Yucatan took from 1526 to 1540. There was one last revolt in 1546.

In late 1523, on Cortes's orders, Pedro de Alvarado set out to subjugate Guatemala. Alvarado was accompanied by some three hundred Spaniards and a large number of Indians, mostly Tlaxcalans.

The population of Guatemala was made up of Quiches and Cakchiquels. The Spaniards gave the latter material assistance against the former, with whom they lived in perpetual conflict, only to discover too late that their allies wanted only to subdue them too. As in Mexico, the country was conquered by playing on its divisions.

The people of Guatemala were more skillful than the Aztecs in defending their cities, which were built on rocky positions accessible only by narrow defiles. The decisive event in the campaign was the taking of the Quiche capital, Uitlan. Allying with the Indians in the neighboring town of Guatemala, Alvarado seized the two paths leading to Uitlan and was able to set fire to the city. He then succeeded in taking the city of Atitlan near the lake of the same name. In 1524, he subjugated the Cakchiquels. The founding of the Spanish city of Guatemala in July 1524, seven months after the beginning of the campaign, marked the end of the first phase of the conquest. But Alvarado and his brothers' cruel methods provoked increased resistance. It took two years to put down the revolts precipitated by the terror that Alvarado unleashed. While he was on leave in Spain in 1527, Alvarado was granted the title of governor of Guatemala. Pedro de Alvarado, whom the Indians called "the Sun" (Tonatiuh), fought victoriously against the Quiches in 1524.

A sixteenth-century document known as the *Titulos de la case*

Uzquin Nehaib (Otzoya) tells in magical terms the story of the struggle that enabled Pedro de Alvarado to defeat Prince Tecum Uman:

> In 1524, the *adelantado*[1] Don Pedro de Alvarado arrived,
> having conquered Mexico and all the lands. He reached the vil-
> lage of Xetulul Hunbatz and conquered the land. . . .
>
> And King Chi Gumarcah sent great Captain Tecun-Tecum, a
> *cacique* who was a native of Quicab. And this captain brought
> with him many people from many villages, ten thousand Indians
> in all, all armed with bows and arrows, slings, lances, and other
> weapons. And before leaving his village, Captain Tecum showed
> his valor and determination in front of the *caciques,* and he grew
> wings with which he flew. . . . The captain flew like an eagle. . . .
>
> Then a man from the village of Ah Xepach, an Indian cap-
> tain, transformed into an eagle, went out with three thousand
> men to fight the Spaniards. In the middle of the night, the Indi-
> ans and the captain who had become an eagle went off to kill
> the *adelantado* Tonatiuh but were unable to because a pure
> white young woman was defending him. [The Indians] all
> wanted very much to go on, but as soon as they saw this young
> woman, they fell down on the ground and could not get up
> again; then many birds without feet came down and surrounded
> the young woman. The Indians wanted to kill the young
> woman, and the birds without feet defended her and picked
> their eyes out. The Indians were unable to kill the Tonatiuh or
> the young woman, so they returned home and sent another
> Indian captain, called Ixquin Nehaib, transformed into lightning
> . . . he went to the place where the Spaniards were . . . to kill the
> *adelantado.* When he arrived, he saw a pure white dove above
> the Spaniards, protecting them . . . then he was blinded, and he
> fell to the ground and could not get up again. This captain came
> down on the Spaniards three more times transformed into light-
> ning, and each time his eyes were blinded and he fell to the
> ground. And when this captain saw that he could not reach the
> Spaniards, he returned and informed the *caciques* of Chi
> Gumarcah, telling them that . . . the young woman, the birds
> without feet, and the dove were defending the Spaniards. Subse-
> quently there was a battle between the Indians and the
> Spaniards.

1. A prestigious military title given to those who pushed the frontiers of the empire
forward.

. . . The Spaniards began to fight with Captain Tecum's ten thousand Indians. And they kept missing each other; they would get half a league away from each other and then meet. They fought for three hours, and the Spaniards killed many Indians. How many they killed is unknown. No Spaniard died; all were Indians who had come with Captain Tecum, and blood flowed, the blood of the Indians killed by the Spaniards at Pachah.

Then Captain Tecum took flight; he had transformed himself into an eagle, covered with feathers: they sprouted from him; they were not artificial . . . and he was wearing three crowns, one of gold, one of pearls, and one of diamonds and emeralds. And Captain Tecum planned to kill the Tonatiuh, who was on horseback. In trying to strike the *adelantado,* [Captain Tecum] cut off the horse's head with his lance. His lance was not made of iron but of small mirrors, and magic enabled him to do this.

Seeing that he had killed the horse, not the *adelantado*, he again took flight to slay the *adelantado*. Then the *adelantado* waited for him with his lance and ran Captain Tecum through.[2]

Then two dogs with no hair came; they were naked; the dogs seized this Indian to tear him to pieces. And when the *adelantado* saw that the Indian was handsome and was wearing three crowns of gold, silver and diamonds, and emeralds and pearls, he came to defend him against the dogs and stared at him for a while. He was covered with quetzals and very beautiful feathers; thus this village was named Quetzaltenango, for this is where Captain Tecum died.

---

2. The *Mahabharata*, India's cosmic epic written *almost fifteen hundred years* before the Indian stories telling of the conquest, describes a similar battle:

When the two armies were quite exterminated, the rakhasa and Iravat, drunk with fighting, faced each other in single combat. When he saw the combat-drunk rakhasa running toward him, the powerful Iravat, furious, also ran to meet him. When the wicked rakhasa got near to him, he cut clean through his shining bow and his quiver with his sword. Seeing his bow broken, the rakhasa quickly took to the air, thus confusing the totally furious Iravat by his magical power. But the invincible Iravat, who knew every vulnerable point and could change form at will, also rose up in space and confused the rakhasa by his magical powers. He riddled all his limbs with cuts and thus the eminent rakhasa was cut to pieces by the arrows raining down on him. (*Mahabharata*, VI, 1–79)

*
*   *

   In the highlands of Guatemala, as in the Aztec world, the Indians
thought that the strangers were gods.

> *Their faces were strange,*
> *the lords thought them gods.*

The Annals of the Cakchiquels say:

> *At that time everything was good*
> *and yet they [our gods] were destroyed.*
> *. . . There were no sins committed*
> *. . . When they arrived here,*
> *they taught fear.*
> *So that their flower should live they blighted and destroyed*
> *ours. . . .*

and later:

> *. . . To castrate the sun.*
> *That is what the strangers came here to do. Their sons'*
> *sons remained*
> *among the people*
> *who are the butt of their bitterness.*

2

ALVARADO'S LETTERS TO CORTES

FIRST REPORT BY PEDRO DE ALVARADO
TO HERNAN CORTES

Written at Utlatan, April 11, 1524

I am writing to Your Excellency of Soncomisco to record all that
happened to me here and, partly, what subsequently awaited me.
After sending my messengers to this place to inform its inhabitants
of my coming to conquer and pacify the provinces that refused to
submit to His Majesty and acknowledge themselves his vassals, I
asked them to look after their land, saying that, in so doing, they
would present themselves as faithful and loyal vassals of His
Majesty, and as such they would be protected and treated justly by
me and my companions; and assured them that, I would wage war
on them as traitors, rebels, and felons to our lord the Emperor, if
they failed to do so. I added also that I would enslave all war prisoners. After dispatching my Indian messengers, I reviewed my troops,
both the foot soldiers and the horsemen.

Another day, on a Saturday morning, I set out to answer a call
from one of your provinces. I rode for three days through a deserted
forest, and as I set up camp, our sentinels captured three spies from
the village of Zaputalan in your lands. I asked them what they had
come here to do, and they said that they came for collecting honey,
where as it was quite obvious that they were spies. However, I did
not want to upset them; quite the contrary, I was nice to them and
gave them instructions and suggestions—as I had before—and sent
them to the lords of their village. But there was no reply. When I
entered their village, I found that all the major roads, both the main
one and those that crossed it, were unprotected, while the tracks that

led into the main roads were blocked. I realized at once that this was done intentionally, and that all had been organized for a fight. At this point, some of the Indians that I had sent told me to advance farther and to take possession of the village, so that they could fight us at their leisure.

I set up camp near the village that day, hidden in the countryside in order to learn their exact plans. A little later, in the evening, unable to conceal their evil designs, they killed and wounded some of my Indian soldiers. As soon as I heard about it, I sent horsemen to scour the fields; they met some armed men and fought them. A number of horses were wounded that night.

Another day, when I went to determine what road we could leave by, I saw so many armed people and a site so wooded with cacao trees and forests that it was all more to their advantage than ours, and I retreated to the camp.

The next day, I went to the village with all my men; on the way we came to a difficult river, where some Indians had taken up position. We fought them and beat them. I waited for the rest of my men, in a plain above a ravine that overlooked the river, because the passage was treacherous, and my men in the rear were carrying dangerous equipment—although I had relieved them of the bulk of the equipment. So I was there, as I say, when Indians attacked me from the forest, leaping out from all sides. We resisted for as long as it took to pass all our equipment. They went home; we fought them, and the fight continued half a league beyond the marketplace. Then we returned and set up camp in that very marketplace, where we stayed for two days scouring the countryside. After that, I went to another village called Quetzaltenango. . . .

On Monday, April 11, I set out for the town of Guatemala, where I intended to wait for a while because of the war at Atitlan, a village on the edge of the water. Four of my messengers were killed there. I believe that with the help of Our Lord I shall subject it to His Majesty very soon, since according to my information, I have much to do farther ahead. Therefore, I shall do everything possible to spend the winter a hundred leagues beyond Guatemala.

SECOND REPORT OF PEDRO DE ALVARADO TO HERNAN CORTES

Written at Santiago de Guatemala, July 28, 1524

I have already sent Your Excellency an account of events that happened to me both in matters of war and in many other areas, and I now want to describe to you the lands I went through and conquered and all that took place. Thus, Lord, I left the town of Utlatan and, two or three days later, I reached Guatemala, where I was received by the notables better than one could be in one's own parents' home. My companions and I were very well provided with every necessity.

After being in the town for a week, I learned from the notables that seven leagues from here, on a very big lagoon, there was a town that was fighting against Utlatan and other towns in the province for control of the waters and their boats.

At night, warriors from that town were making incursions into the lands of my hosts, so the latter, considering the harm they were suffering, told me that as loyal servants of His Majesty they neither wanted war nor to get into it without my permission, and therefore begged me to come to their aid. I replied that I would summon the aggressors in the name of Our Lord the Emperor and that if they responded to the call, I would order them to stop fighting and destroying the lands as they had been doing, and that if they did not, I would join with them to fight and punish them. I immediately sent two messengers to the natives of that town, who massacred them out of hand. When I learned the news and saw the ill intention in their action, I left the town with 60 horsemen and 150 foot soldiers as well as the lords and natives of Guatemala.

I rode so hard that I reached the town on that same day. And when no one came to welcome me as a sign of peace, I decided to advance to the land along the lagoon with thirty horsemen. As we approached some rocks where it was not possible to ride a horse, my companions and I dismounted and together, following the Indians, we entered the rocky area. . . . Meanwhile, my soldiers who had remained behind arrived, and we all reached the rocks together.

The population, which was quite large, began throwing themselves into the water to reach another island, and many of them escaped. We took prisoners, and I sent three of them as messengers to warn their lords that they must present themselves before me as the representative of His Majesty to bear witness to their obedience and submission to the imperial crown; and that if they did not, I would continue the war and drive them into the forest. They replied that never before had their land been violated or trodden by soldiers and that since I had done so, they would gladly put themselves at the service of Your Excellency as I had requested. They then came and placed themselves in my power. I informed them of the greatness and power of Our Lord the Emperor and that in honor of his royal name I pardoned the past deeds and hoped that they would be loyal in the future and make no war on anyone in the provinces, for now they were all vassals of His Majesty. I sent them back, leaving them in peace and security, and returned to Guatemala.

Three days after my arrival in this town, lords, dignitaries, and captains from the lagoon presented themselves to me with presents as evidence of their friendship and satisfaction at being vassals of His Majesty, for that enabled them to put an end to the divisions, wars, and differences that prevailed among them. I made them welcome, made them a present of my jewels, and sent them back home, affectionately, because they are the most peaceful creatures in this territory.

Lords from other provinces on the southern coast came to visit me in this town as a sign of submission to His Majesty, eager to be his vassals and express their desire not to fight with anyone. . . . It goes without saying that I welcomed them and confirmed that they would be protected and aided in the name of His Majesty.

They told me that the inhabitants of the town of which I have spoken were preventing the lords of Iscuintepec province and of other provinces from coming to make their submission to His Majesty as a sign of peace. They told them that it was madness and that it was preferable to let me pay a visit in person to their lands in order to fight them all together. After making certain that what they said was true, I set out with my soldiers, both horsemen and foot soldiers.

We spent three nights in deserted places. In the morning of the next day, as I approached the outskirts of the village of Iscuintepec, surrounded by thick forest, I found all the roads to be narrow, with no way through; they were in fact only paths that led to no open roads. I sent crossbow men ahead, since the horsemen would have been unable to fight because of the marshes. Moreover, it was raining so hard that their scouts and sentinels beat a retreat toward the village. Because they thought that we could not reach the village that day, they somewhat neglected their watch and realized we were there only when we appeared among them in the village.

As we entered, we found all the armed men in the water, enjoying themselves bathing. We did not give them time to re-form, although some were able to wound a few Spaniards and some of our Indian allies. They took refuge in the dense forest. Unable to reach them, we had no choice but to burn the village.

I immediately sent two messengers to ask them to come before me to submit to His Majesty and to say that I would ravage their lands and devastate their maize fields, if they refused. So they came to acknowledge themselves vassals of His Majesty and I welcomed them, calling on them to be loyal in future. I remained in the village for a week, during which people from many other villages and the countryside came to present themselves as vassals of Our Lord the Emperor as a sign of peace.

Because I wished to cross the lands and learn their secrets so that His Majesty would be better served and possess more territory, I decided to leave here and went to a village called Atiepar, where I was welcomed by the lords and natives. They spoke a different language and were different; at sunset, for no reason, the village was completely empty, and not a living soul was to be found there. But since I was afraid of getting caught by midwinter and being prevented from continuing my journey, I left things as they were and went on my way. . . .

Tacuilala inhabitants received me in the same way as those of Atiepar had: they welcomed me peacefully and went away after an hour. From there I came to a very large and populous village called Taxisco, where I was received as previously and where I slept that night.

The next day, I reached Nacendelan, another large village, and because I feared those people, whom I did not understand, I left ten horsemen behind and ten others with the people who were carrying the equipment, and continued on my way.

Two or three leagues from Taxisco I learned that armed men had left there and attacked the group bringing up the rear, where they caused many casualties among the Indian allies and stole a good part of my equipment: all the bow cord and the iron necessary for war. I immediately sent my brother, Jorge de Alvarado, with forty or fifty horsemen to secure what had not been taken. He met many armed men in the countryside, fought them, and routed them, but was unable to recover the stolen goods, because the Indians had already broken everything into pieces. Jorge de Alvarado returned to Nacendelan, but there he found that all the Indians had taken refuge in the woods. So he asked Don Pedro to go and smoke them out with foot soldiers in order to submit them to the service of His Majesty, but that proved to be impossible because of the denseness of the thickets. So he came back. I sent native Indian messengers to order them to come and to warn them that if they did not obey, I would enslave them. Despite my summons, they did not come, nor did the messengers. . . .

Since my aim was to cover the hundred leagues, I set out for the village of Acaxual, on the shores of the southern sea. Half a league from the village, I saw the fields filled with men armed both for defense and offense, wearing feathers and emblems, waiting for me in the middle of a plain. I went as close as an arrow shot of them, halted to await the rest of my forces, and, when we were regrouped, advanced to within half a bow shot, but they did not move. I saw that they were near a wood, where they could easily attack us. So I ordered my force, made up of 100 horsemen and 150 foot soldiers plus five or six thousand Indian allies, to move away. Our forces began to withdraw, and I remained behind to assist the withdrawal.

The Indians were so pleased to see us withdrawing that they followed us, even coming as close as the horses' tails, shooting darts that reached those in the van.

That happened in a plain where we could not trip over anything.

We went a quarter of a league away, and when I saw them within reach with no possibility of flight, I and my force performed an about-face to attack them.

We carried out such a massacre that in almost no time, none of them emerged alive, for they were armed in such a way that anyone who fell down could not get up again. Their three-inch-thick cotton corselets reached down to their feet and their arrows and lances were too long, so they killed themselves as they fell. I was hit by an arrow that went through my horse's saddle and entered my leg, a wound that left me lame, with one leg almost four inches shorter than the other. I and my companions remained in the village for five days to sort ourselves out, then we left for another village called Tacuxcalco. . . .

I came to this town because of its maritime situation, in order to build here, in the name of His Majesty, a Spanish town to be called Santiago, to facilitate the conquest and pacification of this territory, which is so large and has such a big population. This is the heart of this country, and no other place in it has greater or better advantages for conquest, pacification, and settlement.

3

THE CONQUEST OF YUCATAN

When the Spaniards began the conquest of Yucatan, the Maya empire had long since collapsed, and the Mayas were divided into small rival principalities.

In 1526, Cortes sent Francisco de Montejo to conquer Yucatan. The Mayas had no standing army, but they waged a long guerrilla war; unlike the Aztecs or the Incas, they could not be brought down with a single blow removing their leadership. Montejo's troops, 380 men, including 57 horsemen, were decimated, the jungle giving no advantage to mounted troops. It was only a quarter of a century later that, in a second attempt, Francisco de Montejo the younger succeeded in imposing Spanish rule. The revolt of 1546 was brutally put down. Only the Itzas were able to withdraw into the deserts of Peten, where they stayed outside Spanish control until 1697.

The Quiches and Cakchiquels of Guatemala looked on the new arrivals as gods. The Mayas of Yucatan described them as strangers (*dzules*). While it is highly likely that, faced with the suddenness of the attack—and defeat—the Quiches and Cakchiquels were brought down by mortal dread, the conquest of Yucatan was more difficult and took twelve years. Between 1517 and 1519, the Mayas of Yucatan had indeed already had the chance to see whites, on the occasion of shipwrecks. Finally, the fragmentation of the Maya principalities made a single decisive blow impossible.

We owe a very large part of what we know about the conquest of Yucatan and Maya society at the time to the Franciscan Diego de Landa. At the same time as he was compiling a unique inventory of Maya culture in his *Relación de las cosas de Yucatán*, Diego de Landa was the organizer of an auto-da-fé at Mani in July 1562 where, in addition to some five thousand idols, he had twenty-seven manuscripts that he was unable to read burned as "works of the devil." His superior, Bishop Toral, who arrived in Yucatan shortly after the events at Mani, ordered the prisoners incarcerated by Diego de Landa to be freed. He ordered Landa to return to Spain to be tried for his conduct before the Council of the Indies. The *Relación de las cosas de Yucatán* was written in Spain as part of his defense.

Just as the Mexicans had had omens of the coming of the Spaniards, says Diego de Landa in his *Relación de las cosas de Yucatán*, so the people of Yucatan experienced similar phenomena a few years before the arrival of Montejo.

In the district of Mani, in the province of Tutul-Xiv, an Indian named Ah-Cambal (the pupil), who had the job of spokesman (the person who transmits the idols' responses), publicly announced that they would soon be ruled by a foreign race who would preach a new god to them. One of the prophecies of the Chilam Balam of Chumayel puts it thus:

> *This is the face of Katun*
> *the 13 Ahau Katun*
> *the face of the sun will break*
> *it will fall in pieces on today's gods*
> *For five days the sun will be bitten, we shall all see it*
> *Here is the image of the 13 Ahau.*

But the Mayas did not take the strangers for gods. However, the arrival of the Spaniards was preceded by prophecies announcing the advent of strangers "with red beards."

In the course of the eleventh twenty-year period, the 11 Ahau Katun, "the sons of the sun, the fair-colored men" would arrive, say the books of the Chilam Balam of Chumayel and Tezimin.

> *. . . When they arrived, the red-bearded strangers*
> *the sons of the sun*
> *the fair-colored men.*
> *Alas, we weep that they came*
> *they came from the east*
> *to step in our land. . . .*
> *Alas, we weep that they came*
> *Woe unto Itza, the water sorcerer. Your gods shall be worth nothing.*
> *This true God who comes from the heavens will speak only of sin,*
> *his teaching will be only of sin.*
> *His soldiers will be inhuman,*

his wild dogs cruel.
. . . You shall suffer great pain
and great misery from the tribute imposed by violence
. . . That is what shall come, my children,
prepare yourselves for the burden of misery
Which is to come over your people. . .

The Chilam Balam of Mani puts it thus:

. . . The cross will be raised above the peoples
so that it would enlighten the earth.
Lord, there is no more peace.
There is no more envy.
For today the one bearing the sign has come.
Lord, his word shall penetrate the peoples of the earth
from the North, from the east shall come the master.
. . . Receive your guests, the bearded men,
the bearers of the sign of God.
Lord, good indeed is the word of God that comes to us.
. . . Through it there is no more fear on earth.
. . . Lord, the old wood is replaced by the new.

But the strangers are:

. . . big deer that slake themselves on their brothers.
. . . Their kings are false.
. . . Their throat is misshapen.
their eyes half-closed,
slack is the mouth of the king of their land.
. . . There is no truth in the words of the strangers.

The book of Chilam Balam of Chumayel also tells of the trauma of the conquest:

11 Ahau is the beginning of the count, because this was the Katun when the strangers arrived. They arrived from the east. Then Christianity also began. . . .

It was only because of the madness of our priests, the madness of the times that misery was introduced, and Christianity was introduced. Because the Christians came with their true God, and that was the beginning of our agony, the beginning of tribute, the beginning of church dues, the beginning of hidden contention, the beginning of strife with firearms, the beginning of injustice, the beginning of robbery with violence, the beginning of enslavement for debt, the beginning of endless debts,

the beginning of never-ending struggle, the beginning of suffering. . . . This was the origin of service to the Spaniards and
priests.

Diego de Landa records the cruelties of the Spaniards after the
revolt of the Indians in the provinces of Cochua and Chetumal. He
adds:

> [They committed on them] cruelties that were unheard-of,
> cutting off noses, arms, legs, and breasts of women throwing
> them into deep water with weights tied to their feet; stabbing lit-
> tle children for not walking as fast as their mothers, and, if those
> whom they drove along chained together around the neck, fell
> sick or did not move as fast as the others, they cut off their
> heads between the others, so as not to stop and untie them. . . .
> The Spaniards' excuse was that they were few in number,
> and they could not subjugate so many people without instilling
> terror in them by these terrible punishments.

The last revolt in Yucatan on any scale occurred in 1847. From
1712 to 1860 its history is studded with uprisings.

PART III

THE CONQUEST OF PERU

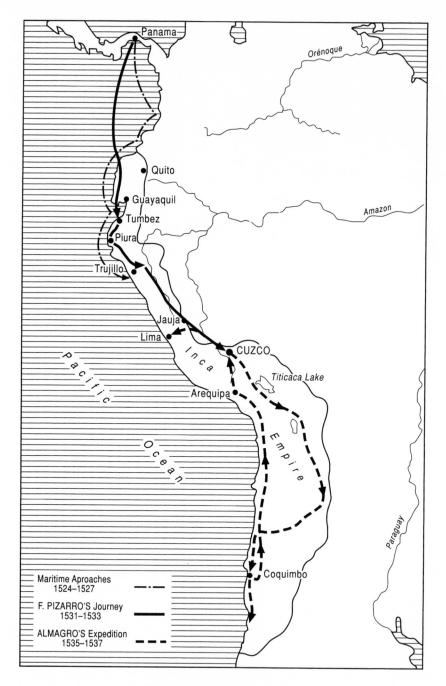

Map 6. *The conquest of Peru*

INTRODUCTION

The conquest of Peru, stretching over forty years, was like a pre-Shakespearean Elizabethan tragedy, with its exaggerated violence, its complicated intrigues, and its unspeakable crimes. Moreover, in the Andes everything unfolded in a tortured environment, with its harsh relief, over great distances and at high altitudes, in climates that were trying even for stolid peasants from the mountains of Estremadura, Castile, and Andalusia, habituated to very harsh living conditions.

Between the coast and the tropical forest, all along the eastern side of South America, the Andes are the backbone of the continent. They are massive, arid, and, as one moves north, form three cordilleras, the most easterly of which peters out in Venezuela. There are few trees, indeed virtually none at all on the altiplano. Divided up into small, cultivated valleys, the Andes are at once a barrier, a refuge, and a reservoir. Peru is a vertical country; Bolivia, a plateau stapled to the Andes with the depression of the freshwater lakes Titicaca (3,800 meters) and Poupo, which lie between the western and eastern Andes. Lake Titicaca is 250 meters deep in places, and its waters are 10–11°C all year round. It is crisscrossed by frail skiffs made from reeds, *totora*, plaited from aquatic fodder plants.

Among inhabited areas, few regions are at once as desolate and harsh as the Andes. At the latitude of Peru and Bolivia, a tropical mountain climate prevails in the Andes, with a dry season from May to September. Above 3,500 meters, it freezes almost every night, while daytime sees the temperature rise to above 40°C. From October to April is the wet season. It rains frequently, but with much smaller variations in temperature. The *puna*, high grassland steppe of a delicate green color, is very beautiful from December to March, a period of light rains reminiscent of the drizzle of Southeast Asia.

Walking in the Andes is a trying activity. Cuzco is 3,500 meters up; La Paz, 4,000; Potosi, 4,200. The mountains are extremely monotonous. But the route taken by Pizarro from Tumbez on the present-day border between Colombia and Ecuador to Cajamarca in the north of Peru between September and November 1532 is not the most difficult one.

We do not have the good fortune to have had in Peru a priest of the quality of Bernardino de Sahagun, who, like some premature ethnographer, collected the stories of the vanquished, nor a chronicler with the breadth of vision, the memory for significant details, and the intellectual probity of a Bernal Diaz. The Nahuatl and Maya sources throw light on the societies of Mexico; there is nothing like them in Peru, where the people had not yet taken even the first steps on the path to writing. On the Spanish side, there are the eyewitness accounts prepared by those who took part in the conquest: Francisco de Jerez, Pedro Pizarro, Miguel de Estete, Diego de Trujillo, Pedro Sancho de la Hoz, Juan Ruiz de Arce, Cristóbal de Mena, and Cristóbal de Molina. Subsequently, four remarkable historians who came shortly after the conquest left works of value: Cieza de León, Agustin de Zarate, Gonzalo Fernandez de Oviedo, and Martin de Murua.

On the Indian side, what we have is chiefly a literature written by mestizos recording the Indian view of things as it was felt or interpreted by the second generation: Guaman Poma de Ayala, Titu Cusi Yupanqui, and Garcilaso de La Vega.

The way I have put together the story of the conquest of Peru, given the sources, differs from what I did for Mexico. In places, especially when dealing with the important episode of the capture of Atahualpa at Cajamarca, I have given complementary versions as they were recorded by different chroniclers. In several places, therefore, the reader will have the feeling of seeing for a second time, as in a film, a sequence that has been slightly altered.

SUMMARY

In 1529, Francisco Pizarro obtained royal "capitulations" to undertake the discovery and conquest of Peru after two expeditions, the first of which was a failure. Thanks to his associates Luque and above all Almagro, he embarked on his third expedition in 1532. After several months of difficulties, he reached Cajamarca, in the north of Peru, with 168 men, 62 of whom were horsemen. At the time, the Inca empire was in the midst of a civil war between a faction led by Atahualpa, who reigned at Quito, and one led by Huascar, who ruled at Cuzco. In a stroke of extreme boldness, Pizarro seized Atahualpa, and to win his freedom, Atahualpa offered a considerable ransom. Meanwhile, Huascar was assassinated by supporters of Atahualpa, who in turn was executed by the Spaniards. The Spaniards were welcomed to Cuzco as liberators and installed Manco II on the Inca throne. Atahualpa's captains were all defeated. Almagro, who had not shared in the booty of Cajamarca, agreed to go and try his luck in Chile, but this proved to be a disastrous expedition. Meanwhile, Manco, humiliated, organized an uprising, laid siege to Cuzco, and seriously threatened Spanish rule when his troops got as far as Lima. But the Indian forces did not succeed in winning either at Cuzco or before Lima, despite a series of successes. On his return from Chile, Almagro seized Cuzco and imprisoned Francisco Pizarro's brothers. Before long supporters of Almagro and Pizarro clashed, and the latter emerged victorious. Almagro was executed. Manco organized a second rebellion, without attacking towns this time. He took refuge at Vilcabamba and waged a guerrilla war. Shortly afterward, in 1541, Almagro's son, with a handful of his supporters, assassinated Francisco Pizarro. The royal troops defeated Almagro's, and Almagro was executed in 1542. The Crown sent a new viceroy charged with implementing "new laws" inspired by Las Casas. These precipitated a revolt by the conquistadors, who found a defender of their privileges in Gonzalo Pizarro, who fought against the Crown. The viceroy was killed in 1546. The conflicts became particularly acute in Peru, especially those between the conquistadors and the Crown. But the Crown regained the upper hand in 1548, and Gonzalo Pizarro was executed. Meanwhile, Manco had been murdered in 1544. His son Sayri-Tupac went over to the Spaniards in 1555. Titu Cusi, the new Inca after the death of Sayri-Tupac, accepted baptism but managed to retain his prerogatives at Vilcabamba. He died in 1571. Toledo, the viceroy, decided to put an end to the enclave at Vilcabamba when the new Inca, Tupac Amaru, raised the standard of revolt again and began persecuting the Christians. In 1572, Tupac Amaru, the last of the Incas, was executed in the great square at Cuzco. Between 1532 and 1572, the Indian population fell by about one-third from its initial figure as a result of epidemics and the various consequences of the conquest.

PREFACE

In a letter written from Guayaquil on January 18, 1803, Alexander von Humboldt asserts: "At Lima, I learned nothing of Peru. People there deal with nothing that has to do with the general good of the kingdom. Peru is farther from Peru than London. . . ."

The Peruvian sociologist José Matos Mar wrote just a decade ago (P*eru Hoy. Desborde Popular y crisis del estado*, Lima, 1984):

> It is vital that two legacies be integrated, the Andean and the Hispanic, to allow the flowering of a unitary society and culture. The conquest marginalized the Andean heritage. That is a crucial problem which, since November 16, 1532 [the date of Cajamarca], has constituted the fundamental cause of a permanent crisis . . . there is persistent discrimination between those from the sierra and those from the coast, the Indian and the Creole, the rural and the urban. . . . One of the fundamental causes of the crisis of republican Peru is the absence of a nation, of identity. For not having been able to forge a synthesis between the Andean heritage and the colonial one, the historical debt from the nineteenth century has become the priority task of twenty-first-century Peru.

Indian revolts, always suppressed, litter the history of Peru, as they do that of Bolivia.

- In 1739, at Oruro (Bolivia), Juan Belez de Cordoba headed an armed movement to restore the Incas.
- In 1742, in the mountains of Jauja (Peru), Juan Santos Atahualpa led an uprising that lasted fourteen years.
- In 1750, Francisco Inca proclaimed himself a descendant of the Incas at Huarochiri (Peru).
- In 1780–1781, José Gabriel Tupac Amaru II led an uprising. He was executed at Cuzco.

- In 1781, Julian Apasa succeeded briefly in laying siege to La Paz (Bolivia).
- In the same year, La Paz was besieged a second time by Andrès Tupac Amaru.
- In 1867, Juan Bustamente proclaimed himself Inca.
- In 1915, Rumi Maqui claimed to restore the Inca empire in Peru.
- In 1923, Carlos Condorena, the leader of the Huancané insurrectionary movement, was executed, like all the earlier insurgent leaders. He had declared:

> We alone have the right to live on the land of our ancestors and to profit from the products of our *altiplano* and the mestizos have no right to continue to steal and exploit our labor. Our aim is to drive them off our lands and we must all together organize an army and reconquer our lands, kill the *principals* and the authorities and return to our old Inca way of life. (in Wilfrido Kapsoli, *Ayllus del Sol*, Lima, 1984)

In the Andean uplands, these millenarian revolts continued for a long time against the background of a tragic landscape. On the altiplano, there is not a single tree; in Peru, there are resinous shrubs and patches of grass between 3,000 and 4,000 meters where most of the people chew coca. Here and there are isolated small towns where an icy wind blows. Higher up, the *puna* becomes a zone of almost total desolation.

In 1953, in Bolivia, agrarian reform gave the Indians the land of which they had so long been deprived. After 1968, the Peruvian agrarian reform affected mainly the coast. Integration is slow. Something pathetic is conveyed by the landscape of these regions and those who live in them. It may seem incredible, but in La Paz, Bolivia has a Museum of the Lost Coastline. On entering, one sees a few, rather fuzzy, black-and-white photographs of Antofagusta and Arica, which were handed over to Chilean rule forever after the Pacific war of 1889. There are a few portraits of defeated generals. Disasters never come singly.

In 1935, defeat in the Chaco war enclosed Bolivia in on itself just a little bit more. In the museum at Potosi, not far from the sinister mines where one freezes at 4,500 meters, there is a long gallery of heads of state who for a century and a half have succeeded one another as one coup d'état followed another, like a farce played by the same people, without anything changing for the inhabitants. Some heads of state stayed in power only just long enough to proclaim that they had seized it.

It is hard to believe, but Lima has no museum devoted to the Indian past comparable to that of Mexico, but it does have a Museum of the Inquisition where instruments of torture are still on display. Lima was once the capital of the viceroyalty and twenty years ago was still a white city, but today the whites cling on, huddled together only in San Isidro, Miraflores, and Baranco. This time, the world of the Andes has come down to the coast. Lima has become the focus of the crisis of Peru.

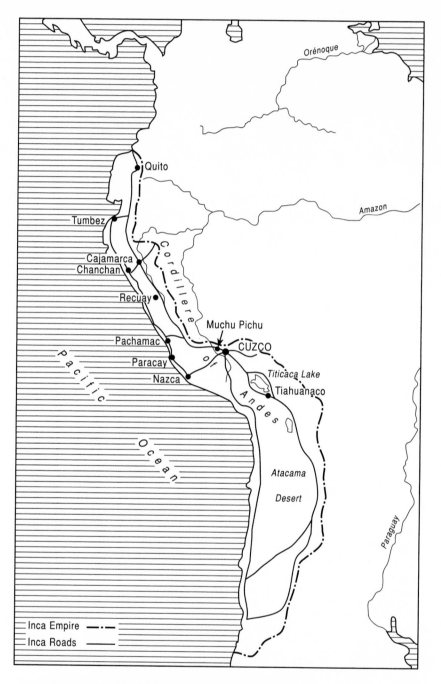

Map 7. The Inca empire and its roads c. 1525

1

CAJAMARCA

The Inca empire covered a million square kilometers spread out over five thousand kilometers along the Andean cordillera, from northern Chile to the border with Colombia. At the time when the Spaniards arrived, this empire, in its then territorial limits, was a recent creation. Its capital was Cuzco, which, as is typical of many cultures, was the center of the Inca world. Its four gates gave onto the cardinal points, and a system of communication that included relay stations enabled messengers to move very quickly despite the lack of ridable animals.

When Pizarro landed on the Ecuadoran coast on May 13, 1532, with just over two hundred men, he was fifty years old. For a conquistador—as for any man intending to embark on an armed expedition into the high Andes—that was the age of a veteran. And although physically very fit, Pizarro was a veteran and indeed had long been. He had served in 1513 under Balboa, the discoverer of the Pacific. He had already led two expeditions. The first—in 1524—was a failure; the second—two years later—was carried through successfully thanks to the pilot Bartolomeo Ruiz and the tenacity of Pizarro and a handful of Spaniards, and at least enabled him to reconnoiter the coast around the equator.

By 1529, Pizarro was in possession of capitulations authorizing him, as the overall leader, to pursue the "discovery, conquest and settlement of the province of Peru." This appointment displeased his associate, Diego de Almagro, and the rivalry between the two men subsequently worsened. By 1530, Pizarro was at Panama with his three brothers—Hernando, Gonzalo, and Juan—whom he had brought from Spain and was preparing the future expedition with Almagro. A third associate was a silent partner.

When the Spaniards landed, they were unaware of their good fortune that after the reign of Huayna Capac, his two sons, Huascar and Atahualpa, were fighting over the succession. Huascar, who held Cuzco, headed for Quito, where Atahualpa was reigning. After a series of battles, Huascar was captured by his brother's troops.

Atahualpa soon learned of the arrival of the white men: they were at Tumbez, a small coastal city. Did he, like Monteczuma, believe that they were gods returning, Viracocha returning? He sent observers and messengers. Five months later, he knew that the Spaniards were heading for Cajamarca, where he was.

Pizarro advanced toward the Inca. He had 167 men, 62 of them horsemen. Atahualpa sent a messenger; presents were exchanged.

On November 15, 1532, the Spaniards entered Cajamarca; the town was almost deserted. Not far away, the Inca's army was deployed, with perhaps thirty thousand men.

The next day, at midday, the sun was shining directly down on the square at Cajamarca, a small town in the north of Peru. One hundred sixty-eight Spaniards, far from their bases, set an ambush of probably unparalleled audacity: it was to attempt to seize the person of the Inca alive while he was surrounded by his troops. The attempt would be made only if success seemed possible or if the Indians seemed threatening. Perhaps Atahualpa could be persuaded to make some gesture of political or spiritual submission, or, if the Indians seemed too strong, perhaps the fiction of cordial relations could be kept up until a new occasion presented itself. However much the chroniclers may have exaggerated in their assessment of Inca Atahualpa's forces, there cannot have been fewer than fifteen thousand warriors camped not far from the town. It was known that when the Inca came, in the late afternoon, he would be surrounded by several hundred dignitaries and his guard. For the time being the Spaniards waited. The Spaniards had been waiting since morning in a state of rising excitement.

There were Pizarro, the leader of the expedition; the almoner, Father Vicente de Valverde; and the interpreter, a certain Felipillo, who spoke Quechua and passable Spanish. The Spaniards were all hidden. The musketeers had dug in their support stand; the crossbow men had stretched their bows and had their arrows ready to fly. The horsemen stood by their horses. Everyone waited anxiously. Early in the morning, a courier from Atahualpa had come to announce that his master was preparing to set out for the interview that had been requested of him. Later, a second one announced that the Indians would come unarmed.

The square at Cajamarca lent itself to the Spaniards' plan: on three sides there were low buildings with numerous doorways opening onto the square. Two of these buildings sheltered the horsemen and their horses, divided into three groups commanded by Hernando Pizarro, Hernando de Soto, and Sebastian de Benalcazar.

Pizarro occupied the third side with twenty foot soldiers. If conditions were right, his contingent would seize the Inca.

The fourth side of the great square was taken up with a mud-brick wall with, in the middle, a tower whose open base formed the entrance to the square. Finally, there was another tower where Pizarro had positioned the bulk of the foot soldiers and, under the command of Pedro de Candia, a Cretan, a dozen musketeers and four small artillery pieces. No one was to fire until ordered to do so by Pizarro. The salvo itself would be the signal for the horsemen to charge.

The cavalry was divided into three squadrons commanded respectively by Hernando Pizarro, the only one of Pizarro's four brothers who would survive the conquest (despite twenty years in prison in Spain); Soto, who would later explore Florida; and Benalcazar, who would go on to take Quito.

The hours went by and the tension rose. The Inca's army slowly got under way. Herrera records in his chronicle that Pizarro watched from the tower as the cortege, moving at a stately processional pace, approached the town. This march, with many halts, took several hours. Between a vanguard and a rearguard made up of a large number of soldiers could be seen the Inca's raised litter sumptuously decorated with feathers. The wait was becoming interminable, and nerves were raw. Pedro Pizarro, from Estremadura, who left an account of the conquest, reports: "I saw several Spaniards wet themselves with fright without even realizing they had done so." Less than a kilometer from the town, the Indians made a last halt. The route to the camp below them was full of warriors. Tents were set up, and it seemed that Atahualpa intended to spend the night near Cajamarca without actually entering the town. For the Spaniards this was the last thing they wanted to hear. Nothing would be worse than a night attack with such a disproportion of forces. The afternoon was ending. Pizarro sent a messenger to invite the Inca to come before nightfall. The Inca agreed. The procession of warriors resumed. It moved forward. The waiting was almost over. On the Spanish side there were 106 foot soldiers and 62 horsemen. Atahualpa had large forces and an elite corps of warriors. The ratio between the forces was at least one hundred to one. They waited.

THE ROAD TO CAJAMARCA

In Peru, as in Mexico, the arrival of the Spaniards was preceded by
bad omens. A thunderbolt struck the Inca's palace. A condor—the
messenger of the sun—pursued by several hawks fell into the great
square at Cuzco. It was sick and died. Or so the chroniclers later
reported.

But above all, what was most worrying was the fatal end of the
Inca world foretold by Viracocha: the empire would be destroyed in
the reign of the twelfth Inca. And the eleventh Inca was the father of
Atahualpa and his brother Huascar. Titu Cusi says:

> Atahualpa heard [the news] from Indians who lived on the
> bank of the Southern Sea. . . . they said that some people, quite
> different in habits and dress, who seemed to be *"viracochas,"*
> which is the name we used to give to the creator of all things . .
> . were coming with large animals that had silver feet . . . and
> also because they had *yllapas* (that was what we called thunder)
> we said that to describe the muskets which we thought were
> thunder coming from the heavens.

As in Mexico, the meeting and clash of two worlds took place in a
world charged with magic. Some of the omens may have been
invented or added after the event, the omen acting as an explanation
for the disaster, making it, in some sense, acceptable.

On several occasions, the chronicles written by the second post-
conquest generation of Indians—for example, Titu Cusi or Guaman
Poma de Ayala—refer to the arrival of the Spaniards as that of gods,
viracochas.

In a very fine book, Nathan Wachtel describes the following
episode:

> As they approached Cuzco, Pizarro's soldiers captured some
> Indian messengers. These had been sent by Chalcuchima, one
> of Atahualpa's generals to Quizquiz, another of Atahualpa's
> generals, and were carrying important news about the nature of
> the invaders. . . . Chalcuchima had sent them to inform
> Quizquiz that they [the Spaniards] were mortal. . . (Wachtel,
> *The Vision of the Vanquished*, Gallimard, 1971).

The conquistadors were not financed by the Spanish Crown. In
that sense, while they explored and fought for the greater glory of
their ruler, they were not simply State adventurers. They were acting

on their own account. Their spirit of enterprise, their personal initiative, their capacity for organization, and their tenacity were what enabled them to succeed or at least embark on this venture.

They invested their own money, they borrowed, and they absolutely had to succeed. In Panama, eight years earlier, three men—Francisco Pizarro, Diego de Almagro, and Canon Hernando de Luque—had come together and pooled their capital. The subsequent financing of the expedition was arranged by Luque through his connections, while the first two looked after the expedition. Pizarro, from Estremadura, not far from Trujillo, was the illegitimate son of a colonel in the armies of Gonsalvo de Cordoba. His childhood had been spent in the countryside. Diego came from Castile, from Almagro, a small town whose central square is rather unexpectedly German in style: under the Hapsburgs, nobles from Germany settled there; the Fuggers had a house there. Obscure as he was when he left his hometown, Diego is today Almagro's sole claim to glory.

In the conquest of the Andes, Panama played the role that Cuba played for Mexico. In 1513, almost twenty years before Cajamarca, it was from Panama that the expedition led by the great Vasco Nuñez de Balboa discovered the Pacific Ocean. Alone, holding his banner, he entered the water to take symbolic possession of it in the name of the king of Spain. Pizarro, who was thirty-five at that time, was one of his captains.

Pizarro's first expedition set out in November 1524. News of the conquest of Mexico, four years before, had greatly excited people. It was a very taxing experience. Pizarro landed at a place to which the Spaniards gave the name the Port of Famine. He lost twenty-seven of his eighty men. Almagro lost an eye. They failed completely and returned home. Undeterred, they attempted a second expedition despite financing problems. At the end of 1526, Pizarro again took to the sea with 160 men, a few horses, and two boats, one of them having the excellent Bartolomeo Ruiz as pilot. The expedition split up. Pizarro set up camp at the mouth of the San Juan River; Almagro returned to Panama to look for reinforcements; Ruiz headed south. Ruiz's ship crossed the equator for the first time on the Pacific side. And he soon came into contact with the Inca world. As he was coasting along, he came upon a vessel with twenty Indians on board. The boat was sumptuously equipped with precious objects that the Incas were going to trade.

Ruiz returned to alert Pizarro. They came back together to the island of Gallo, not far from the estuary of the Tumaco. There was nothing to eat. The climate was unhealthy. Only thirteen men out of eighty-five agreed to stay with Pizarro, thus ensuring that the expedition could continue; without them it would have been simply a second and no doubt final failure. Among those with him were the Cretan Pedro de Candia and Juan de la Torre, who later succumbed to madness in Peru. Five months went by. Bartolomeo Ruiz returned with his ship. After twenty days at sea they reached Tumbez in the Gulf of Guayaquil. This was the first Inca city that they encountered.

The first contact was friendly. Pedro de Candia, whose judgment Pizarro trusted, disembarked and confirmed what the first Spanish emissary, Alonso de Molina, who had been sent with presents, had said; yes, the city was prosperous and all appeared calm. During his visit, Candia created an impression by firing his musket.

In Tumbez, Pizarro asked the *cacique* to give him two boys so that they could be taught Spanish and act as interpreters. They were baptized at Panama and christened Felipillo and Martinello.

The Spaniards sailed farther south to make certain of the importance and wealth of the Indians they had just met. The discovery seemed to be an important one. They brought back vessels of gold, embroidered cloths and clothes, pottery, and llamas. But none of this seemed to interest the governor of Panama enough to make him help finance a follow-up expedition.

It was decided that Pizarro would go to Spain to secure the support of the king and the means to make a conquest. Pizarro was received in audience by Charles V at Toledo during the summer of 1528. His visit luckily coincided with one by Cortes, laden with presents for the Court. The two men met briefly.

The capitulation empowering Pizarro to discover and conquer Peru was executed. Pizarro was named governor and captain-general; Almagro, commander of Tumbez; Luque, protector of the Indians and bishop of Tumbez.

Before leaving, Pizarro returned to Trujillo in Estremadura, which he had left twenty-five years before. He needed reinforcements, men who were reliable. First, there were his brother and half-brothers, although he had never seen at least two of them. Francisco Pizarro was illegitimate; Hernando, the only legitimate son, was thirty; Juan, twenty; and Gonzalo, sixteen. There was also Martin de Alcantara, a half-brother on his mother's side. They got some more men together. These included Francisco de Orellana, who would explore the Amazon; Francisco de Carbajal, who would found Arequipa; and the

Dominican Vicente de Valverde, who would become the first bishop of Cuzco.

Pizarro left Seville in January 1530 with 125 men. At Panama, Diego de Almagro, who considered himself Pizarro's partner, was extremely discontented by what he got out of his associate's intercession with the king. He agreed to continue only because Pizarro promised him a fairer division.

In early January 1531, the third expedition sailed south. Pizarro and Almagro were both over fifty years old.

There followed nineteen months, some of them extremely difficult. Pizarro chose to make landfall on the coast just north of the equator, four hundred kilometers short of Tumbez. This meant grueling marches in a tropical climate and epidemics. They stayed awhile on the island of Puna in the Gulf of Guayaquil. There were clashes; the most serious one occurred when they were sailing between Puna and the continent and, according to the Spaniards, was ordered by Atahualpa. When the Spaniards reached Tumbez, the city was in ruins. There was no news of the Spaniards who had been left there. The Indians explained that the destruction was the result of a civil war.

Meanwhile, fresh troops had arrived: Sebastian de Benalcazar with thirty men from Nicaragua and Hernando de Soto, the future explorer of Florida, with forty. Pizarro left Tumbez in March 1532 and advanced slowly southward. On September 24, 1532, he left San Miguel. He set out accompanied only by those who were resolved to march with him.

Diego de Trujillo reports the beginning of the expedition:

> Those who had accompanied Francisco Pizarro in his first exploration of the coast refused to come, saying that it was a godforsaken land and that those who go with him would go to their death. So many of the ones who came with him from Spain remained behind.

They were suffering from hunger. Diego de Trujillo goes on:

> From there we came to Cancevi, a large village on the coast, which was also deserted. It had many earthenware pots and fishing nets. There were maize fields, and although the grain was hardly formed we ate it, since we were quite short of food. This country has no sweet water, and we suffered from thirst.
>
> Since we did not have a guide who could tell us where we could go and rest, the Governor sent Captain Escobar into the

mountains, to see if he could find an Indian. I went with him. We came to a dry, waterless gully, where we saw smoke; we stayed in that gully until dawn hoping to discover their huts. It rained so heavily at night that the gully was flooded, and one of our soldiers was drowned. The rest escaped by swimming. We found their huts, and there were three or four Indians there. They had slung their beds at the top of high trees, like storks' nests, and were chattering like cats and monkeys. We captured one Indian but had no way of understanding him, or he us. We brought him to the camp, and after two weeks he told us by signs of a populous country ahead, where there was food, and to find food was now all that we wanted.

A few weeks later:

We now had news of Coaque, a large village very rich in gold, silver, emeralds, and other colored stones. . . . It had a large population. That night, while the men were still asleep, the trumpet was sounded for an attack on the village. The attack took place and the *cacique* was captured and imprisoned for a long time. There were large quantities of white cotton cloth there, and the village had big temples with many idols and drums. There was plenty of maize and fruit to eat. . . .

They took eighteen thousand pesos of gold and some low-grade silver in this village. Then the Governor dispatched Bartolomeo Ruiz and Quintero to Nicaragua and Panama, with two ships, carrying the gold, with which he hoped to attract more men. He and his followers stayed at Coaque for about eight months, and during this time many died of sickness. . . .

Meanwhile, the Governor released the *cacique* of Coaque, who then revolted with all his people and burned the village around us, leaving only a single hut in which we all took refuge. We defended this and prevented them from setting it afire. The *cacique* then fled into the mountains with all his people. Taking along an Indian who knew their hiding place, the Governor went searching for them with a few men on foot, since the country was not fit for horses. But as they were crossing a river on rafts, their Indian guide jumped in and was drowned. So the Governor and his men came back, having achieved nothing. . . .

After the ships from Panama and Nicaragua arrived, we left Coaque, although most of our men were sick. We then made for the Cape of Pascio, but being unable to pass the point, cleared a road across the mountain to the village of Pasao and continued until we came to the Bay of Caraquez, suffering from a great lack of drinking water. Here all the sick were put on a ship and sent to Charapoto, a village in the province of Puerto Viejo. . . .

We stayed in the Puerto Viejo country for more than two months. There were maize and fish and a local fruit, the paw-paw.

The Spaniards left Puerto Viejo and came to a port called Marchan. They were suffering terribly from thirst.

From there we went to Santa Elena point. . . . We found that the inhabitants had taken their wives and children and all their animals on their rafts and would not come ashore. We were very hungry when we arrived, but we remedied that. Since the people had put to sea and the villages were deserted, the dogs howled in the night, and we went after them. We kept ourselves alive by eating those dogs; we would have been very badly off without them.

From there we went to the province of Odon in the Guamcavilcas, a land with plenty of food, and both the sick and the sound spent two weeks there recuperating. We then came to the straits of Huayna Capac, so-called because Huayna Capac crossed them to conquer the island of Puna. Tumbala, the ruler of the island, came out with many men and rafts and welcomed us with great feasts and rejoicing. Later we learned that the men steering the rafts intended to untie the cords when we were in the middle of the straits and drown us all. Only the raft carrying the Governor and the ruler of the island was to be left afloat. But the feasting was so excessive that the Governor said to Sebastian de Benalcazar: "All this seems suspicious to me." So he ordered the ruler and other chiefs of the island to stay with him on the mainland, and told us to cross by another way. And so our men got over safely, and the rafts came back to take the Governor and those who had stayed with him.

Pedro Pizarro, who was an eyewitness to the event, describes the landing:

The people of Tumbez . . . offered to carry some Spaniards and baggage on them. Their purpose was treason, as was later shown, for after we had left the island, the balsas carrying some troops and other things . . . put ashore on some small islands that [the Indians] knew. They made the Spaniards go ashore to

sleep, and when they believed them to be asleep, taking the balsas with them, they went away, and later returned with more
[Indian] troops and killed those [Spaniards] whom they had left
there... and the same thing would have happened to Francisco
Martin, Marquis Don Francisco Pizarro's brother, and to Alonso
de Mesa, a citizen of Cuzco, and to me, if it had not been for the
fact that Alonso de Mesa was sick with the *berrugas* and did
not want to get off the balsa . . . where Francisco Martin and I
got off, keeping very close to the shore so that not more than
seventy paces lay between us and the water. At midnight, while
we were sleeping, the Indians pulled up the stone tied with a
rope that served as an anchor. Thinking that Mesa was sleeping,
they intended to go away, leaving us there and killing Mesa
later. And, as I have said, the *berrugas* gave Mesa great pain
and he was awake, and when he saw what the Indians were
doing, he gave great shouts, which awakened Francisco Martin
and I, and when we realized the evil [the Indians] planned, we
bound the chief and the two other Indians, and so we were on
the lookout all night. And the next day we set out and arrived at
the coast of Tumbez, and the Indians, now that we were in the
surf, threw themselves into the water and dragged us into the
waves, which cast us upon the shore very wet and half drowned,
and the Indians, seeing that we were now on shore, pushed the
balsa off into the waves; they took it and went off with it, carrying with them everything that we were bringing with us. They
left us with only what we wore on our backs, and so they
robbed many who had put their belongings on the balsas,
believing that the Indians would carry them safely [to Tumbez].

Pizarro acted ruthlessly to instill fear in the province. He had the
cacique of Almotaje and thirteen lesser chiefs of Lachira strangled,
and then ordered that their bodies be burned. That was terrible for
the Indians, who believed in the survival of the body provided that it
was preserved whole. He thus deprived them of any hope of survival
after death.

Pizarro founded the city of San Miguel de Piura and left sixty
Spaniards there while he turned resolutely southward, on September
24, 1532. Six months had passed since they had left Tumbez, nineteen since they had left Panama.

They followed the coast until November 6. They entered the
foothills of the cordillera. The march to Cajamarca took fifty-two
days. The rearguard was under the command of Pizarro's brother

Hernando. The Spaniards numbered 168, including 67 horsemen; there were three musketeers, twenty crossbow men at most, and perhaps four cannons.

Pizarro's luck lay in the fact that he arrived just as the Inca empire was in the middle of a civil war over the succession.

Until the eleventh Inca, Huayna Capac, the empire had been governed by a single ruler. Huayna Capac waged a long war in southern Colombia, and it was during those campaigns that the Inca heard about the appearance of people who had come from the sea. He never saw them. He was struck down, along with a large section of his army, by a violent illness—no doubt smallpox—that killed him.

His son Huascar succeeded him in Cuzco, the capital. Another son, Atahualpa, took over the imperial army in Quito. He may have been appointed to the post by his brother, or it may be that, as the chronicle has it, Huayna Capac had divided the empire in two, one of his sons ruling at Cuzco, the other at Quito. Whatever the case, civil war between the two brothers broke out within a few years.

Initially, Huascar's forces won a few successes and neared Quito. But they were rapidly pushed back by the Inca generals who had been fighting for years on the northern marches of the empire: Chalcuchima, Quizquiz, and Rumañivi. Not far from Cuzco, Huascar's forces were routed and Huascar himself taken prisoner. Quizquiz, who conquered Cuzco, wiped out all the members of Huascar's family and anyone who could possibly pretend to the title of Inca. Meanwhile, Atahualpa was exterminating the people of the region of Cañaris as punishment for their chiefs' duplicity. Chalcuchima, the commander in chief of Atahualpa's forces, was at Jauja, in the central Andes, while Rumañivi, the third general, was at Quito, the northern capital. Meanwhile, Atahualpa was marching triumphantly southward. He had won. Cuzco was surrounded. Huascar was at his mercy. Those with royal blood and who might lay claim to the title of Inca were almost all dead, murdered. Atahualpa would soon be enjoying the fruits of his victory.

It was just then that the Spaniards appeared, not far from the place where Atahualpa was encamped. He was aware of the presence of the newcomers but had given priority to his dispute. When Pizarro and his men left San Miguel to march south, Atahualpa did not know whether Quizquiz had won the decisive battle before Cuzco or not. But he sent a messenger to make contact with the strangers.

The Inca noble arrived at Cajas when Soto, sent by Pizarro to reconnoiter, was there. He brought as presents dried and seasoned

 EL DOZENO INGA
TOPACVCIGVALPA
GVASCAR INGA.

acaboen Reyn ar
murio en anda

quisquis ynga   an tamarca   challcochimaynga
comingo areuy nay y muro-   guascar

Huascar, the Inca, held captive by his half-brother Atahualpa, is led away by Atahualpa's generals Quizquiz and Chalcuchima.

goose-meat and two pieces of stoneware in the form of castles. He stayed two or three days among the strangers, examining their horses, their armor and their weapons; he pulled a Spaniard's beard, and the Spaniard responded by striking him. The messenger invited Pizarro to go to Cajamarca to meet Atahualpa. Pizarro agreed and sent presents of a fine Holland shirt and two Venetian glass goblets.

Before they reached the Sierra at Cajamarca, the Spaniards had to climb passes 4,500 meters up. They suffered greatly from the change of altitude. They were almost certainly affected by the soroche, a headache that is a reaction to high altitudes. Nowhere did the Inca's forces oppose their advance. But they were closely watched by scouts.

Pedro Pizarro records:

> They could have attacked us there or at another pass before Cajamarca, because the roads were so bad. We could not use our horses on the paths, and away from the paths we could not move either the horses or the foot soldiers. . . . With the third part of his troops which he could have stationed in these passes, [Atahualpa] could have killed all the Spaniards who were going up [into the mountains] or at least the greater portion of them, and those who escaped would have turned in a rout and would have been slain upon the road.

It will never be known for certain why the Inca, who was generally not shy of striking heavily, did not take advantage of such favorable terrain. Did he perhaps half-believe that they were gods? Was he, despite his energy, in the grip of a mortal dread? If he had struck around November 10, 1532, Atahualpa would surely have gained a decade before another wave of Spaniards would come to try and lay his empire low.

The Spaniards reached a high plateau. This was the *puna*. The horses found it hard to adapt to the new temperature. They were covered in sweat, and the cold wind on the plateau caught them.

Two days later, an Inca delegation arrived. It wanted to know when the strangers would arrive so that they could be supplied; so at least they said.

Three days later, on the afternoon of November 15, the Spaniards made their entry into the square at Cajamarca. The town was half-deserted. They were alone, a few kilometers from the Inca whose recent victory had just made him master of the greatest empire that the Americas had yet seen.

Meanwhile, Atahualpa was at the baths with his troops.

What went on in the Inca council of war? Since the landing at Tumbez, all the Spaniards' movements had been watched. Perhaps the council swung between hostility and a curiosity mixed with fear. Perhaps it would have liked to take alive those who had "great rams" and arms with deadly lightning.

Francisco de Jerez records the expedition in detail:

> On September 24, 1532, the Governor left San Miguel in search of Atahualpa. On the first day of his journey, he and his men crossed the river on two rafts, the horses swimming. They spent the night at a village on the farther side, and in three days' march reached the fortress of a *cacique* in the valley of Piura, where they found a captain and some Spaniards, whom the Governor had sent to impose peace on the *cacique* and to prevent him from harassing the *cacique* of San Miguel. The Governor remained here for ten days collecting supplies for his march. On reviewing the Christians in his company, he counted 67 horsemen and 110 foot soldiers, including 3 gunners with guns and some crossbow men. At San Miguel, the Governor learned from his lieutenant that a few Christians remained behind; he proclaimed that any who wished to return and settle in the town should have enough Indians assigned to them to maintain them and the settlers already there. For himself, he intended to advance and conquer with those who stayed with him, whether many or few. Five horsemen and four foot soldiers turned back. Including them, the settlers at San Miguel amounted to forty-five, with ten or a dozen more who remained voluntarily unprovided for. . . .
>
> After making all necessary dispositions, he set out with his men and marched until midday, when he came to a great square surrounded by walls, belonging to a *cacique* called Pabor, where he and his men lodged. He learned that this chief was a great lord, although at present in decline, since Atahualpa's father, "old Cuzco" [Huayna Capac] had destroyed twenty of his villages, killing their inhabitants. . . .
>
> Here the Governor made inquiries about the local villages and chieftains and the road to Cajamarca. He was informed that the village of Cajas was two days' march away, where Atahualpa had placed a considerable garrison to wait for the Christians, should they come that way.
>
> On receiving this information, the Governor ordered Captain

Hernando de Soto to go quietly to Cajas with some foot and horsemen and negotiate honestly with Atahualpa's people if he found them there. He was [to be] careful not to provoke them, and if he could overcome their resistance, he was to bring them into His Majesty's service.

The captain departed immediately. . . .

During the eight days [they spent waiting for Soto to return], the Spaniards reequipped themselves and refreshed their horses for the coming journey of conquest.

Returning with his men, Soto gave the Governor an account of all his observations in the villages. The journey to Cajas had taken him two days and one night, pausing only for meals, and they had climbed high mountains. They had hoped to take Cajas by surprise. But although they had good guides, they would never have gotten there if they had not met some scouts from the place on the road. A few they had captured gave them information. Soto had then marshaled his men and followed the road until they came to Cajas, which lies in a small valley surrounded by mountains. At the entrance to the place they found a military building that seemed to have been used recently. The people were confused, but Soto reassured them, telling them that he had come on behalf of the Governor to receive them as vassals of the Emperor. Then a captain appeared who said that he was collecting tribute from these villages for Atahualpa. Soto asked him about the road to Cajamarca and whether Atahualpa intended to receive the Christians peacefully. . . .

Having established peaceful relations with the village, Soto went on to Nuanca-pampa, a large village a day's journey away. It had better buildings and a fortress of fine masonry built with three foot six or four foot square blocks, so closely joined that there seemed to be no mortar between them. There was a high platform of hewn stone, with two stone staircases and a building on either side. Through both this place and Cajas runs a small river that supplies them with water and is crossed by bridges with well-paved footways. They are joined by the wide road that crosses the entire country, from Cuzco to Quito, for more than three hundred leagues. Where it passes through the mountains, the road is smooth and well built, wide enough for six horsemen to ride abreast without touching. Alongside the road run channels of water drawn from a distance, where travelers can drink. At each stage there is a building where [travelers] may lodge. At the approach to this road from the village of Cajas, a tollhouse stands at the head of the bridge, where a guard was posted to receive porterage in kind from those entering or leaving. . . . No passenger was allowed to take goods into or out of the town by another road. Soto also found in both towns houses stocked with bread and footwear, salt, a food like meatballs, and other stores for Atahualpa's army. He reported that these towns were well ruled and the people lived in an orderly manner.

An Indian chief and some others came with Captain Soto bringing a present for the Governor. The chief said that his master Atahualpa had sent him from Cajamarca expressly to bring the present. It consisted of two drinking vessels carved in stone in the shape of fortresses and two loads of skinned and dried goose meat, which is powdered and burned as incense by the lords of that country. Atahualpa also sent a message saying that he wished to be the Governor's friend and was waiting to receive him peacefully at Cajamarca.

The Governor accepted this present and addressed the messenger politely, saying: "I am delighted to receive you as a messenger of Atahualpa. I have heard such good things about your lord that I long to meet him. I have been informed that he is making war against his enemies. I have, therefore, decided to visit him as a friend and brother and, with the Christians of my company, to aid him in his conquests."

The Governor had food given to the messenger and his companions and ordered that they be provided with all that they needed and be well lodged as ambassadors of so great a prince. Then, after they had rested, he sent for them again and told them that they could either return at once or rest for a day if they preferred. The ambassador said that he would carry the message back to his master immediately. The Governor then answered: "Tell the prince in my name what I have said. Say that I will come to see him quickly and will stop at no place on the way." He gave the messenger a shirt and other articles from Spain to take with him.

The Governor traveled for two days through densely populated valleys, spending the night in fortified houses walled with mud-brick. The village chiefs told him that "old Cuzco" [Huayna Capac] used these houses as lodgings when he travelled. The local population was friendly. A few days later he

crossed a tract of dry, sandy country to reach another well-popu-
lated valley through which ran a large and swift river, which was
in spate. He spent the night there and the next morning ordered
Hernando Pizarro and a few other swimers to cross [the river] to
the villages on the other bank and to convince the inhabitants to
allow the Spaniards' passage. Hernando Pizarro crossed without
opposition, and the people in the villages gave him a peaceful
reception, lodging him in a walled fortress. But despite this
friendly welcome, he found that most of the villagers were
armed and had left their houses, taking their clothes with them.
He therefore inquired about Atahualpa's intentions. Was he
preparing a peaceful or a warlike reception? No one was willing
to answer, for the fear of Atahualpa, until Hernando Pizarro took
one of the chiefs aside and tortured him. The man confessed that
Atahualpa was preparing for war and had divided his army into
three detachments, one of which was at the foot of the mountains, another at the summit, and the third at Cajamarca. He also
said that Atahualpa was waiting with great pride and that he had
heard him boast that every Christian would be killed.

The Captain sent this news to the Governor the next morning.
He ordered trees to be cut down on both banks, so that the men
and baggage could be brought across. Three boats were built,
and in the course of the day all the men crossed over, while the
horses swam. The Governor took a vigorous part in all this
work, and when the passage was complete, went to lodge at the
fortress where the Captain had stayed. He then sent for a
cacique, from whom he learned that Atahualpa was now at
Huamachuco on the other side of Cajamarca with a large army
of about fifty thousand men. Hearing this figure, the Governor
thought that the *cacique* must be mistaken and asked about their
method of calculation. He was told that they count from one to
ten, and from ten to one hundred, ten hundreds making a thousand, and five ten thousands making the number of Atahualpa's
man. The Governor's informant, who was the chief *cacique* of
that river, said that when Atahualpa entered the country, he had
hidden out of fear. Then, furious at not finding him in any of his
villages, Atahualpa had killed four thousand of his five thousand subjects and taken six hundred women and six hundred
boys to be divided among his warriors. He gave Cinto as the
name of the *cacique* of the village and fortress in which they
were standing, and said that he was with Atahualpa.

The Governor and his men rested here for four days. The day before his departure, he took aside an Indian from the province of San Miguel and asked him if he had the courage to go to Cajamarca as a spy and report back what was going on there. The Indian said: "I would not dare to go as a spy, but I will go as your messenger to talk with Atahualpa. I will then find out whether he has an army in the mountains." The Governor agreed. "And if there is an army in the mountains," he said, "as is reported here, send me warning by one of the Indians who will go with you. And when you speak with Atahualpa and his people, tell them how well [we] treat those *caciques* who are friendly to us. Say that we only make war on those who attack us."

The Indian departed with his message, and the Governor continued his journey across these valleys, arriving at a village with its walled and fortified house each evening. After three days he came to [a village] at the foot of the mountains, where he left the road he had been following on the right—since it continued up the valley to Chincha—and turned along the other road that goes straight to Cajamarca. . . .

Some Christians thought that the Governor should follow the Chincha road, since there were difficult mountains to be crossed on the other, and because before reaching Cajamarca they would meet Atahualpa's army, which might harm them. The Governor replied that ever since leaving the San Miguel River, Atahualpa has been aware that they were coming in search of him, and that if they did not follow that road the Indians would think they were afraid to come. . . .

At the foot of the mountains, they rested for a day making preparations for the ascent. After consulting experienced opinion, the Governor decided to leave the rear guard and baggage behind. Taking forty horsemen and sixty foot soldiers with him, he entrusted the rest to his brother Hernando, instructing him to follow at a regular pace until further orders. Having made these arrangements, the Governor began the ascent, the horsemen leading their horses. . . . For the road was so steep that in places it was cut in steps, and the only possible ascent was by following it. They had climbed this pass without meeting any opposition. . . .

The cold in the mountains is so sever that some of the horses, being used to the heat of the valleys, caught cold. The Governor continued on to sleep at another village, and sent a message to those in the rear that they could safely climb the pass. . . .

With his men still climbing the next morning, the Governor pressed on and stopped in a flat place at the top, near some streams, to wait for the rear guard. The Spaniards camped in the cotton tents they carried, kindling fires to protect themselves from the intense cold of the mountains. It is no colder on the tableland of Castile than on these heights, which are bare and covered with a grass like short *esparto*. There are a few stunted trees, and the water is so cold that it gives men a chill to drink it.

When the Governor had rested here for a while, the rear guard arrived. From the opposite direction Atahualpa' messengers came, bringing ten sheep. They paid their respects to the Governor and said that Atahualpa had sent these sheep for the Christians and wished to know on what day they would arrive at Cajamarca so that he could send them food on the road. The Governor welcomed them, saying that he was glad to see them since they were sent by his brother, Atahualpa, and that he would come as quickly as he could. After they had eaten and rested, he inquired about the state of the country and the war in which Atahualpa was engaged. One of them replied that Atahualpa had been in Cajamarca for five days waiting for the Governor, and that he had only a few men with him, because his army was fighting his brother "Cuzco" [Huascar]. The Governor asked him more particularly about the state of this war and how Atahualpa's campaign had begun. . . .

The Governor believed that everything had been said on Atahualpa's instructions to strike fear and terror into the Christians and to impress them with his skill and power. He therefore said to the messenger: "I can well believe that all you say is true. Atahualpa is a great lord, and I have heard that he is a fine soldier. But I must tell you that my lord the Emperor, king of Spain and all the Indies and the Mainland and ruler of the whole world, has many greater lords than Atahualpa among his servants. He and his captains have defeated mightier rulers than Atahualpa, his brother, and his father. The Emperor has sent me to these lands to bring the knowledge of God to the inhabitants and to make them obey Him. With these few Christians of my company I have overthrown greater lords than Atahualpa. If he wishes my friendship and receives me in peace, I will be his friend and help him in his conquests, and he will remain in his high estate, because I am crossing these lands to discover the other sea. But if he prefers war, I will fight him as I fought the *cacique* of the island of Santiago and the *cacique* of Tumbez, and all the others who have opposed me. . . ."

The messengers remained speechless and amazed for a while, unable to believe that so few Spaniards could have performed such great deeds. Then they said they would like to carry this answer to their master and tell him that the Christians would soon arrive, so that he might send them food on the road. The Governor then dismissed them. The next morning he resumed his march, still through the mountains, and slept that night in one of a group of villages that he found in a nearby valley. As soon as he reached it, the same messenger arrived whom Atahualpa had sent to Zaran on the Cajas road with the present of the fortress drinking vessels. The Governor expressed great pleasure at seeing him and asked him how Atahualpa was. He replied, "Well," and that Atahualpa had sent him with twelve sheep for the Christians. He spoke freely and, judging by his expression, seemed an intelligent man.

"But would I not be right to kill this man? He is one of Atahualpa's runners (as I have been told) and yet he speaks with you and eats at your table, while I, a chief, was neither allowed to speak to Atahualpa nor given any food, and only by argument was I able to prevent them from killing me."

Terrified at hearing the other Indian speak with such assurance, Atahualpa's messenger replied: "If there are no people in the town of Cajamarca, it is so that the houses will be empty for the Christians to lodge in. Atahualpa is in the field because that has been his custom since the beginning of the war, and if they did not allow this man to speak to him it was because he was fasting. On his fasting days, he goes into retirement and no one may speak to him. No one dared to tell him that this messenger had arrived. Had he known, he would have had him admitted and would have given him food."

The man used several other arguments to convince the Governor that Atahualpa's intentions were peaceful . . . [and] the Governor said that he accepted his explanations, since he had not lost confidence in his brother Atahualpa. He continued treating the man like before and scolded his own messenger for attacking him in his presence. But secretly he was convinced that his own messenger's story was entirely true, because he knew the deceitful ways of the Indians.

The next day the Governor departed, and slept on a treeless plain that night, expecting to reach Cajamarca at noon the next day, since they told him it was near. Here Atahualpa' messengers came with food for the Christians. And at dawn the next day the Governor set out with his men in battle order and marched to within a league of Cajamarca. Here he waited for the rear guard to arrive. . . .

When they reached the approaches, they saw [Atahualpa's] camp a league away on the lower slopes of a mountain. The Governor reached the town of Cajamarca on the evening of Friday, November 15, 1532. . . .

There is a large square in the middle of the town surrounded by mud-brick walls and lodging houses. Finding it deserted, the Governor halted here, and sent a messenger to Atahualpa announcing his arrival and asking the prince to come and see him and tell him where to lodge. He then sent his men to inspect the town and report if there was any stronger place to camp at. In the meantime, he ordered his troops to stay in the square and the horsemen to remain in the saddle, until he learned whether Atahualpa would come. Those who had inspected the town reported that there was no better position in it. . . .

Entirely walled, the square is larger than any in Spain and has two doorways leading into the city streets. The houses have a frontage of more than two hundred yards and are very well built. The mud-brick walls around them are twenty feet high. The walls and roof are thatched with straw and the walls have wooden cappings. . . . On the field side of the square there is a stone fort, which is connected with it by a stone staircase inside the walls.

Pizarro sent Soto and twenty horsemen to the baths with Martinello as interpreter to invite the Inca to visit him in the name of the king of Spain. Then he began to worry and thought to strengthen this embassy by sending Hernando with another twenty.

The Spaniards moved forward between the silent ranks of the Inca army. They crossed two rivers. Then, along with his interpreter, Soto made for the place where the Inca had his lodgings. He had the invitation interpreted by Martinello. The Inca listened, unmoving. He was an imposing figure, surrounded by his women and his dignitaries. Soto gave him a ring as a sign of peace and friendship. Her-

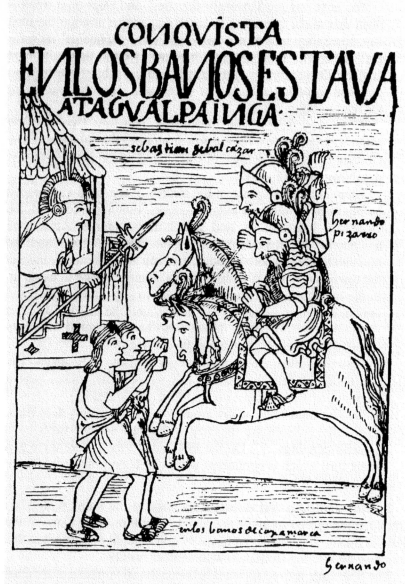

CONQVISTA
EVLOSBANOSESTAVA
ATAGVALPAINCA

sebastian sebal cazar

hernando pizarro

enlos banos de caxamarca

hernando

Hernando Pizarro and Hernando de Soto ride up to Atahualpa to deliver Francisco Pizarro's message. In reality, Atahualpa was sitting in front of his tent during this meeting and not in a litter as shown here by the artist.

nando soon arrived to join Soto, who introduced him as Pizarro's brother. Then Atahualpa spoke. He had received news of the arrival of the Spaniards from the captain of Poechos between Tumbez and San Miguel. "[He] has sent me a message to the effect that you have ill-treated the *caciques* of that province and put them in chains. He . . . tells me he has killed three Christians and a horse."

Hernando replied that the *cacique* was "a rogue. A single Christian would be enough to kill him and all his men. . . . He could kill no Christians, nor a horse either. His men are a lot of chickens. . . . When you see what help the Christians will give you against your enemies, you will know [he] has lied to you."

Atahualpa invited the Spaniards to dismount and dine with him. They declined. He offered them drinks. After some hesitation, they accepted. Two women brought them *chicha* (maize alcohol). The sun was setting, and Hernando begged permission to leave. The Inca wanted them to leave a Spaniard behind, but the two captains replied that that would be a breach of their instructions.

Juan Ruiz de Arce reports:

> He then asked us to dismount and eat. We replied that we had not dismounted even at our lodgings and were pledged not to do so untill we returned. He said that if we would not eat, we must at least drink. And we accepted. . . . The women entered, each carrying two gold cups . . . full of wine.
>
> He was seated on a low chair wearing a sleeveless shirt. . . . He had a cord tied around his head and a red fillet on his forehead. He did not spit on the floor; if he hawked or spat, a woman held out her hand for him to spint into. And any hairs that fell from his head onto his clothes were picked up by the women and eaten. The reason for these customs is known: the spitting was out of majesty; the hairs because he was afraid of being bewitched. He required them to eat his hairs to prevent them from being used in witchcraft.
>
> When we had finished our drink, we begged leave to go, and he asked one of us to remain with him. We replied that we dared not agree, for we did not have the Governor's permission, and if any of us were to stay behind, he would be very angry. Atahualpa gave us leave to go, saying that he would come to see the Governor the next day. He asked us to gallop a horse, before leaving, because he would very much like to see one run. So one of our companions started his mount two or three times. . . . When the horse charged, some thirty or forty Indians who were

near fled out of his way. Immediately after we left, Atahualpa ordered them to be executed, and their heads were cut off.

Pedro Pizarro records:

Atahualpa was at some baths that are more than a league from the town of Cajamarca where he [Atahualpa] had camped, and, according to what we learned, he had more than forty thousand Indian warriors. Then, this same day, the Marquis Don Francisco Pizarro sent Hernando de Soto with twenty horsemen to Atahualpa, [with orders to] tell him that he [Pizarro] had come on behalf of God and the King to preach to them and to have them as friends and to say other words of peace and friendship. . . . Then, having arrived at Atahualpa' place, . . . there was a great tank that they had built, made of hewn stone, and two pipes of water came to the tank, one hot and the other cold, and the one was tempered by the other whenever the Lord or his wives wished to bathe, and no other person dared to enter the water, under penalty of death. Then, having arrived, Hernando de Soto found him [Atahualpa], as I have said, with the troops ready for war. Atahualpa was in this small house, as I have said, seated on his duo [*duho*, seat]; a very fine, thin mantle through which one could see was held before him by two women, and they covered him up with it so that no one would see him, for it is the custom of some of these Lords not to be seen by their vassals except occasionally. When Soto had arrived upon his horse, . . . he [Atahualpa] ordered them to lower the mantle, and he listened to all that he had been ordered to say, which was conveyed to him by the interpreter Don Martinello . . . after having heard the message he replied and told Hernando de Soto to return and announce to the Marquis and the other Christians that in the morning he would go to the place where they were. . . .

Atahualpa ordered those Indians who... had been afraid to be put to death . . . in order to fill his troops with fear and so that none of them would take flight when the time came to fight with the Christians. . . .

Then, as I have said, the Spaniards spent the entire night on guard, with a fair measure of fear, for Soto and those who were with him related what they had seen and the great number of troops that the Indian [Atahualpa] had and because they had no knowledge of how these Indians fought or of their valor,

because up to that time they had not fought with Indian warriors, except in Tumbez and on la Puna, where they did not
number more than six hundred.

Atahualpa was waiting for the people whom he had heard about
and had had watched and spied on for several days already, and of
whose arrival he had learned long before. Now here they were
mounted on their animals, which made a dry, clicking noise when
they ran. They were tall animals, these animals ridden by men with
beards and strange clothes and strange weapons. What was their
strength? Where did they come from? What did they want? Could
they be of use in the war against Cuzco, or would they be dangerous?

Not for a moment could Atahualpa have thought that these
strangers were only a vanguard. Especially the animals. The animals
were fascinating, and the Inca must immediately have been taken by
the idea of owning them. How did they run? He would have wanted
to see how they worked: Who was in control, the animal or the
rider? He noticed how some of the warriors were terrified by the
proximity of the animal and its noise and movement and fell back;
they would be punished.

Atahualpa listened to the interpreter. He was being invited.
Atahualpa wanted to see the strangers on the ground, off their
horses. He wanted to be able to examine the Spaniards for an
evening, to keep one so as to get a proper measure of him. But these
strangers simply came and went. They were proud; they showed no
fear. The desire to see their leader was great. So too was the uncertainty. And, despite all the oracles and all the meetings and talking,
the enigma of the strangers remained total.

Pizarro's patience was infinite.

His first expedition had produced no results. He had made a second one, almost a disaster, in which Pizarro survived with a handful
of men while they waited for food and reinforcements. Time hangs
heavy in the tropics for those with nothing. Fortunately, the pilot
Bartolomeo Ruiz eventually came back. They explored farther
south. And then they returned to Panama with a little gold, some
Indians, and some llamas. There was something there to be taken,
and if anyone was going to take it, Pizarro had no doubt that it
should be he. He had been painfully searching for four years. He
was more than fifty years old. The fever had not gone away, but time
was passing.

So he had gone to Spain and dangled the fruits of exploration and
conquest. Mexico could be repeated. And better perhaps. Cortes had

succeeded. He had enriched the royal treasury. Pizarro wanted to do as much for the Crown. So he went the round of audiences and people of influence, distributing gold to those who counted or for their good works. He secured royal backing: he was now legitimate, he alone. And he would be governor—if at sword point he was able to conquer. There remained to settle the questions of power with Almagro, a partner but not an equal one in Pizarro's eyes.

And he had to ensure loyal helpers when he returned home to Trujillo: there would be the brothers and half-brothers he did not even know, and the sons of those he did know—strapping, devoted young men who would owe everything to him. They talked about what was to be had. Here, there was nothing; there, everything. They set off again from Seville. On the boat, they got to know one another, forged links. On his return, Pizarro landed with his three brothers and more than a hundred men of his own and his titles for the conquest to come.

In his absence, Almagro had pushed things forward, collected money, gotten men together. At one point the association seemed to be unraveling, faced with such inequity in what Pizarro had negotiated for them with the Crown, but it was restored. Open-ended promises on the future were signed on Pizarro's part; they would wait to see on the ground those given on Almagro's part. And anyway, why fight for something that nobody yet had?

January 1531: this time, it was the final departure with a minimum of means—30 horses and 180 men. They hoped for reinforcements.

There is no doubt that the conquest of Peru was physically more demanding than that of Mexico. Just surviving on the first part of the voyage was hard enough. Why did Pizarro land north of Tumbez, which he knew? Illness, hunger, and thirst decimated his men. Contacts with the Indians were more like raids: the first necessity was simply to survive.

Fortunately, Sebastian de Benalcazar arrived from Nicaragua with thirty men and a dozen horses. Then Hernando de Soto came with two ships, one from Nicaragua, the other from Panama: one hundred men and twenty-five horses. That was very few. But they would manage.

Meanwhile, Pizarro and his men had to fight at Puna, where the expedition remained for several months. Everything took time. They lived from day to day, their main concerns being to eat and to stay healthy.

Fourteen months passed before they met up again at Tumbez in April 1532, exactly where Pizarro had been on his previous voyage. In his absence, the civil war—with its inevitable consequences in terms of epidemics—had struck the town and the surrounding region. Two months later, they set out for San Miguel, 150 kilometers south of Tumbez. They founded a town there. More than fifty Spaniards in poor physical shape were left there; nine others soon came to join them when Pizarro let any who did not want to march toward the inevitable confrontation with the Incas free to leave without dishonor.

If we can trust the different figures given by the chroniclers, Pizarro had so far lost about seventy men. When he started out on the last stage, 167 fit men remained. Nothing happened in the week they took to climb up into the cordillera, although in more than one place an ambush would have been disastrous. Having reached Cajamarca and sent messengers to Atahualpa, examined the ground, and weighed the prospects, Pizarro opted for the swift blow, relying on the effects of surprise and fear to carry him through until he had captured the Inca.

During the previous night, the Spaniards had hardly slept; many had only dozed. They had had to be on the alert. They had had the most terrible thoughts. There they were, far from everywhere, so few men facing a multitude about whose fighting methods they did not even know. After all, these were the best Indian troops. They had been carrying all before them, defeating even the Indians of Cuzco. In the night the Spaniards could see the fires of the Indian army.

Cristóbal de Mena reports:

> There was no longer any difference between foot soldiers and horsemen. Everyone did guard duty that night. The good governor did so, too, passing from one point to another to encourage the men. That night we were all horsemen.

Francisco de Jerez reports:

> The Governor and Captain-general inspected the Spaniards' quarters, to make sure that they were ready to come out when necessary. The Governor urged them to make fortresses of their hearts since they had no other, and no other help except from God, who helps his servants in their greatest need. "Although there are five hundred Indians to every Christian," he said, "take courage, as good men would in such times, and trust that God will fight for you. Attack fiercely, but fight steadily and when

you charge be careful that your horses do not collide." Thus, the
Governor and Captain-general heartened the Christians.

The sun slowly set. Atahualpa's procession advanced. The bulk of
the troops were waiting on the plain. The procession entered with
five or six thousand men, say the chronicles. Doubtless the true figure was smaller. But the main point is that they were *unarmed*.

Atahualpa entered on a litter borne by his servants. When he
reached the center of the square, he ordered them to halt. Behind his
litter there were two more litters, carrying persons of importance.
Indians continued to pour into the square. Atahualpa was surprised
not to see any Spaniards. Later, he confided that he thought they
were hiding out of fear. He asked, "Where are they?"

At that moment, Brother Vicente de Valverde, accompanied by
the interpreter Martinello, came forward with a crucifix in one hand
and his breviary in the other. He came up to where the Inca was
seated.

The chroniclers give rather differing versions of the exchange that
followed. Some report that the priest first invited the Inca to talk and
dine with Pizarro, who was awaiting him inside the building.
Atahualpa declined. He said that he would not move until the
Spaniards had returned all the things they had stolen or taken since
they entered his dominions.

Was this a *casus belli*?

Valverde then explained that he was a priest, sent by the emperor
to reveal the true faith to Atahualpa and his people. The summation
that Father Valverde was instructed to deliver by order of the Crown
informed barbarian peoples in substance:

> God created heaven and earth and a man and a woman from
> whom we are all descended, although scattered all over the
> world out of necessity. God gave charge of all these people to
> Saint Peter, so that from Rome he would govern all nations,
> whether Christian, Moorish, Jewish, or pagan. And after him
> and forever this role was passed on to the popes.
>
> One of these pontiffs had assigned the islands and continent
> of the ocean to the Catholic kings of Castile. As a result of this
> assignment, His Majesty the king was master of these islands
> and lands.
>
> Therefore, the holy faith must be accepted without resistance
> and the Church acknowledged as mistress of the world and uni-
> verse and the Pope in her name and the king in her name as

king of the islands and lands by virtue of the assignment; what the priests preach to you must be listened to and obeyed.

Should you consent, His Majesty and I in his name will welcome you with love and affection and will leave you, your wives, and your children free and without servitude; should you not, you will have war and will be subjected to the yoke and obedience of the Church and His Majesty, and I shall take your women and your children and make cruel war on you and all those who do not obey.

I announce that the death and evils that shall come from that will be of your making and not His Majesty's, or ours, or those who have come with me.

The priest declared that revealed truth was to be found in the book he was holding in his hand.

Atahualpa asked him to give him the book so that he could look at it.

Father Valverde gave it to him closed. The Inca tried to open it, without success. The Dominican reached out his hand to help him. The Inca stopped him and wanted to open it himself. He succeeded. He looked at it. Then he threw it on the ground. Martinello bent down to pick up the breviary and gave it to the priest.

The critical moment had arrived. Vicente de Valverde stepped back uttering a few words. At that very moment, Pizarro gave the agreed signal. Pedro de Candia opened fire with two of his cannons. The Spanish horsemen charged to the cry of "Santiago!" while the trumpets sounded and the bells tied to the horses' legs tinkled, adding to the noise.

The Indians' surprise immediately turned to panic. The Spaniards ran through with their swords anyone within reach. The chronicle records: "They were so terrified that they climbed over one another to escape."

Diego de Trujillo reports:

> The next day, Atahualpa came to Cajamarca with all his people in good order. And he stayed long on the road until only an hour and a half of daylight remained. Six hundred Indians in white and colored livery . . . walked in front of him sweeping stones and other obstacles from his path. And the governor, seeing that it was getting late, sent Hernando de Aldena, who knew the language, to tell him to come before it got too late. And Aldena spoke to him, and he [Atahualpa] resumed his march.

There were ten entrances to the Cajamarca square. And at each entrance the governor posted eight or fewer men because of the shortage of men, and the horsemen were divided into three groups: one under Hernando Pizarro with his company, another under Hernando de Soto with his, and a third under Sebastian de Benalcazar with his . . . and the governor was stationed in the fort with 24 men on guard. There were 160 of us in all, 60 on horseback and the rest on foot. . . .

Seeing no Christians as he entered the square, Atahualpa asked: "Where are the men with beards?"

He was told: "They are hiding."

And then, Brother Vicente de Valverde appeared with the interpreter, and he told them why we had come: by mandate from the Pope and the leader of Christendom, the Emperor, our lord. And as he spoke the words of the Holy Gospel, Atahualpa said: "Who says that?"

And he [Valverde] responded: "God says it."

And Atahualpa asked: "How does God say it?"

And Brother Vicente said to him: "Look, it is written here."

And he showed him an open breviary, and Atahualpa asked for it and after looking at it, he threw it down, saying: "Nothing comes from this."

Brother Vicente returned to the governor . . . . Then the governor gave the order and took his sword and dagger and all 24 of us came out with him into the square and charged straight toward Atahualpa. . . . The horsemen came out with their bells. . . . And as the Indians fled . . . they made a breach in the wall. . . . And there, on the square, so many fell on top of one another that they were trampled, and of the eight thousand Indians who died, over half died in that way. We pursued the Indians for more than half a league that evening.

. . . And we put Atahualpa in the fort.

Pedro Pizarro reports:

When his squadrons were formed in such a way that they covered the fields, and when he himself had mounted into a litter, he began to march; two thousand Indians went before him sweeping the road by which he traveled, and these were followed by the warriors, who marched in the fields half on one side of him and half on the other side. . . .

Similarly, many Indians marched before Atahualpa singing

and dancing. This Lord required, to cover the half league between the baths where he was and [the city of] Cajamarca, [the time between] the hour of high mass, as I have said, and three hours before nightfall. When the [Indian] troops arrived at the entrance of the plaza, the squadrons began to enter it, and they occupied every part of the plaza. The Marquis Don Francisco Pizarro, observing how Atahualpa had now drawn near to the plaza, sent Padre Fray Vicente de Valverde, first bishop of Cuzco, . . . and Don Martinello, the interpreter, with orders to speak to Atahualpa and require in the name of God and of the King that he subject himself to the law of our Lord Jesus Christ and to the service of His Majesty. . . .

When they entered the plaza and saw no Spaniard there, he [Atahualpa] asked his captains where were these Christians who failed to appear, and they said to him: Lord, they are in hiding for fear. . . .

When the Padre arrived at the litter in which Atahualpa traveled, he spoke to him and told him the things he had come to say, and he preached to him about the matters pertaining to our holy faith, this being relayed [to the Inca] by the interpreter. The Padre carried in his hands a breviary from which he read what he preached. Atahualpa asked him for it, and he [Valverde], closing it, handed it to him [Atahualpa]. When he had it in his hands he did not know how to open it, and he threw it on the ground. . . .

[Pizarro] gave the signal to Candia, who began to fire, and at the same time sound the trumpets, and the cavalry came out in troop formation, and the Marquis with the infantry . . . and it all happened in such a way that, with the noise of the firing, and the blowing of the trumpets and the bells on the horses, the Indians were confused and cut to pieces. The Spaniards attacked them and began to slay them, and so great was the fear among the Indians, and so great was their anxiety to flee, that, unable to pass through the gateway [of the plaza], they broke down a portion of the wall around the plaza. . . . The cavalry pursued them as far as the baths, where they wrought great havoc among them, and would have wrought much more but for the coming of night.

Returning now to Don Francisco Pizarro, . . . the Marquis attacked the litter of Atahualpa [who would have been killed] had the Marquis not been there, because they were unable to pull him from the litter, and although they slew the Indians who bore it, others took their places at once and held it aloft, and in this manner they spent a great deal of time overcoming and killing Indians, and out of weariness, a Spaniard made as if to strike [Atahualpa] a blow with a knife in order to kill him, and the Marquis Don Francisco Pizarro prevented it, and by his prevention the Marquis received a wound in the hand from the Spaniard who wished to slay Atahualpa. Because of this, the Marquis cried out loudly: "Let no one wound the Indian on pain of death." Hearing these words, seven or eight Spaniards were spurred on, and they rushed upon the litter from one side, and, with great effort, they turned it over, and in this way Atahualpa was taken prisoner.

Francisco de Jerez reports:

As the first troops entered the square, they moved on and made way for others. When Atahualpa reached the middle, he made everyone stop and ordered that they keep holding up his and the others' litters. People were still coming into the square; an Indian captain in the leading group went up to the fort where the artillery was and raised a lance twice as if to give a signal. As soon as the governor saw this, he asked Brother Vicente to go with an interpreter and speak with Atahualpa; he agreed and went forward with a crucifix in one hand and a Bible in the other. He passed through the Indians and reached Atahualpa, and through his interpreter spoke: "I am a priest of God; I teach the Christians the matters of the Lord, and I have come to teach them to you as well; I teach what God has taught us and what is contained in this book. It is as such that I ask you, on behalf of God and the Christians, to be their friend, for that is what God wishes, and you will benefit thereby. Go and speak to the governor, who is waiting." Atahualpa asked to be given the book so that he could see, and it was given to him closed. When he could not open it, the priest reached out his hand to show him how to do it. Atahualpa disdainfully pushed his arm away, and managed to open it himself. He was not surprised to see the characters on the paper, as the other Indians were, and he threw it five or six paces away. . . .

Pizarro put on a cotton-lined breastplate at that moment; he took his sword and his shield and crossed through the middle of the Indians with the Spaniards that he had kept with him, and bravely, accompanied by the only four men who had been able to keep up with him, he reached Atahualpa's litter. . . . The sound of trumpets and the artillery being fired could be heard immediately: all the horsemen and foot soldiers emerged. As soon as the Indians saw the horses galloping, almost all left the square, fleeing with such haste that they broke down part of the town wall, and many fell on top of one another. The horsemen passed over them, killing and injuring them, and pursued them as they fled. The foot soldiers charged those who remained in the square so furiously that in no time most of them were put to the sword.

The governor was still holding Atahualpa by the arm, unable to drag him down from his litter because it was too high. The Spaniards killed enough bearers to overturn the litter, and if the governor had not protected Atahualpa, that barbarian would have paid the penalty for all the cruelties he had committed. In defending him, [the governor] was slightly wounded in the hand.

No Indian used his arms against the Spaniards, during all the action, so great was their fear at seeing Pizarro in their midst and the horses galloping and at suddenly hearing the cannons firing. These were new things for them, and they chose to flee rather than to fight.

Those carrying Atahualpa's litter seemed to be important figures; all were killed, as well as those in the litters. . . . The governor returned to his lodgings with his prisoner, bereft of his clothes, which were torn off him as the Spaniards tried to get him out of the litter.

It was amazing to see such a great and powerful prince taken prisoner in such a short time.

The mestizo Guaman Poma de Ayala writes:

Don Francisco Pizarro and Don Diego Almagro marched toward Cajamarca against the Inca Atahualpa with 160 soldiers against one hundred thousand Indians.

They entered Cajamarca and the Inca Atahualpa was not in the town; he was at the baths. Atahualpa sent his ambassador to the town . . . to tell the Spanish Christians to return to their own land. Don Francisco Pizarro and Don Diego Almagro responded that there was no reason to leave.

The Inca Atahualpa and the great lords and captains and the

The scene in the square of Cajamarca between the Spaniards and Atahualpa. The Peruvian artist, Guaman Poma de Ayala, accurate about the clothing, however, shows the Inca on a throne rather than in a litter and surrounded by armed warriors. European artists, also inaccurate, imagined the Inca almost naked and the city surrounded by crenellated walls.

other Indians . . . were amazed that the Spaniards did not sleep. They were believed to mount guard at night. They and their horses were believed to eat silver and gold, and they were said to wear silver sandals on their feet.

Day and night, [the Spaniards] all spoke with their papers, and they were all shrouded, and their faces were covered with wool, leaving only their eyes visible, and on their heads they wore red pots. . . . They all dressed alike and spoke of others as brothers and all ate at the same table. Only one of them seemed to have powers of command, and he had a dark face, white teeth, and flaming eyes. He often shouted at the others, and they obeyed his orders. . . .

Since Atahualpa was at the baths, Hernando Pizarro and Sebastian de Benalcazar went to visit him. They were in full armor, magnificently mounted on prancing horses, with jingling bells. With the pressure of their thighs, they made the horses to curvet in front of the Indians and then suddenly charged toward the imperial party.

The sound of bells and the hoofbeats produced the utmost shock. The Inca's bearers fled in terror at the sight of the huge animals and riders careering toward them, and the Inca fell to the ground from the litter in which he was sitting. . . . Everyone was terror-struck, and they all fled because such enormous animals were galloping, carrying men, [such as] they had never seen, and all were horrified. . . .

The Spaniards saw this as a good sign. . . .

Inca Atahualpa went from the baths to the town of Cajamarca, and he arrived in all his majesty, surrounded by all his captains . . . on the great square of Cajamarca, with his throne and his seat in the middle. . . . And then Don Francisco Pizarro and Don Diego de Almagro began to speak to him through the interpreter, the Indian Felipe. . . . They told him that they were messengers and ambassadors of a great ruler who desired friendship with the Indians and that this was the only purpose in their coming to Peru. He listened attentively to Don Francisco Pizarro and Don Diego de Almagro and Felipe the Indian. With great dignity the Inca replied that he had no reason to doubt the fact of the Spaniards' long journey or their mission from a great ruler. However, he had no need to make any pact of friendship with them because he too was a great ruler in his own country.

After this reply, Fray Vicente, a crucifix in one hand and his

breviary in the other, began his own [message]. And he said to
Inca Atahualpa that he too was an ambassador and the messenger of another ruler, a great friend of God, and that he must be
his friend and adore the cross and believe God's Gospel to the
exclusion of all others, for all else is mockery.

Atahualpa said that he would worship nobody but the sun,
who never died, and the gods who followed his law: that is what
he believed in. And the Inca asked Fray Vicente what authority
he had for his own belief. Fray Vicente said that the Gospel had
told him so, the Book.

Atahualpa said, "Give me this book, so that it can speak to
me." So it was given to him, and he took it in his hands; he
began leafing through the pages of the book. And the Inca,
speaking from his throne with great dignity, said: "It says nothing to me. The book does not speak to me," and he threw down
the book. . . .

Seeing this, Vicente began to cry: "At them, horsemen, at
these noble Indians who are against our faith!"

Thus, the horsemen began, and they fired their muskets . . .
and the noise of the bells and the weapons and what had never
before been seen on the Cajamarca square which was full of
Indians. The walls of the square of Cajamarca were pushed
down.

They killed one another as they pressed against one another
and the horses stumbled, and many Indians perished, so many
that they could not be counted. . . . Francisco Pizarro seized
Inca Atahualpa [and pulled him] from his throne. They dragged
him without injuring him, and he became a prisoner guarded by
the Spaniards with captain Don Francisco Pizarro. He was
deeply saddened, weeping, deprived of his majesty, seated in
the sun, without his throne and his kingdom.

The procession entered the plaza at Cajamarca. The square filled
up. There were three litters, one of which was Atahualpa's. Why was
the square empty? What sort of reception was that? Was it a trap?
How could anyone set a trap for the great Atahualpa at the head of
his troops? But already a man in a robe was coming forward with a
young Indian beside him. A silence fell on the square. From his litter
Atahualpa looked at the man across the square, who seemed to be
holding something in both hands. The man spoke. He spoke the
unknown language of the strangers. The young Indian translated.

How much of this speech was understood? It included talk of the creation of the world, the Pope, the Emperor, the need for him—Atahualpa—to submit or become a slave. Did Valverde have the time to say everything? Was he interrupted by Atahualpa's question about the claim for revealed religion, which came at the beginning?

Nothing in Atahualpa's attitude suggests submission or visible fear. He was not facing a tribunal deciding his fate. He asked for the book in which these things were written. He looked at the writing; he may even have listened to the book. There was nothing in this message, no intelligible sign.

He asked the strangers to return all that they had taken from his kingdom. He also refused to eat with the leader of the strangers, just as they had declined his offer the evening before.

Now that the Holy Book had been thrown on the ground—a gesture of contempt on the part of Atahualpa but a gesture of breach for the Spaniards—something had to be done. In any case, there was really not much left to say. The Inca worshipped his own gods, who had hitherto been kind to him. The Holy Book was on the ground. Father Valverde opened his mouth. But the Spaniards who were watching, among them Pizarro—who cannot fail to have been observing to gauge the situation—saw what the Inca had done. The Inca had just thrown the Holy Writ on the ground.

The prearranged signal was given by Pizarro. Pedro de Candia ignited his cannons; two balls went off, and the muskets were fired simultaneously. In the rush, two cannons failed to fire. The trumpets sounded and, amid tremendous noise, to the cry of *Santiago y a ellos*, the horsemen emerged with bells attached to the horses' legs.

In less than a minute, the silent square—where it had been possible to hear the words being exchanged—had become a battlefield filled with tumult.

In less than a minute, surprise had been transformed into panic. From the moment the firing started, the noise, the victims in the serried ranks, the pushing and shoving, the cries of fright, and then the horses all heightened the terror: the impact of the horses dominating the situation, the horsemen striking with their swords, the war cries, shock. From the beginning, there was surprise and fear, the shock of the unknown, the suddenness of the attack, the spread of panic.

And people's instinct was to flee, to escape the crush in the crowded square, to get away from the panic. No one could give any orders. No one could hear. The dead and the injured were already being trampled; people were being pushed up against one another, crushed to death, stifled. A compact mass of humanity was pushed against the mud-brick wall with such violence that it crumbled. Amid the cries of those with broken bones, people clambered over one another to get out. The panic of catastrophes makes its own victims. People were terror-stricken.

Followed by just a few men, Pizarro, wearing his cotton jacket, with his sword and his dagger, moved toward Atahualpa. The Inca was in the middle of the square, in his litter. The bearers had not moved. None of those surrounding him had fled. Pizarro wanted to capture the Inca stretched out on his litter. Around Atahualpa the panic was at its peak, but for Atahualpa the circle had closed up. In the midst of the pandemonium there remained this litter surrounded by a group of Spaniards killing the men protecting it or coming anywhere near it.

The other two litters had already been overturned, and the dignitaries closest to the ruler were dead. When the Spaniards killed one of the Inca's porters, another took his place. Then another. This free-for-all was a carnage. In his haste and impatience, a Spaniard tried to strike the Inca with his dagger. Pizarro parried the blow and was wounded in his hand for his pains. He wanted the Inca alive. A group of Spaniards began to push the litter violently from the same side, and it overturned. Atahualpa fell to the ground; he was seized and dragged to the buildings.

The carnage in the square continued, but most of the survivors had already fled. The horsemen pursued them along the road. The Indians had been totally routed. There was no counterattack. No one took charge of the remaining troops. There was no one to do so. On the contrary, panic reigned. The flight of the panic-stricken spread the panic to those who had as yet suffered no harm.

There was a whole valley full of fleeing men pursued by charging horsemen carried forward by their victory.

Soon it was evening. The Spaniards began to withdraw and return to the square. Hundreds of bodies lay there. There were many wounded. In the morning, Cajamarca had been a trap in which the hunter might become the victim; it had become a slaughterhouse. The Inca elite who had been with their ruler at Cajamarca never returned from the abattoir.

In one stroke, without even knowing it yet, the 168 Spaniards had brought down an empire. It was an empire divided by civil war, but the victor in that war they now had at their mercy.

Atahualpa was a prisoner. The Spaniards counted, but not one of them was missing. Not one was wounded, apart from Pizarro's gash.

Surely this was a sign that the grace of God had helped the Spaniards to triumph.

FROM CAJAMARCA TO CUZCO

The Inca was given clean clothes, his own being torn and dirty. Pizarro ordered that any women the Inca wanted among the captured women should be brought to serve him, and then he invited him to dine.

There were three or four more battles; then there were two rebellions, the first a very dangerous one. The empire had not entirely collapsed from a single blow. But it had been brought down. The capture of Atahualpa plunged the Quito faction into disarray. The Cuzco faction preferred the Spaniards to the fratricidal enemy. Such is often the case in civil wars. There is no hatred like the hatred between brothers.

Did Atahualpa want to seize the Spaniards, as he is alleged to have said? Probably so. He had not chosen to annihilate them while they were marching through the valleys on the way to Cajamarca. Perhaps he wanted both the men and the horses alive. But why then did he agree to go to Cajamarca? Why did he not make the strangers come to his own camp? Why did he go into the enemy's territory? Why did he go unarmed? Perhaps he thought that no one would dare attack his army. A surprise attack with no prior declaration or provocation was something outside Indian conceptions. Hostilities were declared; but these strangers so far had only had kind words. His emissaries had deemed the strangers easily conquerable. Was Atahualpa above all a victim of his underestimation of the opponent? Whatever the case, he was certainly a victim of his misunderstanding of the people he was dealing with.

Once he was a prisoner, but alive, Atahualpa's aim was to understand what the strangers wanted and were looking for: gold. He offered to buy his freedom with gold and silver. They could fill his cell so high. According to the chronicle, the room measured seven meters by six, and he promised to fill it halfway up with precious metal. This treasure would be collected within two months.

The Spaniards could not believe their ears. Such a quantity of gold was more than states possessed. The gold was to be gathered together through the good offices of the Inca. Once the fifth reserved for the king had been deducted, the rest would be divided up. The Spaniards began to dream dreams.

Pizarro promised to free Atahualpa in exchange for the quantity of precious metal offered by the Inca. On condition that he not engage in treason, he would be allowed to return to Quito where his father had reigned.

The delay itself was an advantage. So long as the Inca thought that by collecting the treasure he would gain his freedom, Pizarro could send for reinforcements from Panama, where the news of his prisoner and his treasure would cause a sensation. Meanwhile, the imprisoned Inca continued to be treated with respect by his own people. His status was divine.

Pedro Pizarro says:

> He was seated on a duo of wood. . . . The ladies brought his dinner and placed it before him. . . . He indicated that dish which stirred his appetite, and, taking it up, one of the ladies would hold it in her hand while he ate. One day while he was eating in this manner in my presence, while raising the food to his mouth, a drop fell upon his clothing. Leaning with his hand on the Indian woman, he raised himself and went into his room to put on other clothing, and . . . came back.

Another time, Pedro Pizarro saw in the Inca's apartments chests containing everything that he had touched with his hands and garments that he had rejected: everything that he had touched.

> I asked him: Why do you have all these things here? He replied that it was in order to burn them, for each year they burned all these things, because all that was touched by the Lords—who were sons of the Sun—had to be burned, and ashes thrown into the air, for no one must be allowed to touch it.

While he was a prisoner, the leading men of his kingdom came to visit him with every mark of respect. Pedro Pizarro adds: "When they arrived before him, they prostrated themselves, kissing [his] hands and feet. He received them without even so much as glancing at them."

While Atahualpa, a prisoner of the Spaniards but still ruler of his own people, continued to have the treasure collected, his brother Huascar, the defeated party in the civil war, was in the hands of troops loyal to Atahualpa. As for the Spaniards, they were masters of the situation, it is true, but they were vulnerable. They were far from their bases, with no prospect of immediate reinforcements, and were dependent on what Atahualpa's generals decided to do. To the south, there was Quizquiz, the victor of Cuzco, who had considerable forces (perhaps thirty thousand) and was occupying the conquered city. At Jauja, halfway between Cuzco and Cajamarca, there was Chalcuchima, also with large numbers of troops (perhaps thirty-five thousand). To the north, between Quito and Cajamarca, there was Rumañivi, who, unlike the other two generals, was not in hostile territory.

Anxious to eliminate a rival, Atahualpa ordered Huascar to be put to death. He was killed by the guard that was escorting him to Cajamarca. Before Pizarro, Atahualpa denied all responsibility. Pizarro agreed to believe him.

Few of the reigning faction in Cuzco were still alive. Almost all had been killed by Atahualpa's men after the city was taken. For the moment, Pizarro profited from this situation. The civil war was what had given him his chance. Pedro Pizarro argues:

> Had this Huayna Capac been alive when we Spaniards entered this land, it would have been impossible for us to win. .
> . . And similarly, had the land not been divided between Huascar and Atahualpa, we would not have been able to enter or win it unless we could collect one thousand Spaniards for the task, and at that time it was impossible to gather even five hundred Spaniards because of their scarcity and the evil reputation which the country had.

At the beginning of December 1532, the gold began to arrive, but not fast enough for the Spaniards. Atahualpa had dangled before their eyes the treasures of the temple of the sun at Cuzco and the temple of Pachacamac on the coast (south of Lima). He told the Spaniards to go there themselves to see it.

Pachacamac was an old temple that the Incas had preserved as it was, simply adding a building to house the priestesses. This temple delivered oracles. After making certain that no troops loyal to Atahualpa were threatening Cajamarca, Pizarro sent his brother Hernando with a force of several dozen men to Pachacamac. Miguel de Estete accompanied Hernando.

The expedition rode for fifteen days through the mountains before reaching the coastal strip and, shortly after, Pachacamac. But they were disappointed: they found nothing. But they spent a month looking for the treasure that must have been hidden there somewhere.

FROM CAJAMARCA TO JAUJA

Miguel de Estete records:

On Wednesday, January 5, 1533, the feast of Epiphany (or the Magi as it is commonly called), Captain Hernando Pizarro left Cajamarca with twenty horsemen and some harquebusiers, and slept that night in some huts five leagues from the town. The next day he dined at another village called Icocha, where he was welcomed and given everything he needed for himself and his men. . . . The next morning he reached this town, which is a large place lying in a valley surrounded by mountains with fine views and lodgings. Here too, the Captain and his men were well received by the ruler, whose name was Huaman-choro. Here they met a brother of Atahualpa, who was hurrying with a load of gold and told the Captain that Captain Chal-cuchima was twenty days' journey away and was bringing the full quantity that Atahualpa had sent for. . . . The Captain sent for further instructions from the Governor, saying that he would not advance any farther until he received [the gold.] He made further inquiries in the village as to whether the gold was really so far away, and on pressing certain chiefs, he learned that Chalcuchima was actually at the town of Andamarca seven leagues away and was coming with twenty thousand warriors to kill the Christians and free his master. The chief who made this admission said that he had dined with him on the day before. The Captain took one of the colleagues of this chief aside, who said the same thing.

Learning this news, the Captain decided to go and meet Chal-cuchima. Having prepared his men for battle, he started on the road. . . . All the Indians told the same story. Having kept strict watch that night, he continued on his way the next morning, with great caution; and before noon he reached the town of Andamarca, where he found neither Chalcuchima nor any more news of him than Atahualpa's brother had brought in the first place: that he was on his way with a lot of gold and had reached Jauja. At Andamarca, the Captain received the Governor's reply that since Chalcuchima and his gold were far away, he now had in his power the [priest] of the [temple] of Pachacamac and the large quantities of gold that this dignitary was sending. He was, therefore, to inquire about the road to Pachacamac and, if it seemed good to him, to go there, because the gold from Cuzco would arrive in due course.

The Captain inquired about the road and the number of stages to the [temple], and although both men and horses were ill shod and ill equipped for such a long journey, he decided that he would be serving His Majesty if he were to go for the gold and prevent the Indians from hiding it, and also inspect the land to see whether it was fit for Christian settlement. He was informed that the road was long with many difficult places and that there were many rivers to be crossed on woven bridges. But he decided to go, and he took with him a few chiefs who had been in that country.

The journey began on January 14, and on that first day he crossed some difficult passes and two rivers and slept at Totopamba village, which is on a steep slope. There the Indians welcomed him, providing him with plenty of food and all that he needed for the night, as well as porters to carry his baggage. He left the next day and spent the night at another village, called Coronga. . . . The village is subject to Huamachuco. He left the next day and spent the night in the small village of Pinga, which was deserted, since all the inhabitants had fled out of fear. . . . The next day at dinnertime, he reached a large village in a valley. Halfway along the road was a wide and very rapid river that was crossed by two woven bridges; . . . from one side of the river to the other they stretch cables of plaited reeds like willows, as thick as a man's thigh, secured with very large stones. These bridges are wide enough to take a small cart and are formed of tough cords closely woven between the cables. . . . One bridge is for the use of the common people and is kept by a porter who collects a toll; the other is for lords and captains. This is ordinarily kept closed. But it was opened for the Captain and his men, and the horses crossed it easily.

The Captain stayed in this village for two days, since both his men and horses were exhausted from the bad road. The villagers received them well and gave them food and all necessities. . . . On the third day the Captain left that place and dined in a small village, where they provided him with all necessities. Close by he crossed another woven bridge like the last and slept at another village two leagues farther on, where they came out to receive him and gave him food for both the Christians and the Indian porters. . . .

On the next day, the Captain started rather early, for he had been told that the stage was long, and he reached a large village called Suculacumbi, five leagues away. The lord of the village and the inhabitants came out to welcome the Spaniards and gave them enough food and necessities for that day; and at the hour of vespers they set out once more in order to reach the town where the [temple] was the next day. . . . The next day, Sunday, January 30, the Captain marched out and, passing through a number of villages and plantations, reached Pachacamac, where the [temple] stands. . . .

The lord and chief men of Pachacamac came out to welcome the Christians and showed great goodwill. The Captain and his men went to lodge in some large apartments that lie in one quarter of the town. On his return, he said that he had come at the governor's command for the gold of that [temple]. . . . The town chiefs and the servants of the idol gathered and promised to hand the gold over. But they continued to dissemble and delay. Finally they brought a little gold and said they had no more. The Captain then devised a trick. He said that he wanted to see their idol and asked them to lead him to it, which they did. The idol was in a nicely painted house, but in a dark chamber with a close, fetid smell. It was a very dirty, wooden object, which they said was their god who created and sustained them and assured their subsistence. At its feet lay an offering of golden jewels.

This god was held in such veneration that only his attendants and servants, whom they said he himself chose, were allowed to serve him. No one else was considered worthy to enter his house or touch its walls. . . . Before one of his ministers entered to serve him, it was said that he [the minister] must fast for some days and refrain from women. . . .

[This idol] compelled them to accept it as their god and convinced them that offending it or failure to worship it properly could destroy them, and that everything in the world was in its hands.

The people were shocked and alarmed by the mere fact that the Captain went in to see it, for they thought that when the Christians departed it would certainly destroy them all. The Christians explained that they were mistaken and that what spoke from inside this idol was the devil, who greatly deceived them. They admonished the Indians that from now on they should neither believe in him nor follow his counsel, and they said more on the subject of idolatry. The Captain ordered the vault in which the god stood to be pulled down and the god broken up in front of them. He then explained our holy Catholic faith and taught them the sign of the cross, which they must use to defend themselves against the devil. . . .

The lords of the neighboring districts came here to see the Captain, bringing produce of their lands and gold and silver as presents. They were astonished that he had dared to enter the sacred chamber and demolish the idol. . . .

. . . And other lords and chiefs of the surrounding country brought presents of gold and silver, which, added to the amount taken from the [temples], totaled ninety thousand pesos. The Captain spoke most courteously to all these chiefs and thanked them for coming. He commanded them in His Majesty's name always to behave in this way and dismissed them, well satisfied.

Captain Hernando Pizarro received news of Atahualpa's captain, Chalcuchima, while at Pachacamac. He was four days' journey away with the gold and silver and a large army, and was refusing to go any farther. He announced his intention of coming to fight the Christians. The Captain sent him a friendly message, urging him to bring the gold. . . . And . . . he designated a village on the way as a meeting place, where the party arriving first would wait for the other. . . .

Here Hernando Pizarro started on the broad road by which Chalcuchima would be coming. The distance across it is three stages. Here the Captain asked whether Chalcuchima had passed on his way to the agreed meeting place. The Indians all replied that he had and was carrying the entire gold with him. But, as afterward transpired, they had been instructed to give this answer to cause the Captain to march on. But in fact Chalcuchima was still at Jauja and had no intention of coming. Knowing that these Indians seldom spoke the truth, the Captain decided, despite all hardships and dangers, to march as far as the royal road by which Atahualpa's captain would pass, in order to find out whether he had indeed done so and, if not, to go and meet him wherever he was, in order not only to get the gold but to disperse his army, either by winning him over to peace or by attacking and capturing him, if he refused to obey.

The Captain and his men set out for a large village called Pombo, which lies on the royal road. On Monday, March 9, he slept at Cyus, a village in the mountains, whose chief welcomed

the Christians and gave them all that they needed for the night. .
. . The next morning, on Wednesday, the Captain and his men
reached Pombo, where they were welcomed by the local chieftains and some of Atahualpa's captains, who were there with
their troops. Here the Captain found about thirty hundredweight
of gold sent by Chalcuchima, who remained with his army at
Jauja. When the Captain had taken up his quarters, he asked
Atahualpa's captains why Chalcuchima had sent the gold but not
come himself as he had promised. They responded that it was
because he was afraid of the Christians, but also because he was
waiting for more gold that was on its way from Cuzco, and he
dared not come with so little. Captain Hernando Pizarro sent a
messenger from the village to Chalcuchima, telling him in a
friendly way that since he had not come to meet Hernando
Pizarro, Hernando Pizarro would go to meet him, and that he
need not fear. The Captain stayed at Pombo for a day, to rest the
horses in case they might have to fight.

On Saturday, the fifteenth [of March], the Captain left Xacal-
malca and, after marching three leagues, came to a house, where
he was welcomed with a good meal. He marched on to spend the
night at Tarma three leagues away. . . . The chief of this place
received him well and gave him both food and men to carry his
baggage. On Sunday, the Captain left this place early because
the next stage was rather long. Since he suspected that, having
sent no messenger, Chalcuchima intended treachery, he set out
with his men in battle order. At the hour of vespers . . . he
learned that Chalcuchima was not at Jauja, which added to his
suspicions. Being only a league from the town, he resumed his
march soon after the meal and arrived within sight of Jauja,
where he saw from a hill several groups of men who might have
been soldiers or townsfolk. On arriving in the main square, he
discovered that they were townsfolk assembled for a festival.

Immediately on his arrival and before dismounting, the Captain asked for Chalcuchima, and was told that he had gone to
another village and would be back the next day. He had absented
himself on the excuse of some business. . . .

Traveling in the Captain's company was a son of "old Cuzco"
[Huayna Capac] who, when told that Chalcuchima had gone
away, offered to go after him. He departed in a litter. All that
night the horses were kept saddled and bridled, and the chiefs of
the town were instructed to let no Indians on the square, since

the horses were angry and would kill them. The next day "old Cuzco's" son returned, bringing Chalcuchima with him, both in litters and with a large escort. On entering the square, Chalcuchima got down, left his soldiers, and went with a few companions to Hernando Pizarro's lodgings, to see him and present his excuses for breaking his promise and not having come out to welcome him. He pleaded that this was unavoidable since he had heavy duties. The Captain asked him precisely why he had not come to met him as promised, and Chalcuchima answered that his master Atahualpa had sent him orders to stay where he was. The Captain told him that he was not annoyed with him, but that he must now return with him to the Governor, who held his master Atahualpa prisoner and would not release him until he handed over the gold Atahualpa had sent for, for he knew that he had much gold. If Chalcuchima would hand over all of it, then he and the Captain would travel together, and he would be well treated. Chalcuchima responded that his master had sent him orders to stay where he was, and that unless these orders were countermanded, he dared not go, because this was newly conquered country and might rise again in rebellion if he left. Hernando Pizarro urged him strongly, and in the end they agreed that he would consider the matter that night and they would resume their talk the next morning. The Captain was anxious to persuade him by argument in order not to excite the country, since this might endanger the three Spaniards who had gone to Cuzco.

Chalcuchima went to the Captain's lodging the next morning and said that in view of the Captain's wishes, he could not do otherwise than obey. He was, therefore, willing to accompany him and would leave another captain in charge of the soldiers at Jauja. That day he collected about thirty loads of low-carat gold, and they arranged to leave two days later, during which time some thirty or forty loads of silver arrived. Throughout these days, the Spaniards kept a strong guard, and the horses remained saddled day and night, because this captain of Atahualpa's clearly had a large force and would do the Christians great damage if he were to attack them in the night. . . .

Hernando Pizarro left the town of Jauja on Friday, March 20, accompanied by Chalcuchima, on his return journey to Cajamarca. He marched by the same stages as he had come as far as the village of Pombo, where he joined the royal road from

Cuzco. He stayed here on the day of his arrival and one more day. On Wednesday they left Pombo and marched across the plains, on which there were great flocks of sheep and where they spent the night in a large inn. That day there was heavy snow. They spent the next night at Tambo, where there is a deep river with a bridge which is approached by a flight of very steep stone steps. If these [steps] were defended from above, there would be heavy casualties. The Captain was liberally provided by the chief of this village with all that he needed for himself and his men. A great feast was provided in honor of Captain Hernando Pizarro and because he was accompanied by Chalcuchima, who was generally welcomed in this way. . . .

. . . They marched another four leagues along a very rough road, to spend the night at Conchuco. This place lies in a hollow, and half a league before it the road descends in a series of broad steps cut in the rock. There are many difficult places on this stairway, which would make strong defense points. Leaving Conchuco, they marched the next day to a place called Andamarca, which is the point where they had turned off to go to Pachacamac. Here the two royal roads to Cuzco join. . . .

From this place Captain Hernando Pizarro returned to Cajamarca by the same stages as he had entered [Cajamarca] with Chalcuchima on April 25, 1533. Here a scene unparalleled since the discovery of the Indies and impressive even to Spaniards took place. As Chalcuchima entered the doors of the house where his master was imprisoned, he took a fair-sized load from the back of one of the Indian porters and put it on his own. And other chieftains in his company did the same. Thus laden, they all entered their master's presence, and when Chalcuchima saw Atahualpa he raised his hands to the sun, and gave thanks for having been permitted to enjoy the sight. Then very reverently, and with tears in his eyes, he approached his master and kissed his cheeks, his hands, and his feet; and all the chieftains of his company did the same, and Atahualpa preserved so majestic a mien that although he loved no one in his entire kingdom as much, he did not look Chalcuchima in the face or take any more notice of him than of the humblest Indian who might come before him. Taking up a load before entering Atahualpa's presence is a ceremony that has been performed for every lord who has reigned in that land.

While all this was happening, the room set aside for the treasure was filling up. It was learned that some of the treasure was at Jauja. Atahualpa advised Pizarro to send some Spaniards to Cuzco to the temple of the sun.

Pizarro hesitated to split up his forces. News arrived from Hernando. Atahualpa guaranteed the safety of any they sent. In the end, three volunteers left in mid-February 1533. They reached Cuzco and were welcomed by Quizquiz. He had them taken to the temple of the sun in accordance with Atahualpa's instructions. The temple was rich.

Jerez writes: "These buildings were covered with large plates of gold on the side where the sun rises. . . . "

The three Spaniards brought back over 250 kilograms of gold from the temple, in plates 60–70 centimeters wide, about seven hundred of them in all. Although they had not been allowed to visit Cuzco, the Spaniards saw enough to amaze them. Unable to carry all that they had taken, "they placed two seals, one for His Majesty and one for Governor Pizarro, in order to seal a building full of gold and silver vessels."

These three Spaniards were indeed in an odd situation: in a strange city that was controlled by a victorious general and coming, without having struck a blow, to take away booty, assess treasures and seal up safely what they could not carry away, desecrate holy places, and leave escorted by the very troops that were controlling the city.

When the three Spaniards returned, fever once again took hold of their compatriots.

Atahualpa had been a prisoner for several months. Would he be freed? Would the Spaniards keep their word? The initial amazement and surprise had been followed by a period of hope, when the strangers acted as if mad at the idea of getting so much gold.

For they loved gold. Gold was their god to whom they prayed. Who were they? Where did they come from? Why had he agreed to welcome them? Why had he not taken the advice of those who wanted to take them by surprise in a defile in the mountains? Now they had the gold, and they were not talking about setting him free or returning him to Quito.

They were suspicious. What were they going to do? Would they leave now that they had the gold?

Atahualpa, a royal prisoner, still served by his subjects, was uncertain. He did not know what to do to regain his freedom and his empire. Perhaps he felt he had already lost everything except uncertainty, and that was his only hope.

Meanwhile, on his own initiative, Hernando Pizarro decided to meet Chalcuchima, Atahualpa's general, who was at Jauja with a large body of troops, perhaps as many as thirty-five thousand. He established contact. Hernando and his small force of horsemen made the difficult crossing of the snow-covered mountains and reached Jauja in mid-March.

Hernando had with him one of Atahualpa's brothers, whom he sent as a messenger. The next day, Chalcuchima came accompanied by his captains. They spent the day negotiating. Hernando wanted Chalcuchima to come with him while they conveyed the portion of the treasure that had already been brought as far as Jauja. The first day's negotiations were a failure for the Spaniards. The Indian general refused to leave his post; he had received no order from the Inca to do so. But Hernando still insisted, saying that Atahualpa wanted to see him.

It is not known why the next day Chalcuchima agreed to go with the Spaniards to Cajamarca and see his imprisoned master. It is not known what decided him to make himself de facto a prisoner when he could have refused.

Had Hernando promised a terrible death for Atahualpa's brother if he failed to persuade Chalcuchima that his master wanted him to come to Cajamarca? How else can one explain what can only be called a political suicide and a military aberration? No doubt allegiance to the Inca had to come first. He alone was important. It is when it is disguised that servitude is greatest.

Did Chalcuchima perhaps think that by taking prisoner the leader of the strangers' own brother he would have better served his sovereign? It might perhaps have been possible to envisage an exchange. Instead of that here he was returning to Cajamarca with the strangers. For Hernando Pizarro it had been a bold gamble.

After being away for almost three months, the little force returned. It brought with it gold (in modest quantities), but above all it brought a prize catch—one of Atahualpa's three generals—without the loss of a single man. Chalcuchima met his master, still with the same demonstrations of extreme devotion. The sovereign remained unmoved, as was his habit. We can imagine him saying simply, "Why have you come?"

At the end of his "Report to the Royal Audience of Santo Domingo," Hernando Pizarro writes: "We remained here [at Jauja] for five days, and during all that time they did nothing but dance and sing, and hold great drinking feats. The Captain did not wish to come with me, but when he saw that I was determined to make him, he came of his own accord."

Shortly afterward, Chalcuchima was interrogated by the Spaniards. They wanted to know where the gold was hidden.

Meanwhile, Diego de Almagro had at last joined Francisco Pizarro in Cajamarca, five months after the capture of the Inca. He had arrived with one hundred foot soldiers and fifty horsemen. With the return of Hernando Pizarro's force, the Spaniards now had 320 men, greatly reducing fears of an Indian attack; moreover, one of their three generals was a prisoner, and Quizquiz was at Cuzco. The most serious threat might probably be from the north, from Rumañivi.

But the signs were already appearing of what would soon be, over and above the struggle against the Indians, a major part of the history of the conquistadors in Peru—their own internecine rivalries.

Almagro's men, excited by the news of the capture of the Inca and the story of the treasure that was mounting up day by day, learned that they would have no share in its division. Pizarro's men had captured the Inca and they would divide the treasure once the royal fifth had been set aside. Pizarro's position can be defended. Those who do nothing deserve nothing. But Almagro himself had been recruiting and organizing from the very beginning, and he was to have nothing. Pizarro had merely sent him some gold to pay for the ships to transport the soldiers. Bitterness set in.

Soon, the gold and silver were melted down. That took almost four months (March 16 to July 9). Eleven metric tons of gold were melted down to produce 6,000 kilograms of 22-carat gold. There were 12,000 kilograms of silver.

During this period of excitement when the Spaniards faced no problem from the Indians since the Inca ruler was cooperating, there was inevitably a sharp split between Pizarro's men and Almagro's, the former coming to see how their gold and their silver, under constant surveillance, were being melted down, and the latter full of envy and hostility.

But the Spaniards continued to be worried by persistent rumors of Indian troop movements.

On July 16, 1533, Atahualpa's treasure was divided up. Never perhaps have so few men shared so much gold. The Crown received its fifth, half of which had already been taken to Spain by Hernando Pizarro.

On the appointed day, in the presence of a notary, each received what had been estimated as his due. The instrument has been preserved with the names of the 168 men divided into two quite distinct categories: the horsemen, who received 40 kilograms of gold and 80 kilograms of silver, and the foot soldiers, who received half that. The leader of the expedition had more than 250 kilograms of gold and 500 kilograms of silver, plus Atahualpa's throne of 15-carat gold, which weighed 85 kilograms. Two other members of the expedition received much more than their peers: Hernando Pizarro, who received three and one-half times the share of a horseman, and Hernando de Soto, who received double. Four horsemen had more than the rest: Juan and Gonzalo Pizarro, Pedro de Candia, and Sebastian de Benalcazar. Francisco Pizarro received 57,220 pesos; Hernando Pizarro, 31,080 pesos; and Hernando de Soto, 17,740 pesos. The other horsemen received on average 8,800 pesos and the foot soldiers, half that sum.

It was a memorable day. The days that followed were one great gambling spree; the stakes were high, because that was almost the only way to spend one's money in Cajamarca. The foot soldiers also wanted to purchase horses, but their scarcity and the advantage they conferred took their price from 1,500 to 2,500 pesos. Juan Ruiz de Arce, whose horse was killed at Villaconga, writes: "They killed my horse that had cost me 1,600 castellanos. . . ."

And they thought about what they would do with all that wealth. Moreover, twenty men received permission to return to Spain with their spoils. Pizarro surely wanted to create a stir in Spain, and he certainly succeeded. The arrival of these twenty men—able to buy whatever they wanted—produced its effect even on the Crown. Hernando Pizarro, who had brought half the royal fifth, was quickly sent back so that Peru might yield more riches.

Meanwhile the rumors of an attack were becoming more specific. The *cacique* of Cajamarca himself warned Pizarro that Rumañivi was approaching. Other *caciques* confirmed it. Night guards were stepped up. Atahualpa was questioned by Pizarro but denied knowing anything. Nevertheless, he was put in chains. For Atahualpa, the bitterest days were beginning. He had kept his word. The gold had arrived. It had even been distributed. His generals had not threatened the strangers. And yet he was not free. He was in chains, and he was in despair.

Pizarro called a council. Twenty people took part: Hernando de Soto, Sebastian de Benalcazar, his brothers Gonzalo and Juan, the royal officials who had come from San Miguel, the treasurer Alonso

Riquelme, Diego de Almagro and his lieutenant Rodrigo Orgoñez, Father Vicente Valverde, and others. Of the chroniclers, Miguel de Estete and Pedro Sancho were present.

What was to be done? Some wanted to kill Atahualpa, especially Almagro and his men. They felt they should move on Cuzco so that they could carve out their share of the conquest. Atahualpa was Pizarro's prisoner and, in any case, how could they be sure that the Indians would not try every means to free him? With Atahualpa dead, they would have peace. With Atahualpa dead, no new gold they obtained would be a part of the ransom to which they were not entitled. Others, those who were among the first arrivals, wanted to keep him alive, knowing how useful he could be. A small group around de Soto felt that in no event should he be killed, given the promise made to him.

Finally, five men volunteered to go and see whether the rumors had any foundation: Soto, Almagro's lieutenant Rodrigo Orgoñez, Miguel de Estete the chronicler, and two others.

But those who remained did not wait for their return. Other rumors appeared. Another council was held. Those advocating Atahualpa's death became more clamorous. It was decided to put him to death, a decision Pizarro could have opposed had he so wished.

The Inca, it is said, wept. A travesty of a trial was arranged at which he was accused of treason and condemned to be burned alive unless he agreed to convert to Christianity, in which case he would be garroted.

Step by step Atahualpa had been driven back. He had agreed to everything. Now he had to agree to die as his tormentors wished. He converted, so as not to be burned, to keep his body intact. He agreed to everything. He was shattered. The chroniclers report that he even went so far as to entrust his children to Pizarro's care. He was garroted in the square at Cajamarca where he had been captured nine months earlier.

Pedro Sancho records:

> Finally he was taken from the prison and, to the sound of a trumpet, his treason and perfidy were published, and he was brought to the middle of the city plaza and tied to a stake, while the religious was consoling him and teaching him, by means of an interpreter, the things of our Christian faith, telling him that God wished him to die for the sins he had committed in the world, and that he must repent of them, and that God would

pardon him if he did so and was baptized at once. He [the Inca], moved by this discourse, asked for baptism. It was at once given to him by that reverend padre who helped him so much with his exhortation that although he was sentenced to be burned alive, he was given a twist of rope around his neck by means of which he was throttled instead; but when he saw that they were preparing for his death he said that he recommended to the governor his little sons. . . .

His body remained in the plaza that night [because he had died in the late afternoon], in order that all might learn of his death, and on the next day the Governor ordered all the Spaniards to be present at his interment, and, with the cross and other religious paraphernalia, he was borne to the church and buried with as much solemnity as if he had been the chief Spaniard in our camp. All the principal lords and *caciques* who served him were pleased at this, considering as great the honor which was done them, and knowing that, because he was a Christian, he was not burned alive, and he was interred in church as if he were a Spaniard.

Guaman Poma de Ayala writes:

When they seized the Inca Atahualpa, Francisco Pizarro and Don Diego de Almagro took away all his possessions . . . and they took all the riches of the temple of the Sun and of Curicancha and of Vanacauri, plus millions in gold and silver beyond counting, since all the walls, the roof, the floor, and the windows at Curicancha were covered with gold. . . . And when he saw himself so maltreated and robbed, a great sadness entered his heart . . . and there were loud cries in the city, Indians who sang. . . . A perverse warrior has imprisoned us . . . robbed us . . . and now we must die.

Titu Cusi, who occupied the throne of the Incas at Vilcabamba from 1557 to 1570, dictated an *Account of the Conquest of Peru* to the Spanish priest Marcos Garcia, who had come to catechize him. These are the words he attributes to Atahualpa's captains addressing the Spaniards:

What has this man done to you? Is this how you repay him for his considerable service in allowing you to enter his land against our will? What do you want of him? What more can he do that he has not done already? Did he not allow you to enter this land in peace and with every honor? . . . Did he not send all

his people to pay you a tribute? Did they not pay it to you? . . .
Did he not give you a house full of gold and silver to ransom
himself, the day after you captured him? And from us nobles
and everybody, did you not take our wives, and sons and daughters? What more do you want? Every time you have asked for
gold, silver, or to collect this or get that together, has it not been
done? . . . Did not you yourselves deceive him by claiming that
you came with the wind, on the orders of Viracocha, that you
were his sons, and that you came to serve the Inca, love him,
treat him and his people as yourselves? . . . Although he does
not deserve it and has never given you the least occasion to do
so, you torment him at every turn. . . .

Everyone here is so shocked and angry at what you are doing
that they are at a loss for words and do not know where to turn,
because they see themselves deprived of their memory, their
wives, their sons, their ties, and their lands . . . and in their situation, there is nothing left except to hang themselves and abandon everything.

Atahualpa's tragic end evoked literature in the Quechua language,
such as this *Tragedy of the End of Atahualpa* still performed today:

> *Bearded enemy, the red man,*
> *from where did you come?*
> *What wind brought you here,*
> *and what do you want*
> *here in my house, here in my land?*
> *On your way here*
> *the heat of the sun did not burn you*
> *and the cold did not freeze you*
> *and the mountain recoiling from your trampling did not*
> *crush you beneath its pain*
> *and the land did not open up beneath your feet to swallow*
> *you up*
> *and the ocean bearing you*
> *did not make you disappear.*
> *How did you come*
> *and what do you want from me?*
> *Go, return to your country! . . .*
> *Manco's son, Sayri-Tupac, says to Atahualpa:*
> *I cannot understand the language of the enemy, the flash*
> *of his sling fills me with fear.*

Only you, my Lord, my Inca,
powerful as you are,
only you can see him and speak to him as an equal.
Perhaps you will be able to make out
his thundering language?

Felipillo the interpreter translates to Atahualpa what is said by
Pizarro, who simply moves his lips: "He came down to this land
solely to lead you to his all-powerful Lord. For that and for no other
reason." Atahualpa replies:

Woe unto me, my beloved Lord,
you who are as Viracocha,
I am in your hands now.
Why are you getting angry already?
Perhaps you are tired,
rest a little,
perhaps you are overcome by the sun,
take a little shade.
. . . You see me bent
at your feet, submissive to your rule.

Atahualpa reminds Pizarro of the meeting at Cajamarca:

Alas, my bearded enemy, Viracocha,
at our meeting yesterday,
you saw me among my countless vassals
honored, borne in the royal litter of gold.
And now you see me at your feet
humiliated,
you speak to me arrogantly.
But do you not know that all depends on my will,
that silver and gold are subject to my order?
Ask me for what you desire to carry away,
I will give it to you with my own hands.
. . . But, powerful Lord, do not take away my existence.

The most beautiful funeral song—devoted by an anonymous
author to the death of Atahualpa—is known as *Apu Inca Atahualpa-
man.* It is of unknown date. The Spanish version is by the Peruvian
writer José Maria Arguedas.

On every side a sinister
hail is falling.
My heart felt it coming,

in my very dreams I was assailed,
in my rest
the blue fly foreshadowing death,
never-ending pain.

The sun is turning yellow, night is falling
mysteriously,
it buries Atahualpa, his body
and his name.
The death of the Inca reduces time
which lasts but a flicker of the eye.

Already the fearsome enemy
envelops his well-beloved head.

A river of blood flows,
spreads out into two streams.
. . . His eyes which were like the sun have become leaden
the eyes of the Inca.

Now the great heart of Atahualpa
is frozen.
The tears of men of the four regions are stifling it.

. . . The Spaniard,
rich with the gold of the ransom.
His frightful heart eaten by power.
They are killing each other,
with ever darker lusts
as of game in fury.

You gave them all that they asked for
but they killed you
. . . You alone
and by dying at Cajamarca
you destroyed your line.

And in your veins
the blood has now come to an end.
The light in your eyes
has been put out,

your look has fallen to the bottom of the brightest star
. . . Under a foreign rule, all sufferings combined,
surprised, lost, memories destroyed,
alone,
dead the shadow that protects
we weep
we rage
without knowing whom to turn to
or where to go.

The Inca's death was received as a catastrophe by the Indian population.

It was only after the Inca's death that Soto's reconnaissance expedition returned. There was nothing at all to report. All was calm. There were no troop movements. Soto was furious that the Inca had been killed. He said that he should have been sent to Spain and that he himself would have accompanied him to the port.

With Atahualpa dead, there remained only to set out for Cuzco and its riches: the three Spaniards' account of them had excited everyone's imagination. The men who had come with Almagro were naturally the keenest on moving forward.

The duly registered instrument relating the division of Atahualpa's treasure is a document that makes it possible to know more about "the men from Cajamarca" than about any other group of conquistadors, whether in Mexico, Colombia, Central America, La Plata, or Chile.[1]

Among these men, apart from two or three, there were no veterans of wars in Europe. But many had long experience in fighting against the Indians. Out of 101 men whose careers are known, 37 had no experience prior to their expedition to Cajamarca. But 64 of them did, and of these, 52 had previously lived in the Americas for periods ranging from five to twenty or more years (twenty-five in the case of Pizarro). It is thus likely that at least half of those who were involved in capturing Atahualpa were veterans of the wars in the Americas (Soto and Benalcazar had twenty years' experience).

The age of participants depended on their experience: the captains were well over thirty: Benalcazar over forty and Pizarro over fifty. But the average age of the troop was naturally much lower. Out of 103 men whose age is known, 70 were in their twenties, 5 under 20, and 28 in their thirties. In fact, 89 out of 103 were aged 20–35.

1. The patient work of John Lockhart, *The Men from Cajamarca* (University of Texas Press, 1972), established the statistics that follow.

The expedition contained 166 Spaniards; 1 Greek, Jorge Griego; and 1 Cretan, a gunner, Pedro de Candia. Castilians and Andalusians, with men from Estremadura, made up the overwhelming majority. Andalusians accounted for more than a quarter, Castilians for 36 percent, and men from Estremadura 28 percent, their high proportion being due, in the case of Peru, to recruitment by Pizarro.

The Andalusians came predominantly from the west of the province (Seville-Huelva): 26 out of 34. Most of the men from Estremadura came from the Trujillo-Caceres region (21 out of 36), doubtless because of Pizarro's connections there.

The regional origin of 131 of the men from Cajamarca is known: Estremadura, 36; Andalusia, 34; Old Castile, 17; New Castile, 15; Leon, 15; Biscaya, 8; Navarre, 2; Aragon, 2; Greece, 2 (including 1 Cretan).

The social background of the participants is extremely interesting. Of course, there were no nobles of any consequence. But of the 135 whose social background is known, there were 38 hidalgos (and 6 close to that status) and 91 commoners. Only 20 of these latter could be considered to belong to the lowest social strata in terms of their origin and life-styles. The rest, according to Lockhart, would have no problems mixing with hidalgos.

Of the 141 individuals considered, 51 were literate, 57 could sign their names, and 33 were definitely illiterate.

Of those who had a trade before enrolling in the expedition, the occupations of 47 are known: 1 ecclesiastic, 6 clerks or notaries, 6 accountants, 13 men of affairs (merchants, managers, entrepreneurs), 17 artisans (among whom were 6 tailors, 2 horseshoers, and 2 carpenters), 2 artillerymen, and 2 seamen.

Contrary to an idea widespread among certain moralizing nineteenth- and twentieth-century writers, the conquistadors were thus not all punished for their ill-gotten goods.

The reality is that between 1534 and 1535, over a third of the men of Cajamarca—sixty—returned to Spain, having made their fortune. Among the first group of twenty, who left immediately after the division of Atahualpa's treasure, were Francisco de Jerez and Cristóbal de Mena, both of whom wrote accounts. Subsequently, between 1535 and 1550, a dozen others left the Americas. Generally, those who returned home were horsemen whose fortune was considerable. Two horsemen returned to Spain for every foot soldier. A sizable proportion of the foot soldiers remained in Peru; among the horsemen who stayed, most were veterans, whose career had largely been on the continent and whose links with the mother country had become tenuous.

Those who returned wanted to be members of municipal councils or magistrates in their hometowns or in the nearest large town.

Fifteen years after Cajamarca, when Gonzalo Pizarro's rebellion had been put down (1548), some twenty-five survivors of the sixty or so men present in Peru immediately after Cajamarca remained in the country, which, at a time when life expectancy was about forty years, was, for conquistadors, an excellent average.

2

THE ASSAULT ON CUZCO

Once Atahualpa had been executed, Pizarro's and Almagro's forces marched on Cuzco. Pizarro sought above all to appear as a liberator, since he had just decapitated the faction of Quito.

The eldest of Huayna Capac's sons, Tupac Hualpa, was under Pizarro's protection at Cajamarca and had thus escaped the series of assassinations of possible claimants that Atahualpa had ordered. Tupac Hualpa, one of Huascar's brothers, was to serve Pizarro's plans. Pizarro would make him an Inca in the service of the Spaniards. Indirect rule seemed to be the best solution to establish both peace and Spanish control.

Losing no time, Pizarro called together the Indian dignitaries to tell them that Tupac Hualpa would now be Inca, to which they agreed. Great festivities were organized. All the Indians, including Chalcuchima, swore allegiance to the new ruler.

On August 11, 1533, the Spaniards set out from Cajamarca. In three weeks they passed through Huamachuco, Andamarca, and Huaylas. They had to cross the Santa Marta River on a hanging bridge, which was difficult for the horses. But they succeeded in crossing, one by one.

Pedro Sancho reports:

> To one who is not used to it, crossing [the bridge] appears dangerous because, the span being long, the bridge bends when one goes over it, so that one goes continually downward until the middle is reached, and from there he keeps going up until he has finished crossing to the other side, and when the bridge is being crossed, it trembles very much.

They rested and then resumed their journey. During the two months that Pizarro took to cover half the journey, all was calm.

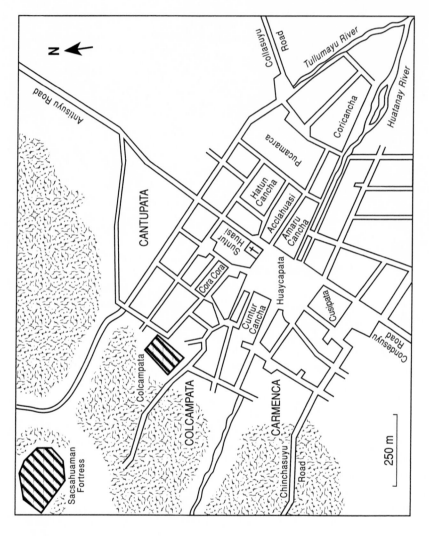

Map 8. *Cuzco at the time of the conquest*

Nevertheless, they continued to mount guard and be on the alert. But while the new Inca was only too content to see Cuzco's power restored, they had little confidence in Chalcuchima, who was with them. Rumors abounded of a possible attack by the latter's troops, and as a precaution the Indian general was put in irons.

By the beginning of October, the rumors seemed to be getting more definite as they reached the imperial road of the Incas at Junin.

Pizarro decided to speed up the march. He sent ahead of the column an elite force of seventy-five horsemen (including Almagro, Soto, Juan Pizarro, and Pedro de Candia) and twenty foot soldiers to watch the prisoner Chalcuchima.

While they were welcomed as liberators by the ordinary citizens of Cuzco, Pizarro and his men had their first armed encounter with the forces of Quito on October 10, 1533. *This was the first military confrontation with the Incas since they had left San Miguel seventeen months before!* It was short. It occurred at Jauja, where six hundred Indians of the army of Quito were cut to pieces by one hundred Spaniards.

The remaining Indian forces sought to link up with Quizquiz's forces at Cuzco. Pizarro sent his horsemen after them. They caught up with the rearguard which put up a short defense and was then overcome. The rest of the troops fled, and in a pursuit over some fifteen kilometers many Indians were killed. Prisoners and booty were also taken.

Pizarro halted for two weeks at Jauja, time to found a symbolic Spanish settlement and declare it the capital of Peru. He left eighty Spaniards there—the bulk of his troops had caught up with him during his halt—and wanted to press forward with the best of them only. At this point Inca Tupac Hualpa died of an illness.

The situation once again became highly unstable. Who should succeed him? The supporters of Huascar advanced the candidacy of a brother of Tupac Hualpa; those of Quito preferred a son of Atahualpa.

Meanwhile at Quito, no one knew who would have power, Atahualpa's brother or General Rumañivi. At Cuzco, General Quizquiz favored one of Atahualpa's brothers, Paullu, who appeared not to be too hostile to the faction of Quito.

The empire was falling apart. Dynastic disputes were helping the process, and ultimately Pizarro remained the arbiter of the situation as long as he retained the military advantage. The first thing was to get to Cuzco: the city exercised an irresistible attraction; its riches fascinated. After that, they would see about conquering Quito.

The welcome from the inhabitants of Jauja, supporters of Huascar, was significant. The Spaniards were hailed as liberators. Soldiers of Quito were handed over to them when they were captured. The forces of Quito were fighting less against a foreign invader than against the allies of those men of Cuzco who had executed Inca Atahualpa.

They resumed their march, following the imperial road of the Incas. Pedro Pizarro reports: "The road through the mountains is worth seeing. Nowhere in the whole of Christendom can one see such a magnificent road in such wild country."

The imperial road, of which the Spaniards were in fact using only one section, ran almost 6,000 kilometers from Colombia to Chile through the Andes. Feeder roads linked it, especially in its central section, to a second imperial road along the coast.

The forces of Quito retreated southward, destroying the hanging bridges and pursuing a scorched earth policy. Pizarro sent Soto with seventy horsemen with the best horses to try to seize the bridges before they were destroyed. On October 25, 1533, Pizarro and Almagro set out with thirty horsemen and the remaining thirty foot soldiers.

In eleven days, Soto's horsemen covered almost 400 kilometers. They caught up with the forces of Quito at Villas. The Spaniards seized the town and garnered a rich booty, but the Indian soldiers who were away hunting returned and gave battle. Pedro Pizarro reports:

> At the hour of vespers . . . they attacked us from all sides, and we did the same. Because of the hilly terrain, they rather had the advantage over us, although some of the Spaniards distinguished themselves, for example Captain de Soto, Rodrigo Orgoñez, Juan Pizarro, de Orellana . . . and a few others who reached some high ground and defended themselves there against the Indians.
>
> That day, the Indians killed a white horse which belonged to Alonso Tabuyo. We had to withdraw toward the square of Villas and spend the whole night under arms. The next day, the Indians launched a fierce attack. They carried banners made from the mane and tail of the horse they had killed. We were forced to return to them the spoils that we had taken and the women, and Indian men who had been tending their flocks. After that, they withdrew.

The Spaniards lost one horse and suffered a few wounded. The Indians had many dead. This was the second encounter with the Indians, who, despite their numerical superiority, were unable to carry the day.

Soto unwisely decided that, instead of waiting for Pizarro and Almagro at Vilcashuaman as agreed, he would continue on his way in order to take control of the bridge at Apurimac to prevent the troops from Jauja from linking up with those of Quizquiz. Pedro Pizarro reports: "As we had suffered all these difficulties, it was fair that we should have the pleasure of entering Cuzco without the reinforcements following us."

Soto crossed the Andahuylas and Abancay rivers without trouble. After passing through Vilcas, Pizarro became worried and urgently sent Almagro with thirty horsemen to catch up with Soto. He kept with him only ten horsemen and thirty foot soldiers with his prisoner Chalcuchima.

Soto reached the Apurimac, an imposing river. The bridge that would have enabled him to cross it had been destroyed, but the Spaniards, taking advantage of the season, were able to ford it.

On November 8, they crossed the heights of Vilcaconga. They numbered seventy-six, having left ten horsemen to escort the spoils taken at Vilcashuaman. Juan Ruiz de Arce reports: "We were moving along without any thought of a battle order. . . . We had forced our horses to ride very long stages, so we were leading them by the bridle through the defile in small groups of four."

Just before reaching a river, Soto, who was in the van, saw enemy troops along the crest of the mountain. Suddenly, after first pushing down large rocks on the Spaniards, three or four thousand Indians charged. Those who had the time to mount their horses tried to get to the top of the hill so as to be able to maneuver on the level ground. Juan Ruiz de Arce continues:

> The horses were so tired that they did not have the strength to push through such a host. . . . They [the Indians] rained down lances, arrows, and stones. They wore out the horses so much that the horsemen could hardly make them trot and some of them could barely walk. . . . The Indians then attacked furiously . . . five Spaniards were killed.

Diego de Trujillo reports:

> We were making our way . . . when we received what seemed like a fall of rocks . . . and they killed five and wounded seven-

teen of the forty horsemen that we had. . . . And that night we suffered a great deal, because it snowed . . . and the Indians were all around us with their fires.

Soto and his troops were able to retreat to ground more favorable to the horses. After taking some losses, the Indians prudently remained on the hills. But the Spaniards' situation was bad: seventeen horsemen and fourteen horses wounded. Night fell, and it was cold. Sentinels were posted, and they waited anxiously for morning.

Unfortunately for the Indians, it was not their custom to attack at night. This would have been fatal to the sixty uninjured Spaniards, who kept watch anxiously through the night.

Suddenly, in the middle of the night, could be heard the sound of Spanish troops. Almagro's thirty horsemen, who had met up with the small force left behind by Soto, were arriving. Diego de Trujillo continues:

> At midnight . . . the trumpet sounded. When we heard it our hope returned . . . and those [Indians] who must also have heard the trumpet, understanding that help was coming to us, abandoned their fires and withdrew toward Cuzco. . . . And soon Diego de Almagro came.

The relations of force had changed.

From being the hunted, the Spaniards had become the hunters. They put hundreds of Quizquiz's warriors to flight. Quizquiz had been unable to exploit the situation. But Soto had lost more men in a day than the expedition had in a year.

They waited for Pizarro. Once the Spanish troops were reunited, Pizarro held Chalcuchima responsible for the attack. He was condemned to be burned alive. Father Valverde offered him the garrote in exchange for his conversion. But the warrior rejected the trade-off that the Inca had accepted.

On that very day one of Huayna Capac's sons, who had escaped the massacre perpetrated by Quizquiz, came to seek refuge with the Spaniards. Pizarro realized the advantage he could extract from this meeting and told him that he had come to liberate the people of Cuzco from rule by the people of Quito. Pedro Sancho writes: "The Governor made him all these promises in order to please him."

Quizquiz's forces engaged in one last battle before Cuzco. The day was won by the Spaniards at the cost of several wounded and three horses killed. From beginning to end the superiority of the Spaniards, thanks to the horse, was total, and when the first blows came, the Indians had no time to adapt to the techniques of the invaders.

Later, as in Chile when the Indians were commanded by a leader who knew the Spaniards, such as Lautaro, who was the invaders' interpreter before becoming their most determined opponent, the Spaniards were held to a standoff. After this last battle before Cuzco, Quizquiz's forces disintegrated.

Pedro Pizarro reports:

> At dawn, the next day, the Governor set out for Cuzco with the horsemen and foot soldiers. They were in battle order, ready for anything, since they were sure that the enemy would attack them on the road. But no one appeared. And thus the Governor entered the great city of Cuzco without any resistance or fighting at the hour of high mass on Saturday, November 15, 1533.

CUZCO AS SEEN BY PEDRO SANCHO DE LA HOZ

The city of Cuzco is the principal one of the cities where the lords of this land have their residence; it is so large and so beautiful that it would be worthy of admiration even in Spain; and it is full of palaces of lords, because no poor people live there, and each lord builds his house there, and so do all the *caciques*, although the latter do not dwell there continuously. The greater part of these houses are of stone, and others have half the facade of stone. There are many houses of adobe, and they are all arranged in a good order. The streets are laid out at right angles; they are straight and paved, and down the middle runs a stone gutter for water. The main defect of the streets is that they are narrow, so that only one horse and rider can go on each side of the gutter. The city is located on a mountain slope, and there are many houses on the slope and others below on the plain. The plaza is rectangular, and the greater part of it is flat and paved with small stones. Around the plaza are four houses of noblemen, who are the chief men of the city; [the houses] are of stone, painted and carved, and the best of them is the house of Guaynacaba [Huayna Capac], a former chief, with a marble door [colored] white and red and other colors; and there are other sightly buildings with flat roofs. In this city, there are many other buildings and grandeurs. Along the two sides [of the city] pass two rivers which rise a league above Cuzco, and from there down to the city and, for two leagues below it, they run over stone flags so that the water may be pure and clear. . . . They have bridges for those who enter the city. On the hill which is rounded and very steep, toward the city, there is a very beautiful fortress of earth and stone. Its large windows over-looking the city make it appear still more beautiful. Inside, there are many dwellings, and a chief tower in the center, built square, and having four or five terraces one above another. The rooms inside are small and built of stones that are very well worked and so well adjusted to one another that it does not appear that they have any mortar, and they are so smooth that they look like polished slabs. . . . Five thousand Spaniards might well be within it. . . . On the city side, which is a very steep slope, there is no more than one wall; on the other side, which is less steep, there are three, one above the other. The most beautiful thing which can be seen in the edifices of that land are these walls. . . . The Spaniards who have seen them say that neither the bridge of Segovia nor any other of the edifices which Hercules or the Romans made is so worthy of being seen as this. . . .

Around the city, many houses are seen from this fortress, a quarter of a league, half a league, and a league away, and in the valley, which is surrounded by hills, there are more than five thousand houses, many of them for the pleasure and recreation of former lords and others for the *caciques* of all the land who live in the city. The others are storehouses. . . . There are houses where the tribute is kept which the vassals bring to the *caciques*; and there is a house where more than a hundred dried birds are kept, because they make garments of their colorful feathers. . . . Each dead lord has his house and all the tribute paid to him during his life here; for no lord who succeeds another [and this is the law among them] can, after the death of the last one, take possession of his inheritance. Each one has his service of gold and of silver, and his things and clothes for him-self, and he who follows takes nothing from him.

CUZCO AS SEEN BY PEDRO PIZARRO

The city is the largest and the most beautiful one seen in this country or any other part of the Indies. We can assure Your Majesty of its magnificence and that there are so many fine buildings that it would appear remarkable even in Spain. . . . At Cuzco there was such a press of people to see us that the surrounding fields were covered with them. . . . But we entered the city without meeting any resistance as the Indians received us kindly. . . .

. . . On the top of a hill they had a very strong fortress surrounded with masonry walls of stones with two very high round towers. And in the lower part of this wall, there were stones so large and thick that it seemed impossible that human hands could have set them in place. . . . And they were so close together, and so well fitted, that even the point of a pin could not have been inserted in one of the joints. . . . There were so many rooms that ten thousand Indians could go within them. All these rooms were occupied and filled with arms, lances, arrows, darts, clubs, bucklers. . . . This fortress would have been impregnably strong had it been provided with water. . . .

Now I shall tell about the people who live in Cuzco and the vices which they had. There were so many drums heard during the night in all parts [of the city], and there was so much dancing and singing and drinking by the dead and by the living, that the greater part of the night was passed in this way.

This was the daily custom of these Lords and Ladies and *orejones* [long ears], for the rest of the Indians were innocent of it except at certain times of the year when, with the permission of the *orejones* who governed them, they celebrated according to their nature, but most of the year they were occupied with work for their Sovereign.

CUZCO AS SEEN BY DIEGO DE TRUJILLO

> At Cuzco, we found a larger quantities of silver than gold,
> although there was a lot of gold. We saw military magazines
> with lances, arrows, clubs, and slings, storerooms filled with
> ropes of varying sizes, from string the thickness of a man's fin-
> ger to cable the thickness of a man's thigh that the natives use to
> drag stones for building. Other storerooms were full of copper
> bars tied up in bundles of ten; elsewhere there were piles of
> cloths, stocks of coca. . . . There were even places where flayed
> Indians were kept.

Although no rumors had been circulating about an attack by
Quizquiz's forces, for a month Pizarro stationed his troops in the
great square with the horses ready, night and day, as a precautionary
measure.

The leaders divided up the palaces on the great square among
them: Francisco Pizarro, Almagro, Soto, and Hernando Pizarro
housed themselves sumptuously. Sites were chosen for the church
and the municipal building.

Pizarro soon decided to have Manco enthroned. By restoring the
legitimate authority of Cuzco, they could pass themselves off as liberators, and Pizarro encouraged the formation of an army to fight
Quizquiz's forces with the help of the Spaniards.

Five thousand Indians and fifty horsemen under Soto's command
set out in pursuit of Quizquiz and his men, who had withdrawn 40
kilometers southwest of Cuzco. While not conclusive, the encounter
discouraged the troops from Quito, very far from their bases and in
hostile country. They retreated northward.

At Cuzco, Manco was enthroned Inca shortly before Christmas
1533.

There remained to divide up the treasure of Cuzco—without
excessively upsetting the Indians of whom the Spaniards were officially the allies and protectors.

Melting down the gold and silver took three months. The division
was made in mid-March. This time everyone got a share whether
they were present or absent, the men at Cuzco as well as those left at
Jauja—among them the royal treasurer Riquelme—and those who
had returned to the port of San Miguel with Sebastian de Benalcazar.
This time it was Almagro's share that was the largest, Pizarro con-

tenting himself with a more modest share. There was only half as much gold as at Cajamarca but four times more silver. The total value of the booty from Cuzco was slightly higher than that from Cajamarca.

The gold flooded into Spain.

The sack of Cuzco was experienced as a dispossession by the Indians. Pedro Pizarro describes the Indians' reaction when the Spaniards were about to melt down the statue of Manco Capac: "In a cellar . . . a bundle of gold was found, on account of which the Indians were much afflicted, for they said it was the figure of the first Lord who conquered this land."

The Spaniards entered the Temple of the Sun, which among other things housed precious objects that had belonged to Huayna Capac, the father of Atahualpa and Huascar. Diego de Trujillo reports: "As we entered, Villac Umu, one of their priests, cried out: How dare you enter here? Those who enter here must have fasted for a year and must enter barefoot carrying a load! But we paid no attention to him and went in."

Cristóbal de Mena, who later became a priest, writes: "Their sole concern was to grab the gold and silver and become rich . . . without thinking that they were causing harm, spoiling, and destroying things. And what they were destroying was more perfect than anything they ever owned."

Pillage was the reward for victory. As it ever was in this type of war of conquest.

The instrument dividing the spoils was signed on March 19, 1534. Four days later, Cuzco was officially founded as a Spanish municipality. The taking of possession was so total that it involved the complete symbolic eradication of any previous existence and the beginning of history again with a new dawn.

Pizarro writes:

> To mark the foundation and the fact that I am taking possession on this day, Monday, March 23, 1534, by this gibbet that I ordered to be constructed a few days ago in the middle of the square, on these stone steps that are not yet finished, I, Francisco Pizarro, using the dagger that I carry in my belt, cut a sliver of wood from the gibbet and mark one of the stones forming the steps.

Ninety-eight Spaniards chose to become citizens of the city thus founded: the most noble and great city of Cuzco.

The first phase of the conquest was officially over.

Capac Inti Raymi *(Supreme Sun Feast) was the name given to the last month of the year in Inca civilization. It contained the great feast and ceremonial festival of* Inti, *the Sun.*

3

THE INCA EMPIRE

The Inca empire was barely a century old when it collapsed under the assault by the Spaniards, who took advantage of a civil war. It was formed in the fourteenth and fifteenth centuries largely through the efforts of two Incas: Pachacutec and Tupa Yupanqui. At the death of the father of Atahualpa and Huascar, who were fighting over the empire when the Spaniards arrived, the empire stretched from southern Colombia to central Chile. It was highly centralized politically and had a common religion and language imposed by the Incas.

Like the Aztecs and the Mayas, the Incas believed that four worlds—four "suns"—had preceded their own and that each of the previous worlds had been destroyed by a cataclysm.

The Inca empire was at the peak of its power at the beginning of the fifteenth century. At the base there was the Ayllu, or small rural community claiming descent from a common ancestor, but the state structure was centralized. The population was divided by age and sex. Men aged between twenty and fifty were required to perform public labor. In exchange for submission, the population benefited, in the event of famine, from food stores. For counting they used the *quipu* (knotted string).

The religion of the Incas was built around the cult of the sun. Inti, the sun, the mythical ancestor of the dynasty, was the god of the empire, and his great temple was at Cuzco. The Inca was a semidivine figure during his life on earth and became a god after his death. His mummified body was carried onto the great square at Cuzco on the occasion of ritual festivals. The high priest was a member of the imperial family.

The religious pantheon included the sun, the moon (his sister-wife) and thunder. The nobles alone had a special cult devoted to Viracocha, the creator.

In terms of the Americas, the Incas were formidable warriors. They had subjugated hundreds of tribes in less than a century and had built up an extensive empire. Once subjugated, the people were ruled directly.

All fit men had to undergo military training and were liable to service from the ages of twenty to fifty. But, like the Aztecs, the Incas did not have a standing army. The army was organized on a decimal system and could produce corps of up to ten thousand men: the Incas could raise armies of up to one hundred thousand men and perhaps more.

An elite corps of several thousand men acted as the Inca's personal guard. It was made up solely of nobles who had undergone four years of training crowned by a trial at the end of which their ears were pierced and a heavy gold pendant hung in them. Over time, their lobes became excessively distended, causing the Spaniards to nickname them *orejones* (long ears).

The leading figures were distinguished by their casques and feathers, among other things. The weapons the Incas and their allies used included slings, bows, *bolas* (three stones held together by strings attached to a rope that could knock out an animal as it ran), lances, clubs, stone- and copper-headed axes, and copper-edged wooden swords.

After declaring war and collecting information about the opponents' forces and organization, the classic battle consisted in seizing the enemy's leaders in order to cause resistance to collapse. After the yelling designed to intimidate and the launching of missiles, the Incas would attack and try to unbalance the enemy by knocking out its command center. A force would be kept in reserve to deal with any eventuality: to reinforce a corps in difficulties, take the enemy from behind, cut the enemy's lines of communication, or protect their own.

Before declaring war and attacking, the Incas gave their enemies the choice of surrendering or fighting. If the enemy resisted, the repression was harsh. Whole tribes were massacred. This happened to the Cañaris, decimated by Atahualpa; their desire for revenge made them into allies of the Spaniards.

The Incas' military and administrative system depended on their road infrastructure. Two parallel roads—one along the coast, the other through the Andes—crossed the empire for almost 6,000 kilometers in the case of the longer, inland one. These two roads were connected by a series of minor roads. The total Inca road network must have been of the order of 15,000 kilometers. They were built in straight lines, and about every 20 kilometers they had depots where the army could get supplies. Messengers had a network of relay points every 4 or 5 kilometers, enabling runners to cover up to 250 and even 300 kilometers a day. The Incas did not have the wheel, and thus the army's baggage had to be carried by human porters or llamas. Throughout their empire the Incas had built a network of fortifications.

The initial collapse of the Incas, from Cajamarca to the attack on Cuzco, was primarily the result of the civil war and its consequences. In the case of Cajamarca, one should also add the fact that the Incas underestimated the Spaniards as a result of erroneous information and the effect of surprise. Subsequently, the military tactics used by the Indians, notably during the uprising led by Manco in 1536–1539, showed an effort to adapt on the part of the Incas, but at the same time also showed their limitations.

The successful operations were all ambushes in which hand-to-hand fighting was excluded. In frontal combat, the Spanish horsemen appeared invincible even when they had no more than twenty horses. The most effective Indian tactic was to attack by throwing stones and pushing rocks and other missiles down on a body of Spanish horsemen in a defile from which exits had been cut off. But it is striking that at the siege of Cuzco, tens of thousands of Indians were unable to overcome fewer than two hundred Spaniards who had been isolated for several months.

After 1539, Indian guerrilla warfare simply survived and lasted only until 1572 because it was quite marginal in character, and the Spaniards hoped they would succeed in winning the Indians over. The year 1534 saw the annihilation of Atahualpa's forces. In that year, the Spaniards realized that with the capture of Atahualpa they had delivered a mortal blow.

Yet the Spaniards were holding Peru with barely three hundred men and only three secure bases: San Miguel in the north, Jauja in the center, and Cuzco in the south. The whole region of Quito—modern Ecuador and part of northern Peru—was controlled by Rumañivi. Quizquiz had withdrawn toward Quito. He was thus nearly 2,000 kilometers from his base. On the way he tried to capture Jauja, where eighty Spaniards were stationed along with a large part of Peru's treasure. But the surprise effect did not work, coordination was poor, and—thanks to the Huanca allies who remained loyal to the Spaniards—the latter carried the day with a few cavalry charges. That was in mid-February. Two months later, Pizarro, accompanied by Manco, arrived in Jauja. He founded the town's municipality, while Soto and Gonzalo Pizarro—at the head of fifty horsemen, thirty Spanish foot soldiers, and several hundred Indian allies—went in pursuit of Quizquiz. He avoided confrontation. The conquest of Peru seemed to be almost over.

In April 1534, Pizarro allowed those conquistadors who wished to return to Spain to leave. Sixty men left, almost all from among those who had shared in the spoils of Cajamarca. Diego de Trujillo, Juan Ruiz de Arce, and Miguel de Estete went home. Francisco de Jerez had already left. The sole chronicler of the conquest who remained was Pedro Pizarro.

In accordance with the capitulations, Pizarro began to distribute *encomiendas*. These were large, since anyone who agreed to settle permanently received up to five thousand serfs for two generations.

In Cuzco, the ban on pillaging issued by Pizarro was not observed. He delegated powers to Soto to put an end to something that might easily precipitate a revolt in a country as yet only loosely held.

Fifty Spaniards became citizens of Jauja, the capital, in exchange for *encomiendas*. But the following year, in January 1535, Pizarro founded the definitive capital of Peru, Lima, on the coast, Spain being a maritime empire.

A few years later, in about 1550, Cieza de León, the great historian of Peru, visited the capital, which was still called the "city of the Kings."

> After Cuzco, this city is the largest one in the country; it possesses solid houses some of which are superb, with towers and terraced roofs. The square is large and the roads wide. There is running water in most houses. It is used to water many delightful gardens. The abundance of administrative services involves a continuous movement of visitors and the traders have well-stocked shops.

In 1545, Lima was elevated into an archbishopric. After 1543, the viceroys governed all the states from Colombia to Argentina from there. In 1551, the University of San Marcos was established.

4

THE EXPEDITION TO QUITO

The territory of Quito lay in the north of the territory granted to Pizarro by royal document. Rumañivi, who had had one of Atahualpa's brothers assassinated, held sway there. The *adelantado* Pedro de Alvarado—who, after the fall of Mexico, had become the conqueror of Guatemala—landed in late February on the coast near the equator with 500 men, including 119 horsemen, a considerable force. As soon as he heard of the landing, Sebastian de Benalcazar, who was at San Miguel, without waiting for Pizarro's agreement set out for Quito with some 200 men, including 62 horsemen.

There was no chronicler of this campaign. But it is known that at the first encounter between the forces of Quito and the Spaniards, the sight of the horses put the Indians to flight, and Benalcazar won the support of the Cañaris, a tribe hostile to Inca rule.

In May, Rumañivi fought two battles with an army of perhaps twenty thousand warriors. They were defeated on both occasions. Nine Spaniards were killed. Three other battles were fought up to June, when the Spaniards reached Quito.

The Spaniards were exceedingly disappointed not to find any significant booty. The city had been evacuated and put to the torch. Benalcazar sent his fastest horsemen after Rumañivi, but he was able to execute a turning movement and attack Quito by night. The Spaniards learned of the imminent attack from the Cañaris and were thus able to withstand it; at dawn they won the day with a charge.

Before long, Almagro arrived, anxious to ensure that Benalcazar did not have all the limelight. As for Alvarado, after losing eighty-five men and a number of horses crossing the Andes, he met up with Almagro and his forces. They negotiated hard in a tense atmosphere. Finally, for 100,000 pesos—twelve times the sum collected by a

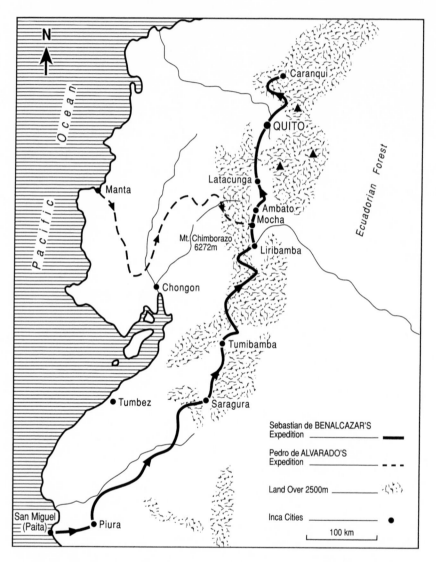

N

Ocean

Pacific

Caranqui

QUITO

Manta

Latacunga

Ambato
Mocha

Mt. Chimborazo
6272m

Liribamba

Chongon

Ecuadorian Forest

Tumibamba

Tumbez

Saragura

Sebastian de BENALCAZAR'S
Expedition _____

Pedro de ALVARADO'S
Expedition _____

Land Over 2500m _____

Inca Cities _____

100 km

San Miguel
(Paita)

Piura

Map 9. The Quito campaign, February–July 1534

horseman at Cajamarca—Alvarado agreed to abandon the conquest of the continent, and his men were given permission to join Pizarro's service. Meanwhile, the resistance of the men of Quito disintegrated, while, after a long retreat, Quizquiz's forces were nearing Quito without even knowing that it had fallen. Quizquiz's vanguard was surprised by the Spaniards, who decided to strike at the main body of the Indian forces. One night, with all the available horses, Almagro and Alvarado went to take the enemy by surprise. Horses that cast their shoes in the stony ravines were reshod by torchlight to save time. But the alarm was given on the Indian side, and Quizquiz put up a stiff resistance and then escaped. His troops' morale collapsed. The news that the very sanctuary of their empire had fallen was too heavy a blow after a retreat of 2,000 kilometers. The troops broke up in disorder and went to their homes. Quizquiz refused to surrender and was murdered by his own men.

Shortly afterward, Rumañivi was taken prisoner. Other local chiefs were defeated or surrendered. All organized resistance in the province of Quito soon ceased. Rumañivi, the last of Atahualpa's three generals, was executed on the great square at Quito.

The Inca empire now belonged to the Spaniards.

Agustin de Zarate writes:

> After the capture of Atahualpa, [Pizarro] sent Captain Benalcazar . . . as his lieutenant to San Miguel.
>
> On his arrival, the Cañaris Indians came to him to complain about Rumañivi and other captains from Quito continuously attacking them. Just then a great number of men arrived from Panama and Nicaragua; and Benalcazar took two hundred of them, including eighty horsemen, and advanced toward Quito, both to protect the Cañaris Indians, who had signed a treaty with him, and because he had received a report that Atahualpa had left great quantities of gold at Quito.
>
> When Rumañivi heard of Benalcazar's approach, he came out to block his advance and fought him with more than twelve thousand Indians at many dangerous passes. He laid ambushes on the road, all of which Benalcazar avoided with great prudence and cunning. He would himself remain facing the Indians, but would send a captain with fifty or sixty horsemen riding through the night either above or below the road to seize the narrow place before daybreak. Thus he drove the Indians back onto the plains, where the horsemen could inflict great losses on them. They waited for his attack because they had dug deep and

wide pits set with sharp poles and stakes and covered with turf
or grasses on thin canes. . . .

The Indians could never deceive Benalcazar, no matter what
they did; his men did not fall into any of these traps, and
received no harm from them. He never attacked the Indians
from the front when they faced him, but made a detour of a
league or two and attacked them from the rear or the flank. He
took great care not to ride over turf or grass that had not grown
naturally on the spot. . . .

[Rumañivi] decided to leave the city, but first he set fire to a
room full of rich clothing left from the time of Huayna Capac;
and before he fled he made a surprise attack on the Spaniards at
night, but inflicted no damage. Benalcazar then took possession
of the city.

Agustin de Zarate writes about the meeting of Diego de Almagro
and Pedro de Alvarado with Quizquiz:

As Don Diego de Almagro and Don Pedro de Alvarado were
on their way from Quito to Pachacamac, the *cacique* of the
Cañaris informed them that Atahualpa's captain Quizquiz, having collected all the Indians and flocks that he had found from
Jauja onward, was approaching with an army of more than
twelve thousand warriors. He promised to deliver Quizquiz into
their hands, if they would wait. But, putting no trust in this
promise, Don Diego continued on his way, and when they
reached the province of Chaparra, they suddenly encountered
two thousand Indians marching two or three stages ahead of
Quizquiz under a captain called Sotaurco.

Quizquiz's dispositions were as follows: Sotaurco and his
troops marched ahead; on the left flank was another three thousand men gathering food from the neighboring districts; and in
the rear, two stages behind, were another three or four thousand
men. Quizquiz himself marched in the middle with the main
body, the llamas, and the prisoners. His army, therefore, covered
more than fifteen leagues of country from front to rear. As
Sotaurco was preparing to occupy a pass through which he
thought the Spaniards would be coming, Don Pedro de
Alvarado arrived and captured him. Learning Quizquiz's dispositions from Sotaurco, he made a night march with his horsemen who could follow him. They had to stop at night, however,
because as they rode down to the river, the horses cast their

shoes on the great boulders and had to be reshod by torchlight. Then, they continued on their way with great speed fearing that some of the Indians whom they had met might go back to Quizquiz and tell him of the Spaniards' approach. They did not stop until late the next day when they came in sight of Quizquiz's camp.

When Quizquiz saw the Spaniards, he went by one road taking all his women and servants, and sent Atahualpa's brother, Guaypalcon, with the soldiers by another, rougher road. Don Diego met those soldiers on the slopes of a hill, where he outflanked Guaypalcon and attacked him from the rear. Finding themselves surrounded, Guaypalcon and his men fortified themselves in a wild and rocky place and defended themselves until night. Don Diego and Don Pedro then gathered all their Spaniards and Indians and went out in the dark in search of Quizquiz, whom they found, but not before the three thousand Indians of his left flank had beheaded fourteen Spaniards they had taken in an attack. During their march, the two Spaniards ran into Quizquiz's rearguard. The Indians took up a defensive position on a riverbank and prevented the Spaniards from crossing all day. They themselves crossed the river upstream of the Spaniards and seized a hill. Although they would have preferred to retire, the Spaniards advanced to fight them. But they could not do so because the ground was covered with thorny shrubs. So they suffered heavy casualties. . . .

Throughout the night the Indians kept careful watch. But when dawn came they had retired from the river crossing and fortified themselves on a high peak, where Don Diego de Almagro, not wishing to stay any longer, left them in peace. That night the Indians burned all the clothing that they could not carry with them. Remaining in the camp were more than four thousand men and women, Quizquiz's prisoners, who came over to the Spaniards.

5

THE GREAT REBELLION

Hernando Pizarro dispatched his brother Juan with seventy horse-men to the valley of Yucay, where reports indicated a large concen-tration of Indians. But the Indians were already massing around the capital. When Juan Pizarro returned to Cuzco, the city was almost completely surrounded.

The encirclement lasted several weeks. The high priest Villac Umu argued for an immediate attack. Manco preferred to await the arrival of reinforcements so that his numerical superiority would be overwhelming. But Villac Umu obtained agreement to seize the citadel of Sacsashuaman, the city's strategic point, and destroyed the irrigation canals vital for the fields all around the city.

Throughout the siege, the Spaniards were cut off from all outside help. There were fewer than 200 of them, 196 precisely, including 80 horsemen. Hernando Pizarro, who was in overall charge of military operations, divided the horsemen into three groups and, at the begin-ning of the siege, sought to use the Spaniards' usual tactic—a charge. But this failed to achieve the usual breakthrough. The number of Indians trampled was so great that the horses were unable to maneu-ver and were threatened with encirclement each time the Indian host launched one of its sporadic counterattacks. The chronicles, ever quick to exaggerate the figures, speak of at least fifty or one hundred thousand Indians. In any event, the rebellion was massive and was the most considerable act of resistance by the Inca empire.

There were Indians on each side, although far fewer among the allies of the Spaniards: Cañaris and Chachapoyas, as well as Incas. Among the latter were two of Manco's brothers and their followers. In every respect, the conquest of the Americas by the Spaniards was the first colonial war in the modern sense of the term.

Without giving the alarm, Manco had been able to collect thousands of warriors not far from Cuzco. The revolt against the intruders had spread from village to village. The traditional Inca chiefs had raised peasant units in the old way. The troops had armed themselves with whatever came to hand. There were those who had been pressured by the Spaniards, those who followed their chiefs, those, around Manco, who wanted to rule again. Inca glory was still very recent. People could remember it, ten years ago before the civil war, just a few years before the intrusion of the strangers. When the Spaniards first arrived, Manco had seen in them the men who had laid Atahualpa low. Atahualpa, the conqueror of Cuzco, had ordered the assassination of all those of royal blood who might have challenged him for the throne. In the beginning, Manco had been treated with respect. This was because the strangers were still unsure of their victory. They were still drunk with the gold of Cajamarca, drunk with the gold of Cuzco.

And then others had come: all wanted ever more gold. They were insatiable. They applied pressure; they kept on looking, they wanted more. Soon their rule became more and more arrogant. They were the stronger party. Gradually, Manco began to plan his flight; he wanted to stop being their prisoner and to be the Inca not of the strangers but of his own people.

But he had been caught. The strangers had shown themselves in their true colors. He had been put in irons, humiliated. A group of them would come to see him: they had raped his wives in front of him, and he could say nothing, do nothing. Once, when they were drunk, they had urinated on him and burned his eyebrows with a candle. He had stayed silent. And he had had to pretend that he had forgotten everything, to continue playing at serving them, to be compliant—until the day when he was able to leave the city for a religious ceremony, promising to bring them back a statue made of gold. He knew them well: gold was all they wanted. Why did they love it so?

Now the Indians would be able to get their revenge for everything at once—the humiliations and the defeats—and put a permanent end to the Spaniards' pretensions.

Villac Umu, the high priest, wanted to attack at once, taking advantage of the fact that the Spanish forces were scattered. But Manco wanted to wait until reinforcements had arrived and launch a general attack so powerful that it would carry all before it. They needed to be many to overcome the strangers. Again, the omens

were unfavorable. It would be better to wait. But Villac Umu, acting
on his own accord, seized the citadel of Sacsashuaman, which dominated the city and was undefended.

And then the propitious day to launch the attack came, shortly
after the reinforcements arrived. Everyone was ready. The city had
been surrounded by clinging to the escarpments where horses could
not go and then, as more and more men arrived, they had established
themselves in the plain. The city was surrounded by a host.

Within the city were the Spaniards, fewer than two hundred in
number, with several hundred Indian allies. There was growing anxiety. There were so many Indians that their fires could be seen at
night as far as the eye could see. By day, they enveloped the city in
the noise of their drums. The Spaniards attempted a charge without
success. There were too many bodies trampled underfoot, which
prevented the horses from galloping. The Indians were too many. So
the Spaniards waited for the attack. There would be no reinforcements; presumably no one knew that Cuzco was encircled. There
was no way to send a messenger. It was impossible to leave the city
except in strength.

And the Indians did attack. In a few days, the situation had
become dramatic. They had set fire to the roofs of the houses.
Unable to do anything about it, the Spaniards had to fall back around
the great square where the stone buildings were intact.

A large part of the city was taken over by the Indians, who built
barricades to prevent the horses from advancing. The Spaniards had
the impression of being unavoidably caught in a trap. Keeping watch
night after night was exhausting but necessary, even if the Indians
did not attack at night. The Spaniards had to keep their boots on permanently. They were always ready for the worst. And the worst
came when food had to be rationed.

The Indians were exultant. Victory seemed close. The Spaniards
were caught in an ever-narrowing space. They were still dangerous,
still fearsome with their horses and their firearms, still dangerous in
hand-to-hand fighting with their swords and their way of advancing
in tight groups that caused the Indians to fall back. But the Indians
were making progress; now they were moving on the walls without
roofs above the horsemen, raining stones and arrows down on them.
The Indian leaders exhorted. The omens were favorable. Soon they
would take Cuzco. Soon they would once again be in control.

But the Spaniards tried not to give way to despair; they simply
had no choice. They had to hold out. They became angry. They

wanted to use terror to force the grip to relax. They were prepared to do anything. They cut off the right hands of Indian prisoners and sent a hundred of the mutilated prisoners to strike fear into the rest. The Spaniards had to hold out or they would die there horribly, for the hatred against them was now very deep. Some suggested falling back to the coast; others, taking refuge in an impregnable building. After consulting his advisors, Hernando Pizarro refused. They would not flee; they would be massacred on the road. They would not let themselves get caught in the trap of a building, however solid.

The only alternative was to attack and start by retaking the citadel of Sacsashuaman, which they should never have allowed the Indians to take. The first task was to remove the barricades, a job that was handed over to the Spanish foot soldiers and the Indian allies. They said prayers and commended themselves to God. And they came out in force led by Juan Pizarro, who, although wounded in the jaw by a stone, took command of operations.

Playing on surprise, he came out at the gallop. They forced their way through, giving the impression of fleeing by taking the long way around the citadel. They advanced as best they could along paths deliberately broken up by the Indians to make the horses stumble.

They attempted to enter the citadel by force, but it was too well held. There were still more barricades. The Indians had worked hard to put up traps and obstacles everywhere. The Spaniards had to await nightfall. Meanwhile, Hernando Pizarro, along with the foot soldiers and the remaining horsemen, fought off the Indians' attempt to penetrate into the great square.

In the night, the Spaniards managed to get through one barricade before the alarm was given. They penetrated into the courtyard of the citadel. The Indians at once threw stones and darts, while the Spaniards struck out with clubs and maces, creating a space around themselves.

Villac Umu and other chiefs left the citadel to alert Manco to send reinforcements.

Juan Pizarro was wearing no helmet because of the injury to his jaw, and he was struck on the head by a large stone. He managed to hold up for a few moments and then collapsed. He died not long after. He was twenty-five years old. They concealed his death from the Indians. They sent to inform Hernando.

There was much grief. How had it happened? Hernando went to the citadel. It was dawn, the dawn that saw his brother die. He took command of the siege. His strategy was to attack the higher levels, the towers, or at least to wear them down, counting on the lack of arrows and stones and the shortage of water. The Indians could not hold out for long. The course of events altered as they buried Juan Pizarro, who had received absolution.

A few days later, they resorted to an assault using ladders. The Indians, all peasants, could stand no more. Alone, a noble warrior, the "long ears," the one they called in Quechua *pakayoc*, inspired the struggle, running everywhere a threat appeared, firmly clasping a Spanish sword. They would not take him alive. He threw himself from the top of the tower, his tunic over his face like a Roman.

Perhaps the sandglass counting the Spaniards' days had just reversed direction?

Yet countrywide the news was good for Manco. Runners arrived to announce victories. They had taken Jauja in the center of the country; Manco's captains controlled the country. The Indians celebrated: they drank; they gave thanks to their gods; they rediscovered hope. Manco savored these moments. He was the Inca. Now that there were no more Spaniards except at Cuzco and Lima, a decisive blow had to be struck. They had to take Lima and kill these strangers or make them leave forever. He sent his runners to have done with it.

But have done with it they could not. The reinforcements sent to Cuzco to save the Indians besieged in the citadel arrived too late. The strangers were now solidly dug in. The Indians could only count on starvation and time.

But there again the Indians failed to starve them. The strangers had come with their horses and had seized supplies and llamas brought by Manco's troops. How had they allowed themselves to be taken by surprise? News had arrived from Lima. The Indians had not been able to have done with the strangers. The captains commanding the attack were dead. On the plain, the Spanish horsemen had recovered all their capacity to hit hard. They broke the vanguard where Manco's captains were. The troops fled. How could it be that despite their numerical superiority the Indians could not defeat these strangers? What magic did they have that Manco had been unable to discover during his stay in Cuzco?

And then the Indians had to retreat. Almagro had returned with his troops from Chile, with fine words. The strangers always had fine words in the beginning. They could not be trusted. Other Spaniards had come from the north. They had had to retreat. Now the couriers reported that they were fighting among themselves. May they all end up killing each other!

The Indians had to withdraw into the Andes at Vilcabamba, which was almost inaccessible, and prepare a new attack next year, when all those who worked in the fields would have finished their work. Nothing was yet lost. They retained the hope that, next time, they would finish the Spaniards off, especially if they weakened themselves by fighting each other over gold.

In those years, Manco's warriors came back in large numbers. His captains were in the north and the south. Some tribes, previously subjugated, refused to join his war, but others agreed to do so. In those years they killed many Spaniards. They would catch them like game in a defile, where their horses stumbled, and crush them with rocks. They knew how to deal with them. All they had to do was finish off the wounded and carry their heads in triumph on pikes so that everyone could see how vulnerable the Spaniards were and how brave the Inca was. In those years, Manco's war brought back the great armies of earlier years.

And then the strangers became more numerous; they came from abroad. They arrived in strength. They gave no quarter. They massacred all those who had participated in any way, however slight, in the revolt—women and children too. They wanted to strike fear. Manco's captains had been defeated or had surrendered or were dead. And the strangers did cause fear. Now Manco had withdrawn into a region very difficult of access; he launched raids on roads. He harassed communications whenever the enemy was few in numbers. He now simply wanted to stay free and not be told what to do by strangers. As the years went by—seven had passed—he became no more than the ruler of an inhospitable mountain, but he still had followers. He lived with them outside the world of the strangers who had subjugated the land of his ancestors. From time to time he attacked them. And then there were long periods when nothing happened. Manco and his followers lived as best they could. They spread fear and they suffered in turn when the Spaniards came in strength to hunt down the Inca in his lair. And twice Manco succeeded in escaping them. They attacked both Vitcos and Vilcabamba, but each time Manco fled just in time with some of his loyal supporters, his wives, and his children. Among them was Titu Cusi, who would later tell with all due respect—as is right—the heroic and sad story of his father, who was betrayed by the Spaniards whom he had welcomed into his land and protected, the story of his father who lived free despite the twilight of the Incas.

And time passed over Vilcabamba. Two Incas followed Manco.

The first, Sayri-Tupac, ended up going to Lima, was received with full honors, and died the following year. Who knows whether the Spaniards did not themselves kill him in some way? The second was Titu Cusi, who negotiated with them continuously without leaving his secure retreat; he agreed to be baptized and entrusted to a priest an account in which he denounced the Spaniards' injustice toward his father and his people and accused them of loving gold more than the God of whom the priest spoke to him and [God] who was just.

In the late afternoon of September 24, 1572, it was cold at Cuzco. The last of the Incas, Tupac Amaru, was about to be put to death. He was not a Christian. He worshiped his own gods. He had declared war on the strangers again. He was an Inca. He caused the envoys of the Crown and the Pope to be executed. He wanted to return to the old order. He said no.

Spanish troops hunted him down for a long time. They clashed with his men and beat them. Only a handful of them was left, and their redoubt had been besieged, but Tupac Amaru had already left. They pursued him along rivers and through the jungle. Tupac Amaru fled with his pregnant wife. He wanted to escape the Spaniards, but in the end they caught up with him after a long chase.

He was their prisoner forever. Before long, all that remained of him would be the echo of revolt, always so difficult to stifle—the murmur, ten times repeated, of the refusal to be subjugated.

In the great square at Cuzco, the Inca was to be beheaded, the method of execution then reserved for great criminals. He was guilty of treason. He was the last Inca of a world whose death had begun at Cajamarca forty years before.

Guaman Poma de Ayala speaks thus of the Spaniards:

> Day and night the men from Castile . . . said in their dreams: "The Indies, the Indies, gold, silver, gold, the silver of Peru."
>
> This lust for gold and silver is still alive today, and the Spaniards kill one another, and they skin the poor Indians for gold and silver, and much of the kingdom is now desolate. . . .
>
> The Spaniards spread out all over this kingdom, in pairs and sometimes alone, some with their Indian *yanaconas,* who were all looking for their own benefit, causing great harm and suffering to the Indians, demanding gold and silver, seizing clothes and food. And they [the Indians] were terrified to see these people they had never seen before, and so fleeing the Christians, they hid. . . .
>
> After conquering and stealing, they [the Spaniards] started to

seize the women and rape the young women, who were killed like dogs, if they refused, punishing them without fear of God or justice. There was no justice.

Manco Inca reigned at Cuzco under the control of the Spaniards. One of his younger brothers, Paullu, was also in the capital. He was later to play an important role as an ally and collaborator of the Spaniards.

But by the beginning of 1535 frictions between Almagro and his men, backed by Alvarado's men and Pizarro's, reached the boiling point. The Crown had granted Pizarro northern Peru, and Almagro received the southern part as far as northern Chile. This left the status of Cuzco uncertain. Pizarro proposed a compromise that opened up to Almagro the prospect of exploring, conquering, and ruling the lands in the south. Pizarro even agreed partly to finance the expedition. To him, this had the merit of removing from Cuzco many men who had nothing to do and were keen to make their fortunes. In the meantime, Cuzco was full of intrigue. Manco had one of his brothers assassinated, then sought Almagro's protection, his relations with Juan and Gonzalo Pizarro being bad.

Almagro set out for Chile in July 1535, in the middle of the southern winter—it was not long before he realized his mistake—with 570 men and several thousand Indians under the command of Paullu and the high priest Villac Umu. Their presence would ensure that the expedition enjoyed the cooperation of the local people.

But the expedition to Chile was a failure. There was no gold, and nature was pitilessly harsh. They lost many men, some Spaniards but mostly Indians, and horses. Chile was the conquistadors' Ultima Thule. To reach there, they had to cross the cordillera—the Bolivian plateau—in the middle of the southern winter, then the desert of Atacama between the hostile mountains and the freezing rollers of the waves of the Pacific. Few landscapes are more tragically desolate.

The historian Francisco de Oviedo writes:

> There was no wood at all to make a fire. There was no shelter. The Indians collapsed in the snow, froze to death while leaning on a rock, catching their breath. Thirty horses died. The hunger was such that the Indians were eating their fellows who had frozen to death and the Spaniards, their frozen horses. If they halted, they succumbed to the cold.

The Spaniards, especially Almagro's men, behaved extremely cruelly. Cristóbal de Mena reports:

Every native who refused to accompany the Spaniards was
taken in chains or tied up. They were locked up at night, and
during the day they carried heavy loads, dying of hunger. . . .
When the mares of the Spaniards foaled, they made Indian
women carry the foals in litters. Others had themselves carried
in litters, leading their horses by the bridle to fatten them.

Atrocities became an everyday affair.

The high priest Villac Umu escaped in October at Tupiza (in
Bolivia) and returned to Cuzco. Before long most of the Indians had
fled.

While Pizarro founded Trujillo in the north of the country, at
Cuzco there was an influx of arrivals from Central America and the
Caribbean. The vanquished were increasingly badly treated. The
arrogance of the victors was given free rein. Juan and Gonzalo
Pizarro and other Spanish captains treated the Inca Manco in a
humiliating way. The situation became intolerable. Soon Manco
attempted to flee. He was caught and put in irons. They urinated on
him and raped his wives in front of him.

Hernando Pizarro returned to Cuzco in January 1536 after two
years' absence in Spain, and, in accordance with the policy laid
down by the Crown, sought to regain Manco's friendship and loyalty. But it was too late. After he was freed, Manco, who pretended
to accept his fate, successfully deceived the Spaniards by pretending
to absent himself for a religious ceremony in April, at the end of the
rainy season. It was two days later that the Spaniards became certain
that Manco had escaped and was fomenting a rebellion. The troops
were to meet at Calca in the valley of Yucay. There they would be
protected from the Spanish horsemen by the Yucay River and would
be only 25 kilometers from Cuzco.

Titu Cusi imagined what his father Manco said to the Spaniards:

And now, alas, this is the second time that you have so irrev-
erently and sadly offended me . . . holding me in prison for a
long time, since I have been in irons like a dog for two months
now. And I will repeat again and again that you have done this
not as Christians and sons of God as you claim, but as the devil
whose path you follow, doing evil to those who do you good.
And I will even say that you are worse than one who is not
looking for gold or silver . . . whereas you seek them and want
to take them by force even from places where there is none. You
are worse than the Yungas [devils] who would kill their father

and mother for gold and even destroy the world. And you have completely forgotten the favors you received from me, and the fact that I loved you with all my heart and desired your friendship, which you rejected for gold, treating me worse than you treat your dogs. . . . You seem to cling more to your gold than to the friendship of men, since for love of gold you lost my friendship and the friendship of the people of my land.

Garcilaso Inca writes:

The Inca [Manco] summoned warriors to go to Cuzco and the city of the Kings [Lima] to fight and defeat the Spaniards. He sent them to kill all those who were sucking the country dry and taking gold from the mines, those who, thanks to the Indians' hard work, were behaving as if they were in their own land while killing Indians all over the country. Thus, for this purpose they secretly went to Cuzco . . . and more than two hundred thousand Indians came, most of them with bows and arrows and incendiary materials. They fired on all the houses in the city, not even sparing the royal dwelling places, except for the Temple of the Sun with all that it contained.

Pedro Pizarro reports:

When Hernando Pizarro learned that a force of warriors was being assembled at Yucay, he ordered his brother, Juan Pizarro, to take seventy cavalrymen and disperse the gathering being made there; and after we went there [we saw] on the other side of the very large river that is in this [valley of] Yucay some ten thousand Indian warriors, who did not believe that we could cross the river. Seeing this, Juan Pizarro ordered all of us to throw ourselves into the river and swim across it with our horses, and, with him doing so first, we all followed him, and in this way we crossed the river by swimming and attacked the Indian warriors and routed them, and the Indians withdrew to some high peaks toward the mountains where the horses could not climb.

While we were here for three or four days, Hernando Pizarro called us to return with all speed, giving us to understand that a great force of troops was marching upon Cuzco, and so it was that, when we returned, we found many squadrons of troops who were arriving continually, and were camping in the roughest spots around Cuzco, waiting for the rest [of their troops] to come, and when they had all arrived, they camped on the plains and the heights. So numerous were the troops here that they covered the fields, and by day it looked as if a black cloth had been spread over the ground for half a league around Cuzco. At night there were so many fires that it looked like a very serene sky full of stars. There was so much shouting and din of voices that we were all amazed. When all the troops that Inca had sent to assemble had arrived, . . . one morning they began setting fire to all over Cuzco, and by means of this fire they were gaining many portions of the town, making palisades in the streets so that the Spaniards could not go out through them. We Spaniards gathered in the plaza and in the houses adjoining it, such as Hatuncancha . . . and here we were all assembled, and some were in tents in the plaza, because the Indians had burned all the rest of the town. And in order to burn down these dwellings where, as I say, we were, they used the stratagem of taking several round stones and throwing them in the fire, where they became red hot. Wrapping them up in cotton, they threw them by means of slings into the houses that they could not reach when thrown by hand, and in this way they burned our houses before we understood how.

At other times they shot flaming arrows at the houses, which, being of straw, soon took fire. While we were in this confusion, Hernando Pizarro divided the troops into three parties of cavalry, assigning captains for them. He gave one to Gonzalo Pizarro, his brother, another to Gabriel de Rojas, and the third to Hernando Ponce de León.

The Indians had us so hard pressed and in so much confusion that it is certain that our Lord delivered us by his own hands, because [we would surely have perished] on account of the many Indian warriors there were and the small number of us Spaniards—not even two hundred all told, and of these, only seventy or eighty cavalrymen did the fighting, because the rest were nonfighters and infantrymen, and these last did but little, for the Indians hold them in slight account; and it was certainly true that an Indian could fight better than a Spanish foot soldier, because the Indians are very free [in their movements] and they shoot at the Spaniards from a distance, and before the Spaniards can catch up to them, they have dashed off to some other place than that from which they fired the first shot, and so they [the Indians] wear them out, and the Indians being so many, they would kill them [the Spaniards]. . . .

But they feared the cavalry greatly, because they [the cav-
alry] could catch up to them and kill them as they swept by.
Hernando Pizarro agreed, therefore, not to use the infantry,
making use [instead] of the cavalry for this business, because
the majority of the infantry were thin and debilitated men. He
ordered them to go by night with some leaders who were named
for the purpose, Pedro del Barco, Diego Mendez, and Villa-
castin, and some friendly Indians, some fifty or sixty Cañaris,
who had remained in the service of the Spaniards and who were
enemies of Manco Inca, to throw down the palisades that the
Indians were building by day. . . .

Cuzco is overhung by a hill on the side of the fortress, and
the Indians came down on this side to a spot near the plaza that
belonged to Gonzalo Pizarro and his brother, Juan Pizarro, and
from here they did us much harm, for with slings they hurled
stones into the plaza without our ability to prevent it. This place
being steep, as I say, [and accessible only] through a narrow
lane that the Indians had seized, so that it was not possible to go
up through it without all those who entered it being killed, and
while we were thus in a state of uneasiness, for there was certainly much din because of the loud cries and alarms that they
gave and the trumpets and flutes that they sounded, so that it
seemed as if the very earth trembled, Hernando Pizarro and his
captains assembled many times to discuss what to do, and some
said that we ought to desert the town and leave it in flight; others said that we ought to establish ourselves in Hatuncancha,
which was a great enclosure where we might all fit, and which,
as I have already said, had but one doorway and a very high
wall of stone masonry. None of this advice was good, for if we
had sallied from Cuzco, they would have killed all of us in the
bad passes and mountain fastnesses there, and if we had taken
refuge in the enclosure, they would have imprisoned us with
adobes and stones because of the many troops that there were.
So Hernando Pizarro was never in agreement, and he told them
that we would all have to give up our lives and not desert
Cuzco. These meetings were attended by Hernando Pizarro and
his brothers, Gabriel de Rojas, Hernan Ponce de León, and the
treasurer Riquelme. Then, after several meetings, Hernando
Pizarro agreed [to attempt] to capture the fortress, for it was
from there that we received the most harm, as I have said,
because at the very beginning an agreement was not reached to

take it before the Indians laid siege, nor was the importance of holding it realized. This being agreed on, a task was set us, and we in the cavalry were ordered to be ready with our arms to take [the fortress], and Juan Pizarro, his [Hernando Pizarro's] brother was ordered to go as leader, and he gave the same orders to the other captains already mentioned. Hernando Pizarro remained in Cuzco with the infantry, all gathered together where he ordered them to be.

Then, a day before this sally, it so happened that they [the Indians] shot a big stone from an *anden*, and it hit a soldier named Pedro del Barco, striking him on the head so that he fell upon the ground unconscious, and, seeing it, Juan Pizarro, who was nearby, rushed to aid him, and then he was hit in the jaw and injured by a large stone. I wanted to tell this in order [to explain] what I shall relate farther on, concerning him.

The cavalry having set out, as I said, in order to take the fortress, with Juan Pizarro as chief of all of them, we went up through Carmenga, a narrow road, bordered on one side by a declivity and on the other by a gully, deep in some places, and from this gully they did us much harm with stones and arrows, and in some places they had broken down the road and made many holes in it. We went by this way with much effort, because we kept stopping while the few friendly Indians, not even one hundred, whom we had with us filled up the holes and covered the road with adobes. Having climbed, with a sufficient amount of hard work, up to a small flat place . . . we went around some small hills and difficult places in order to capture the flat part of the fortress where the principal gateway and entrance is, and in these little gullies we had encounters with the Indians, because they had almost captured two Spaniards who had fallen from their horses.

As we arrived at the plain and gateway by which we were to enter, it was so well barricaded and so strong that, although we tried twice to enter, they made us retreat, wounding some horses; and so the captains agreed to wait until midnight to attack them, because at that hour the Indians are sleepy.

Going back now to Hernando Pizarro, who remained in Cuzco, the Indians came out into the streets and entered the houses, for they believed that we were deserting the city. Elsewhere, they saw that Hernando Pizarro and the infantry were all together. They could not understand what was happening, so they were surprised until they saw us attack the fortress from one side, and then they understood what we were doing. . . .

While Juan Pizarro and those of us who were with him were waiting for the nightfall, it grew dark, and Juan Pizarro ordered his brother Gonzalo Pizarro and the other captains to enter [the fortress] with half of the cavalry, whom he ordered to alight, and the others to be on horseback ready to aid them; and Juan Pizarro remained with the mounted men, because he was not able to wear armor on his head, which had been torn by the wound he had received on his jaw, as I said, on the day they attacked him.

Then, entering [the fortress], those who were on foot began very slowly to throw down the first gateway, which was barricaded with a wall of dry stone, and when it was taken down, they began to go forward up a narrow path. On arriving at the barricade of the other wall, they were spotted by the Indians, who began to throw so many stones that the ground was torn up, and this caused the Spaniards to grow cool and they stopped and did not press forward. While things were in this state, a Spaniard cried out to Juan Pizarro, saying that the Spaniards were retreating and were fleeing. Hearing this cry, Juan Pizarro placed a shield on his arm and hurled himself into the fortress, ordering those of us who were mounted to follow him, and so we did; and with the arrival of Juan Pizarro and the mounted men at the second barricade and gateway, it was won, and we entered as far as a courtyard that is in the fortress. Then, from a terrace that is on one side of this courtyard, they showered us with so many stones and arrows that we could do nothing, and for this reason Juan Pizarro incited some infantrymen toward the terrace that I mentioned, which was low, so that some Spaniards might get up on it and drive the Indians from there. And while he was fighting with these Indians in order to drive them away, Juan Pizarro neglected to cover his head with his shield, and one of the many stones that they were hurling hit him on the head and broke his skull, and he died of this wound in less than two weeks. Even though wounded, he was fighting with the Indians until this terrace was won, and when it was gained, they took him down to Cuzco. . . .

Learning about the disaster that had befallen his brother and of the state in which the capture of the fortress was left, he [Hernando Pizarro] soon went up there, leaving Gabriel de

Rojas [in charge] in Cuzco. When Hernando Pizarro arrived [at
the fortress] it was already dawn, and we spent all of this day
and the next fighting with the Indians who had gathered
together on the two topmost levels, which could be gained only
by means of thirst, waiting for their water to give out, and so it
happened that we were here two or three days until their water
came to an end, and when it had given out, they hurled themselves from the highest walls—some in order to flee, and others
to kill themselves—and others surrendered, and in this way they
began to lose courage, and so one level was gained. We arrived
at the last level, [which] had as its captain an *orejon* so valiant
that the same might be written of him as has been written of
some Romans. This *orejon* bore a shield on his arms and a
sword in his hand . . . and a helmet upon his head. This man had
taken these arms from the Spaniards who had perished on the
roads. . . . This *orejon*, then, marched like a lion from one end
to another of the highest level of all, preventing the Spaniards
from mounting with ladders and killing the Indians who surrendered, for I understand that he killed more than thirty Indians
because they [wanted] to surrender and to glide down from the
level. . . . Whenever one of his men warned him of some
Spaniard climbing up in some place, he rushed at him like a
lion, with his sword. . . . Seeing this, Hernando Pizarro commanded that three or four ladders be set up, so that while he was
rushing to one point, they might climb up at another, for the
Indians this *orejon* had with him had all now either surrendered
or were lacking in courage, and he alone was fighting. Hernando Pizarro ordered those Spaniards who climbed up not to
kill this Indian but to take him alive, swearing that he would not
kill him if he had him alive. Then, climbing up at two or three
places, the Spaniards won the level. This *orejon*, realizing that
they had conquered him and had taken his stronghold at two or
three points, threw down his arms, covered his head and face
with his mantle, and threw himself down from the level to a
spot more than one hundred *estados* below, where he was shattered. . . .

The taking of the fortress was the reason the Indians withdrew a little, giving up the part of the city that they had gained.
In this manner we were on the alert during more than two
months.

Despite their considerable numerical superiority, the Indians were unable to win, either in frontal attack or in a war of attrition. They were unable to break the Spaniards' morale, and the fall of the citadel at the end of May 1536 signaled the failure of the siege, although it actually continued for a further two months.

In a dialogue that he imagines between Manco and his captains, Titu Cusi has Manco say:

> You deceived me. You were so many and they so few, and yet they have escaped you . . . you knew that they are our greatest enemies and that we must always be theirs since that is how they have willed it. . . .
>
> The captains answered: We are so ashamed that we dare not look you straight in the face. We do not know why, except for that we were wrong not to have attacked [the Spaniards] in time, and you did not allow us to do so.

With hindsight, the Indians had a better appreciation of the effect of surprise. The Incas' conceptions of war contained many other shortcomings, such as no nighttime attacks except on nights when there was a full moon, which, being ritual, were predictable. As for the Spaniards, with their backs to the wall and nowhere to turn except prayer and faith, they fought with admirable resolve and tenacity. Hernando Pizarro proved himself a skillful and energetic leader in war, and his two brothers, leaders of men and magnificent fighters.

The Spaniards suffered heavy losses. On both sides the war was extremely cruel. Alonzo Enríquez de Guzman writes:

> As I know from experience, this was the most fearful and cruel war in the world; for between Christians and Moors there is some feeling of fellowship, and both sides, acting in their own interests, spare their prisoners for the sake of the ransom. But in this Indian war there is no such feeling on either side; both kill as savagely as they can.

The Spaniards impaled their enemies or burned them alive. Women were not spared, particularly during the siege, when they actively helped the warriors. Gonzalo Pizarro had the right hands of two hundred prisoners cut off in order to strike terror into the Inca fighters. When they could, the Indians did just the same.

The rebellion, largely involving peasants, was not limited to Cuzco. In the center of the country, around Jauja, other operations were conducted by Manco's captains, such as Tiso, Quizo Yupanqui, Illa Tupac, and Puyu Vilca.

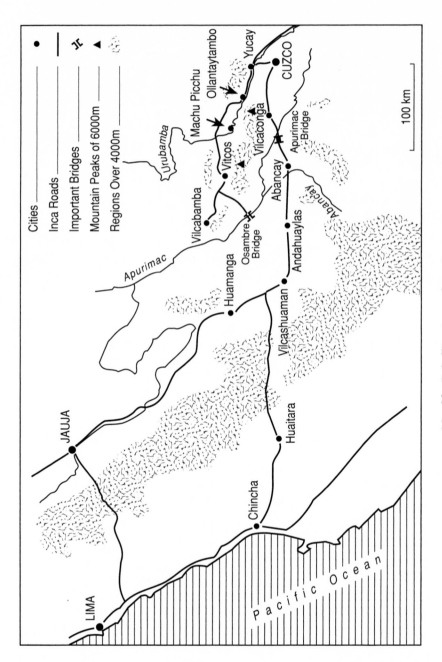

Map10. Rebellion in southern Peru

It was only at the beginning of May that Francisco Pizarro, in Lima, learned of the siege of Cuzco. He immediately dispatched thirty horsemen under the command of Morgovejo de Quiñones and then seventy as reinforcements commanded by Gonzalo de Tapia. These latter fell into an ambush in the cordillera. Quizo Yupanqui was waiting for them in a pass whose exit had been blocked by rocks. From the heights, the Indians rolled down large boulders. Not a single Spaniard was able to retreat. Near Parcos, the same Quizo Yupanqui did the same to sixty Spanish horsemen.

Subsequently, Pizarro sent two more detachments to Cuzco. The first was composed of thirty horsemen of whom only one survived, and a second of thirty men who fell back to Lima when they realized how difficult their task would be.

Agustin de Zarate writes:

> Now as the Marquis received news of the Indians' rebellion . . . he began sending reinforcements to Hernando Pizarro at Cuzco, little by little as he could collect them. . . . But, hearing of these reinforcements, the Indians posted large numbers of warriors at the narrow and dangerous passes on the road to intercept them. And so, all those sent by the Marquis at different times were defeated and killed; which would not have happened had he taken the precaution of sending them all together. . . . The Marquis sent Diego Pizarro with seventy horsemen to reinforce Cuzco, and they were all killed at a very dangerous pass, called the Parcos hill, fifty leagues from the city; and Gonzalo de Tapia, one of his brothers-in-law, whom he sent afterward with eighty horsemen met with the same fate. The Indians also defeated Captain Morgovejo and Captain Gaete and their followers on different days, and hardly a man escaped. Those who were riding behind were unaware that those ahead had been overwhelmed, since the attack took the following form: the Indians let the Spaniards enter a very deep and narrow valley, and blocked both the entrance and the exit with great numbers of men. Then from the slopes, they hurled so many stones and boulders down on them that they killed almost all of them without coming to close quarters.

Meanwhile, buoyed up by his victories, Quizo Yupanqui launched a surprise attack on Jauja. The town was held by a few dozen Spaniards.

Martin de Murua writes:

Quizo Yupanqui arrived at dawn. He arrived so unexpectedly that the Spaniards were surrounded, even before they realized what was happening. They were still in bed and did not even have time to get dressed. In this chaos, they regrouped in a temple that had been turned into a fortress with whatever weapons they could pick up in their haste. One can imagine the confusion, for they would never have believed that the Indians could attack them. . . . The fighting went on from morning when the Indians arrived to the hour of vespers . . . and the Indians killed everyone, as well as their horses and Negro servants.

Quizo Yupanqui's forces had virtually wiped out the Spanish presence between Cuzco and Lima. The small detachment of thirty men commanded by Morgovejo de Quiñones, the first sent by Pizarro to relieve Cuzco, was ambushed twice in the cordillera. As they were retreating toward the coastal road, they fell into a third ambush in a defile. Five Spaniards—including the leader of the expedition—were killed. Of the four detachments sent by Pizarro as reinforcements, not one was able to fulfill its mission, and almost three-quarters of the men died.

Pizarro had to call for outside help. In July, he wrote to Pedro de Alvarado, the powerful governor of Guatemala: "The Inca has been besieging the city of Cuzco for five months and I have no news of the Spaniards there. The country is in such disarray that no Indian chief will agree to serve us and they have won many victories over us." Soon reinforcements were being organized in Nicaragua, Panama, and elsewhere.

Manco ordered Quizo to leave the cordillera and head for Lima to deliver the final blow. After a few preparations, Quizo approached the foothills. News of the arrival of Indian troops soon hit the city.

Although the rebellion had failed to overcome the determined resistance of the defenders of Cuzco, it was proceeding satisfactorily in the rest of the country. The Spaniards had their backs against the wall.

Meanwhile, in Cuzco, Hernando Pizarro was attempting a bold maneuver: to come out in force from Cuzco with seventy horsemen, thirty foot soldiers, and a strong detachment of Indians to try to strike at the head.

The target was Manco. He was at Ollantaytambo in a fortresslike temple in very mountainous country. Hernando's forces occupied a band of plain between the Yucay River and the foothills. Now it was the Indians' turn to take the offensive. Numerous bowmen rained down their darts on the Spaniards, who tried unsuccessfully to charge. Nor was it possible to take the high ground that dominated the fortress, since there were too many Indians, and they were pushing down so many rocks. The Indians were even beginning to have a few metal weapons taken from the Spaniards. Manco himself appeared on horseback to encourage his men. One day, the Indians succeeded in diverting the waters of a nearby river, intending to flood the plain where the Spaniards were. The water came up to the horses' knees, and the Spaniards had to retreat. "And the Indians attacked us with great cries, catching the horses by the tail. . . . They attacked us furiously as we tried to cross the river at night with our torches."

The next day, however, Hernando Pizarro's forces succeeded in getting back into Cuzco.

Encouraged by the Spaniards' setback, Manco tried to assemble a larger army to attempt a new assault on Cuzco.

Hunger was becoming chronic among the besieged, and it caused more deaths than the military operations. They tried to grow some maize, but there was not enough. However, Hernando Pizarro learned that the Indians had just received a large quantity of llamas and maize. He sent seventy horsemen to try and seize them.

Pedro Pizarro records: "We went there and remained absent for twenty-five or thirty days and after taking almost two thousand head of cattle, we returned to Cuzco without being intercepted." The besieged thus escaped starvation.

Yet once or twice Manco just missed victory. Two detachments totaling thirty-five horsemen led by Gonzalo Pizarro and Alonso de Toro were ambushed while on a reconnaissance operation, and their lives were saved only by the fact that Hernando Pizarro made a sortie at the head of a dozen horsemen.

However, even at the darkest hours, the Spaniards always took the initiative. Their strategy remained essentially offensive even when they were besieged.

The Indians increasingly had the feeling that they would not be able to take the city by a direct assault. There remained the hope of annihilating the bulk of the horsemen when they made a sortie or if they could be engaged on unfavorable terrain.

Spanish reinforcements flooded into Lima. Men arrived from Nicaragua; Hernando Cortes sent arms from Mexico; the governor of Panama sent several detachments. One hundred horsemen and two hundred foot soldiers arrived from Santo Domingo. There was a continent behind the men in Peru. And while Manco gathered together his men for a final assault after the rainy season, two Spanish forces were marching on Cuzco. Whenever they encountered resistance, they resorted to terror tactics aimed at discouraging any spread of the rebellion. They renewed ties with Indian tribes opposed to the Incas and ready to cooperate with the Spaniards. Fresh forces sent by Pizarro amounted to almost five hundred men.

From the south the survivors of Almagro's expedition to Chile were also heading for Cuzco.

Almagro returned from northern Chile where the expedition had suffered a severe setback, after being away for twenty months. According to Oviedo, 1,500 Indians, 200 Spaniards, 150 blacks, and 112 horses died of cold. This was in the spring of 1537.

When Almagro left for Chile, Pizarro's hope was that he would find there enough gold and other riches to satisfy him. The division set out in the royal decrees gave Pizarro 270 leagues of land south of his point of entry at Puna. Did this include Cuzco? That remained undecided. Almagro and his men, bitter and having paid dearly without results, wanted Cuzco.

Grasping the situation at once, Almagro tried to resume his alliance with Manco and wrote to him acknowledging that Manco had reasons to revolt and assuring him that the guilty would be punished by the Crown and that doubtless his own rebellion would be pardoned if he immediately renounced it. Finally, Almagro vaunted his own power and offered Manco his friendship.

Almagro reached Cuzco first. If he were to succeed in forming an alliance with the Inca, perhaps he might be able to make the Pizarro brothers carry the blame for Manco's revolt and himself appear as the restorer of order to the benefit of the Crown. But the negotiations with Manco marked time. Hernando Pizarro sent Manco a letter telling him not to trust Almagro. In any event, how *could* Manco trust the Spaniards, the very people who, when he was Inca in Cuzco, had humiliated and abused him? Doubtless after some hesitation, Manco took counsel, questioned the oracles, and decided not to embark on an alliance over whose implementation he would have no control whatsoever once it was sealed.

Having no time to waste, Almagro launched his attack. On April 18, 1537, the capital was taken without too much difficulty. Only the Pizarro brothers and a handful of their most ardent supporters fought. For the rest, Almagro was better than the Indians.

It was only in July that the troops sent by Pizarro arrived. Almagro's lieutenant, the remarkable Rodrigo Orgoñez, confronted them on the banks of the River Abancay and easily won a battle against inexperienced troops with little loss of blood.

That was a severe blow for Pizarro, who lost half his forces. He then tried to have the conflict arbitrated. A first embassy failed. Pizarro organized the defense of Lima. A delegation of notables from Central America headed by Gaspar de Espinosa, who knew both governors, went to see Almagro. He rejected any compromise. Espinosa left him with this premonitory phrase regarding the conflict: *El vencido vencido y el vencidor perdido* (the vanquished vanquished, and the victor undone).

As for Manco, he had no choice but to withdraw to places as remote as possible. The Spaniards could not be beaten. But they could be resisted in mountainous areas. He withdrew to Vitcos, a position from which it would be difficult to dislodge him, not far from the valley of Vilcabamba. Almagro sent Orgoñez after the Inca. He reached Vitcos and seized a great amount of booty, but the Inca had had time to flee. Orgoñez brought back several thousand prisoners. From now on, the Inca Manco was a sovereign without an army. Now he survived only by fleeing. His army, made up mainly of peasants who returned to their villages when the time for sowing or harvesting came, had been unable to overcome a handful of Spaniards by means of a frontal assault. From now on Manco would pursue a war of attrition from a sanctuary.

When he was master of Cuzco, against the advice of Orgoñez, Almagro refused to execute the two Pizarro brothers, thinking that to do so would create a breach and prevent any compromise with Francisco Pizarro. Gonzalo succeeded in escaping and Hernando was released during the negotiations.

Once the three brothers were together again, they rejected all negotiations. War would decide the outcome.

Hernando Pizarro himself took command of the forces that would face Almagro's. His second in command was Pedro de Valdivia, a veteran of the Italian wars, who was later to win fame as the conqueror of Chile. The Pizarros had eighty muskets; Almagro, only fifteen.

The die was cast on April 26, 1538, at the battle of Las Salinas, where the aging Almagro, who was sick (he had syphilis), was present in his chair. Rodrigo Orgoñez fought valiantly, but the Pizarros' superior firepower carried the day. Orgoñez was wounded and captured and was beheaded. To his great surprise, Almagro, who had spared the brothers, was condemned to death and garroted. He was sixty-three years old.

Hernando Pizarro returned to Cuzco. Almagro had had the support of one of Manco's brothers, Paullu, who now agreed to serve these new masters. The chances of a successful Indian rebellion looked more remote than ever.

The conflict between Manco and his successors and the Spaniards was overshadowed after 1538 by the rivalry between the supporters of Almagro and those of the Pizarros. The war in Peru became triangular, the Indian threat being marginal. With hindsight, the most important aspect of intra-Spanish rivalries was, however, less the struggle to the death between the Almagro faction and the Pizarro faction (1537–1542) than the very bitter confrontation between the Pizarro faction, made up of men who were conquistadors and settlers, and the Crown.

When the king sought to put an end to the most scandalous abuses and use new laws to regulate the exploitation of Indian labor, which previously was unrestricted, a conflict broke out that went on for ten years (1544 –1554). In the course of it, a viceroy met his death before the royalist camp gained the upper hand and Gonzalo Pizarro was executed (1548). The years 1553 and 1554 saw a final uprising by the last remaining supporters of the Pizarros led by Hernando Giron.

THE END OF THE INCAS

Unable to engage in frontal combat, Manco resorted to guerrilla warfare. His forces created insecurity over much of the country's communications. In the north, his general, Illa Tupac, still had troops. But in the center, the Huancas, who had suffered under Inca rule, refused to join the rebellion.

In late 1538, Francisco Pizarro sent troops to the area of Andaguaylas to capture the Inca. They fell into a trap. In the same area, Manco's forces won a second victory. He took advantage of it to punish the Huancas by destroying their temple. But at the beginning of 1539, one by one the leaders of the rebellion in the south surrendered, the last of them, to the Spaniards' surprise, being Tiso, who was undefeated. On March 19, 1539, Gonzalo Pizarro returned in triumph to Cuzco with his prisoner, the last survivor of Huayna Capac's generals. It was not until October 1539 that the high priest

Villac Umu agreed to surrender. The resistance fighters' morale had broken.

Yet in the north, the rebellion continued. Illa Tupac controlled the cordillera from Jauja. The Spaniards, wanting to put the rebellion down finally, organized a hunt. At the head of seventy horsemen and several thousand Indian allies, Gonzalo Pizarro went off in pursuit of Manco, who had set up camp at Vilcabamba. Gonzalo's troops fell into an ambush and suffered heavy losses. Once they had reinforcements, the Spaniards attacked and took the fortress of Vilcabamba. But, once again, Manco had escaped.

Out of spite, Francisco Pizarro had Manco's wife, who had fallen into his hands, cruelly put to death. He also executed Villac Umu, who had surrendered, and Tiso, along with fifteen other Inca military leaders. The second rebellion was crushed, except for Illa Tupac, who continued to operate in the north, and Manco, who was still alive and free.

Gonzalo Pizarro was named governor of Quito in 1539. He set out from Quito in search of Eldorado, sailing along the Napo River. It was on this occasion that Francisco de Orellana descended the Amazon.

Hernando Pizarro returned to Spain in 1539. He was imprisoned the following year and remained incarcerated, in very liberal conditions, for twenty years before being released. Of the four Pizarro brothers, he alone survived to die a natural death.

In Cuzco, the Spaniards now relied increasingly on Manco's brother, Paullu. But for Pizarro, the newly restored peace was of short duration. Almagro's supporters, bound together by a shared history and a shared frustration, plotted and came together behind Almagro's mestizo son, Diego de Almagro (el Mozo), to assassinate the aged conquistador.

On Sunday, July 26, 1541, in Lima, twenty of Diego de Almagro's men forced the doors of the palace and, after a sharp skirmish in which Pizarro, now more than sixty years old, showed himself to be still tough, did what they had planned. Today, Pizarro's tomb lies in Lima cathedral, and an equestrian statue of him stands in the great square, opposite the cathedral.

Diego de Almagro and his men occupied Lima for a year and sought to establish their control over the country. They were defeated in September 1542 at the battle of Chupas by troops of the king's licentiate, Vaca de Castro. Diego de Almagro was executed.

It was about this time, in November 1542, that new laws were decreed creating the Council of the Indies. For the past three years, under the influence of Las Casas among others, a series of questions about the Indians had been debated, and the new laws were largely in favor of these latter. Slavery was to be abolished. The *encomienda* system (there were slightly fewer than five hundred *encomiendas* in Peru) was to be reformed. A new royal representative was sent, Blasco Nuñez de Vela, who tried to enforce the new laws strictly; that provoked a revolt by the Spaniards in Peru led by Gonzalo Pizarro.

The viceroy, Blasco Nuñez de Vela, was killed in January 1546, and Gonzalo became master of Peru. The Indians were no longer a danger. At most they were something to be fought over by the strangers, and the victor would be their master. In fact, by as early as 1539, there was no longer any Indian threat of any significance. As for Manco, he was killed by some Spaniards, supporters of Almagro, to whom he had offered refuge.

Faced with the new situation, the king of Spain partly revoked the new laws and delegated a new representative, Pedro de La Gasca, who pursued a skillful policy that gradually isolated Gonzalo. On April 9, 1548, not far from Cuzco, the two armies—the legitimists' and Gonzalo's—faced each other. The bulk of the latter's army went over to the royalist side. Gonzalo was captured; he was executed the next day.

Manco continued to fight on until his death in 1544. When pressure from the Spaniards grew too strong, he withdrew to Vilcabamba.

Guaman Poma de Ayala relates the end of the Incas thus:

> Manco and his captains and many Indians fled to the village of Tampo. . . . But, he did not feel safe in Tampo and he withdrew further into the mountains around Vilcabamba. He had with him his captains. . . .
>
> A new Cuzco was populated and built as well as a new temple of Curicancha. . . . Few people, Indians of various classes, remained in the city of Vilcabamba; few fields were sown and there was little cattle, and Vilcabamba remained very poor. . . .
>
> On Inca Manco's orders, his captains took over of the gorge of the Apurimac at the point where the highway from Cuzco to Lima crossed the river. Their mission was to attack all parties of Spaniards and their friendly Christian Indians who tried to cross the river with their herds of cattle or merchandise. The Spaniards were to be killed and their goods, clothes, and all

their possessions taken; their attendant Indians were to be taken prisoner. In this manner, Manco Inca was able to survive in Vilcabamba for many years. . . .

A mestizo named Diego Mendez tricked his way into the city of Vilcabamba and, deceiving Inca Manco, he assailed and killed him with dagger blows. . . . The captains then killed this mestizo, and the heir was Inca Sayri-Tupac, who died at Cuzco and was succeeded by Tupac Amaru.

On the death of Manco, Sayri-Tupac was proclaimed Inca. La Gasca sought to negotiate with him so that he would come to Lima of his own free will, but without success. Sayri-Tupac remained in Vilcabamba. Meanwhile, in Cuzco, Paullu died. Negotiations with Sayri-Tupac resumed but proved very difficult. They lasted until 1557, when he left Vilcabamba. He reached Lima in great state in January 1558. He was twenty-nine years old. He was given several large *encomiendas* and these were granted to him not for two generations as with other proprietors, but in perpetuity. Sayri-Tupac went to Cuzco and was acclaimed by the Indians on the way. For the Spaniards this represented a considerable diplomatic victory.

But Sayri-Tupac died barely two years later.

When Sayri-Tupac had left Vilcabamba, his elder half-brother, Titu Cusi, had succeeded him. He supplanted a younger brother of Sayri-Tupac's, Tupac Amaru. Titu Cusi resumed the belligerent policy of Manco and harassed the Spaniards. In late 1564 to early 1565, he even succeeded in starting a revolt by the Indians in the Jauja region. The Spaniards entered into negotiations with him. Titu Cusi was aware of his own weakness and played for time. In 1566, he agreed to sign an agreement with the Spaniards. He converted to Christianity, strengthened his legitimacy by marrying the Inca's daughter, and obtained permission to stay in Vilcabamba, keeping the Indians who were with him in exchange for refraining from fighting. The treaty was ratified the following year. In 1570, he dictated his *Account*.

In reality, by 1570 Vilcabamba had been independent for almost thirty-five years. An Inca enclave survived, even if numerically weak.

The new viceroy, Francisco de Toledo, settled the Inca problem step by step. In 1570, he launched a great survey. His *informaciones*, sent to king Philip II (Charles's successor) in 1571, showed that the Incas had reigned over the empire only for a short time before the arrival of the Spaniards. A second survey, a "moral" one it might be

called, was conducted in 1571 regarding the Indians' customs and
the Spaniards' manner of treating the vanquished people. It was at
this point that Titu Cusi died. For Toledo, the fact that Titu Cusi's
successor was not his son but his brother Tupac Amaru was doubtless a determining factor. The latter, unlike Titu Cusi, was not a
Christian and was even very hostile to Christianity. Churches and
church paraphernalia in Vilcabamba were destroyed. Spaniards were
killed and converts persecuted. Coexistence was finished. The
viceroy hesitated to initiate an expedition, because the royal instructions were against a resumption of war against the Indians. But when
Tupac Amaru's supporters killed the viceroy's emissary, who was
bearing letters from the Pope and from the king, Toledo put an end
to his hesitation. He issued a declaration of war on April 14, 1572.

The operation against Vilcabamba was prepared carefully . The
main column had 250 well-equipped men. Two smaller columns
were sent to Abancay and Apurimac to cut off the Inca's retreat. On
June 1, the main column reached Coyao-Chaca, where Tupac
Amaru's men had set an ambush. The Spaniards lost two men in the
fighting.

The column continued toward Vitcos, which the Indians had
abandoned for Vilcabamba. The Spaniards headed there. On the
way, they passed by the places where, twenty-three years before,
Manco's forces had inflicted heavy losses on Gonzalo Pizarro's
forces. But the Indians no longer had the same manpower. The most
the Indians could do was harass the Spaniards at difficult places.

On June 20, the Spaniards reached the fort of Huayna Pucara. The
approach to the place was extremely difficult and could be very
costly. So they opted for a turning movement carried out in such a
way that the departure of fifty foot soldiers was not observed by the
Indians. The maneuver succeeded, and the surprise was such that the
Indians abandoned easily defensible outposts and withdrew into the
fort. At the agreed signal, the main Spanish force set off. A few
salvos were enough to take the place. On June 24, the expedition
reached its goal and took possession of Vilcabamba. But it was
deserted; some of the houses had been burned.

Martin de Murua writes:

> The entire city had been pillaged so systematically that the
> Spaniards and their Indian [friends] could not have done worse.
> All the men and women had fled and hidden in the jungle, car-
> rying with them whatever they could. They had burned the
> maize and foodstuffs left in the depots which were still smoking

when the expedition reached there. The temple of the sun that housed their principal idol was burned. They had done this before, when Gonzalo Pizarro entered the city. . . . They hoped that finding no food or anything else, the Spaniards would return. . . .

The town stretches or rather stretched over almost half a league, rather like Cuzco, but bigger. . . . The houses were covered with solid roofs. The Incas had a palace on several stories covered with tiles and painted with variety of paintings in their style—which is really worth seeing. There was a large square—large enough to hold a sizable crowd—where they held their festivals. . . . The doors of the palace were made of fine cedar, a tree which grows abundantly in the region.

It was learned that Tupac Amaru and Titu Cusi's son, Quispa Titu, had fled the previous evening toward the northwest. This time, the Spaniards were determined finally to bring the rebellion to an end. Several detachments of the fastest men were sent out. One of them found Quispa Titu. The Inca was still fleeing.

At the head of forty men, Martin Garcia de Loyola descended the Masahuay River in Mañaris country for more than 250 kilometers. They were already in the Amazonian forest, and the hunt continued, obstinately, thanks to a few scraps of information gleaned from the Mañaris Indians. These became more precise, and they left the river and moved into the jungle. To make up the delay, Loyola sometimes made night marches by torchlight. They covered about 80 kilometers in the jungle.

One evening, the Spanish vanguard saw a fire a little way off. The Inca, accompanied by his pregnant wife, had been caught.

Guaman Poma de Ayala writes: "They fought Tupac Amaru and put the Indians to flight. . . . Nothing happened, being young and knowing nothing, the Inca did not defend himself, he fled, and he was taken on the edge of the river, alone, with no Indians."

Tupac Amaru, the last of the Incas, was beheaded in the great square of Cuzco on September 24, 1572.

Tupac Amaru, the last of the Incas, is being led through the streets of Cuzco, barefoot, with a golden chain around his neck. He was beheaded in the great square of Cuzco on September 24, 1572.

CONCLUSION

No society has a monopoly on cruelty or justice. The terrible population loss that the Indian world experienced was first and foremost the consequence of epidemics in 1546, 1549, 1566, and so on. Bad administration and forced labor, especially in the mines in Peru, also played a role, as did the collapse of all the values that underpinned the balance of Indian societies. Broken, these societies took refuge in passive resistance (while their elites collaborated), sometimes exploding into revolts that were harshly put down. From the civil war between Quito and Cuzco followed by the conquest, Manco's rebellions and the struggles between Spaniards, Peru experienced a period of upheavals lasting more than a quarter of a century. The fertility rate itself collapsed.

I do not share the opinion of those who, basing themselves on the admirable but sometimes excessive denunciation by Las Casas, attribute a "black legend" to the conquest. The conquest unfolded in conditions that we, with our colonial experience, know to be quite classic. It is anachronistic to blame the Spaniards for having engaged in "ethnocide."[1] The Spaniards were convinced that they were bringing the true faith and saving the Indians from the shadows of idolatry. They were natural proselytizers. While it is true that the conditions of the conquest were very harsh, it is also true that laws were issued by the Council of the Indies in an endeavor to protect the Indians. Later, no other colonial power would decree anything comparable. The Franciscans, the Dominicans, and the Augustinians took on a role as protectors of the Indians: in Mexico, Bishop Zumarraga, the Franciscan Toribio "Motolonia," the bishop of Michoacan, the great Vasco de Quiroga.

Las Casas arrived in the Americas in 1502 and began to devote himself to the service of the Indians in 1510. By his own tenacity, he

1. Only people like Montaigne and La Boètie had become aware of such a reality.

later achieved the promulgation of "new laws" suppressing slavery and laying down that the Indians must be treated as subjects of the Crown (1542). These laws were bitterly opposed by the Spaniards in the Americas. Ten years later, his *Very Brief Account of the Destruction of the Indies* was printed in Seville. An important debate took place on the initiative of the Council of the Indies in which Ginès de Sepulveda clashed with Las Casas. At the end of this debate, the Council did not come down on one side or the other. But Sepulveda's writings were banned, while Las Casas's were not. Las Casas is not unique in Spain; one has only to mention the admirable figure of Francisco de Vitoria.

What does Las Casas say? That he feels it

> . . . proper that the Indians should no longer be subject to the regime of *encomienda* and that all establishments of this type should be closed immediately; that they should cease to distribute the natives among the Spaniards to be employed in their service or as they saw fit. Unpleasant experience has proven that this system has led to the greatest cruelties committed and it has delivered men, legitimately as free as we are, to the horrors of famine and terrible tortures; [men] whose race is on the point of disappearing in these provinces, as it has already disappeared in the Spanish island [Santo Domingo].

In his second memoir, he adds:

> . . . that your Majesty should have the general courts of his kingdom decree that all Indians presently subject to his power and those who shall be hereafter shall be considered free and subjects only of the Crown, [since] obviously no power on earth has the right to deprive a man of his freedom, except in case of an offense which justifies such a measure. The Indians must therefore remain free, since their conduct has never given grounds for others to become masters of their persons. No man can be dispossessed of his goods without a trial and judgment; therefore, no one can be deprived of his freedom, which is his first possession.

In his *Very Brief Account of the Destruction of the Indies*, Las Casas notes the atrocities committed by the Spaniards: their bleak cruelty is so reminiscent of the usual exactions that occur in wars of this type. Man's inhumanity to man is all too human.

Conversely, with regard to the Indians, Las Casas is very short-sighted. He uses such terms as *tender sheep* and *very tender lambs* to

describe them, as if they were of a different species. Marcel Bataillon, who is not unsympathetic to Las Casas and admires his courage,
writes: "Beneath his Dominican habit, taking on the role of God's
spokesman, he prophesies. At his height, in 1542, he dared to prophesy that, through the incalculable harm they had done in the Indies,
the Spaniards were exposing Spain to terrible punishment, even total
destruction." Las Casas's prophetic excesses do not diminish his
role, but he was not alone—far from it: priests, senior Spanish
authorities, even the Crown itself were concerned with protecting the
Indians, and in this respect Spain was in the vanguard. "Compared to
other colonial regimes, the Spaniards stand out by their efforts on
behalf of the natives," writes the American John Hemming.

In his introduction to *Récits aztèques de la Conquête (La Conquête de l'Amérique. La question de l'autre)*, Tzvetan Todorov, basing himself on the continent's demographic decline in the decades
that followed the conquest (which were the result of a variety
causes, and the Spaniards were not directly responsible for all of
them), writes: "If the word *genocide* is ever applied accurately to a
case, it is this one." And he adds: "None of the great massacres of
the twentieth century can be compared to this hetacomb, so it is easy
to understand how vain are the efforts being made by some writers
to dissipate what is known as the 'black legend' establishing Spain's
responsibility in this genocide and tarnishing its reputation. Much
indeed was black, but there was no 'legend.'" And he adds further:
"If religious murder is a sacrifice, massacre is an atheistic murder
and the Spaniards seem to have invented (or rediscovered—but not
borrowed from their immediate past: the pyres of the Inquisition par-
take more of sacrifice) precisely this type of violence."

It is most odd to accuse the Spaniards of the golden century of
being atheists; as for massacre, it is typical of wars to the death
between sharply differing societies, although it cannot be said that
the Spaniards (who were in any case too few to indulge in it) systematically massacred the Indians. Todorov seems to forget that in
the modern concept of genocide, the key criterion is intention. This
intention never existed among the settlers, who were eager to exploit
a servile labor force. The Crown or its representatives in the Americas are even less open to such an accusation. The conquest of the
Americas by the Spaniards cannot be judged, without making some
reference to other ancient conquests, in the light of our contemporary views alone; one cannot simply ignore the world of values in
which another society than ours lived. Otherwise one finishes up
with this sort of retrospective view:

The Spaniards won the war. But this victory from which all of us, Europeans and Americans alike, derive, delivered a heavy blow to our capacity to feel ourselves in harmony with the world, as belonging to a preestablished order; it had the effect of profoundly repressing the communication of man with the world, creating the illusion that all communication is inter-human; the silence of the gods weighs on the Europeans as much as it does on the Indians. What he won on the one hand, the European lost on the other; by imposing his will on the entire earth by what was his superiority, he crushed in himself his capacity for integration into the world. During the centuries that followed, he would dream of the noble savage; but the savage was dead or assimilated and this dream was condemned to remain sterile. The victory was already heavy with his defeat. (Todorov, p. 103)

The Incas were defeated, like the Aztecs, for a series of reasons, the principal one being the overall inferiority of their level of development. Weakened by civil war, the very hierarchically organized empire collapsed once its head had been stricken. The Spaniards were seen as allies by Huascar's followers, and the Cañaris, among other people, joined the Spaniards to shake off the Inca yoke. Manco's great rebellion failed in part because the Huancas and the Chachapoyas refused to align themselves with the Incas.

The defeat of the Indians was not only a military disaster but also a cosmic one. Resort to magical explanation transformed the vanquished into the victim of fate. "Like the sun, total disaster cannot be looked at directly: it is unbearable" (B. Mangin).

What the Indians suffered was an Apocalypse: "and they were given power over a fourth of the earth, to kill with sword and famine and with pestilence and by wild beasts of the earth" (Revelation, 6.7). The old order had changed. Gradually, the Church brought another truth, and everything that had previously given meaning to the world had to be hidden in people's memories, where it was slowly forgotten. Rarely has defeat been on such a scale.

Insofar as the traumatic shock of defeat can be eliminated only by adopting the behavior and language and faith of the Spaniards, it remains present, consciously or otherwise, in the marginalization and silent humiliation of the Indians in the Andes, the last echo of which perhaps resonates in the *quema*, the Indian flute with its desperately melancholy sound.

Ayacucho — Paris
1985–1989

BIBLIOGRAPHY
OF SOURCES

In putting together this book, I used the following texts, almost all contemporaneous with the conquest: Indian sources and chronicles by conquistadors or by historians who collected the accounts of the actors themselves.

Among the accounts of the conquest of Mexico: above all the *Codex florentinus or Histoire générale des choses de la Nouvelle-Espagne* (French ed., La Découverte, 1980) by the Franciscan Bernardino de Sahagun, who arrived in Mexico in 1529. He began to learn Nahuatl in 1536. In about 1547 he embarked on his work as an ethnographer and, mainly between 1550 and 1555, collected a series of accounts from Indian informants in Tlatelolco. He completed his *General History of the Affairs of New Spain*, an essential source of our knowledge of Mexican society, in 1568. His manuscript, in Nahuatl and Spanish, ended up in Florence, where it was discovered in 1793. Between 1950 and 1974, two American researchers, Charles E. Dibble and Arthur J. O. Anderson, published the Nahuatl text accompanied by an English translation. The passages dealing with the Indian perception of the conquest make up Book XII of the *General History*.

In French, the most complete work on the Aztec accounts of the conquest is *Récits aztèques de la conquête*, a collection of texts chosen and presented by Georges Baudot and Tzvetan Todorov, translated from the Nahuatl by Georges Baudot and from the Spanish by Pierre Cordoba (Seuil, 1983). This work includes the *Codex florentinus*, Book XII of the *General History of the Affairs of New Spain,* the *Codex Ramirez (Account of the Indians who populate New Spain);* Aubin's *The (anonymous) History of Tlatelolco 1528*; the *History of Tlaxcala* by Diego Muñoz Camargo; and a few passages from Diego Duran, *History of the Indies and New Spain and the Islands of Terra Firma.*

I have especially used the remarkable work by Miguel León Portilla and Angel Maria Garibray, *Vision de los vencidos* (Mexico, 1961). This work has been translated into French with the title *Le Crépuscule des Aztèques. Récits aztèques de la conquête* (Brussels, 1965). This work includes Book XII of Bernardino de Sahagun's *General History of New Spain* and a large selection of other accounts relating to the conquest of Mexico, Yucatan, Guatemala, and Peru. See also M. León Portilla, *El Reverso de la conquista* (Mexico, 1964); French translation by J.-P. Cortada (Federop, 1972).

On the conquest of Yucatan and Peru, the Indian sources are:

Adrian Recinos, ed., *Memorial de Solala—Annales de los Chakchiqueles* and *Titulo de los Señores de Tutonilapan* (Mexico, 1950). J. A. Villaloria, *Memorial de Telpan-Atitlan (Anales de los Chakchiqueles),* (Guatemala, 1936). *Libros de los libros de Chilam Balam* (published by Alfredo Barrera Vasquez, Mexico, 1948). French translation of the *Chilam Balam de Chumayel* by Benjamin Peret (1955), and more recently by J.-M. Le Clezio (1976). See also the *Chilam Balam de Tisimin. Le Codex Perez*, translated by E. Solis Alcala (Herida, 1949). Adrian Recinos,ed., *Cronicas indigenas de Guatemala* (Guatemala, 1957).

On the conquest of Peru, where there are few Indian sources:

Guaman Poma de Ayala, *Nueva Cronica y Buen Gobierno* (illustrated, 3 vols., Madrid, Edition 16, 1988).

Garcilaso de la Vega, *Comentarios Reales* (2 vols., Madrid, 1980), French translation, La Découverte (1982).

Yupanqui Titu Cusi (Diego de Castro), *Relación de la Conquista del Peru y hechos del Inca Manco II* [1570] (Lima, 1916).

Indigenous folklore:

Apu Inca Atawalpaman, Elegia quechua anonima, translated into Spanish by José Maria Arguedas,(Lima, no date).

Tragedia del fin de Atahualpa, monograph and translation by Jesus Lara Cochabamba (1957).

La Conquista de los Españoles, Drama indigeno quechua-castellano, ed. and trans. Clement Hernando Balmori (Tucuman, 1955).

On the conquest of Mexico, as transmitted by the Spaniards who took part in it, I have above all made extensive use of the account by Bernal Diaz del Castillo, *Historia verdadera de la conquista de la Nueva España* (1 vol., Madrid, Alianza, 1989). A shortened French version of this account was published by F. Maspero in 1980.

Bernal Diaz was born in Castile in about 1495 into a very modest family; his education was rudimentary. He was about twenty when he arrived in Cuba, and he participated in the first two expeditions on the continent before joining Cortes's expedition. He became a *regidor* (municipal councilor) of Santiago de Guatemala, and decided to write his account in 1552 in reply to the biography of Cortes written by Gomara, which he found hagiographical. He ended his chronicle of almost 600 closely written pages in 1568: he was seventy-three years old. The book was not printed until 1632.

Another key document:

Hernando Cortes, *Cartas de relación de la Conquista* (Madrid, 1988). These dispatches, the first three of which relate to the conquest of Mexico up to the fall of the city of Mexico, were published in French by La Découverte (1988).

The other accounts by conquistadors suffer by comparison with the two works cited above: Andrea de Tapia, *Relación sobre la conquista de Mexico;* B. Vasquez de Tapia, *Relación;* Francisco de Aquila, *Relación breve de la conquista de la Nueva España* (brought together in a single volume by Editorial 16, Madrid).

Among historians contemporary with the events: Diego Duran, *Historia de los Indios de la Nueva España e Islas de Tierra firme* (2 vols., Mexico, 1867–1880). Juan de Acosta, *Historia natural y moral de los Indios* (1st ed., Seville, 1590; Mexico, 1962). Toribio de Benavente (Motolinia), *Historia de los Indios de la Nueva España* (Mexico, 1941).

I have not made use of the complacent *Historia de la conquista de Mexico* by Francisco Lopez de Gomara, despite its various merits. See also *Historia general de las Indias* (2 vols., Madrid, 1941). The historian Gonzalo Fernandez de Oviedo y Valdes collected a large number of testimonies from Cortes's companions in his *Historia general y natural de las Indias* [1557] (5 vols., Madrid, 1959).

On Yucatan, see the key testimony of Diego de Landa, *Relación de las cosas de Yucatán* (Merida, 1938); English translation by W. Gates, *Yucatan before and after the Conquest* (New York, 1978; reprint of Maya Society edition of 1937).

Chroniclers of the conquest of Peru:

Pedro de Pizarro, *Relación del descubrimiento de los reinos del Perú* [1571] (Lima, 1978). He was a nephew of Pizarro and the chronicler who was present longest during the conquest.

Pedro Sancho de la Hoz, *Relación para Su Majestad de la sucecido en la conquista y pacificación destas provincias de la Nueva Castilla* [1543] (Madrid, 1962).

Diego de Trujillo, *Relación del descubrimiento del reino del Perú* (Seville, 1948).

Cristóbal de Mena, *La Conquista del Perú llamada la Nueva Castilla* (Seville, 1934).

Francisco de Jerez, *Verdadera Relación de la conquista del Perú* [1534], presented by P. Duviols, A. M. Metaillé (Paris, 1976).

This edition of Jerez chronicle includes the account by Miguel de Estete of an episode in the conquest (published in Seville in 1534).

Juan Ruiz de Arce (c. 1543), *Advertencias que hizó el fundador del vinculo y payorazgo a los sucesores de él*, (Madrid, 1933). Cristóbal de Molina (El Chileno), *Relación de la conquista y población del Perú* [c. 1553] (Lima, 1943).

For this part devoted to Peru, except for Francisco de Jerez's *Conquête du Pérou*, there is nothing in French. I have therefore translated fragments of the following chroniclers and historians: Pedro Pizarro, Diego de Trujillo, Pedro Sancho de la Hoz, Juan Ruiz de Arce, Cristóbal de Mena, Agustin de Zarate, Pedro Cieza de León, Martin de Murua, and others.

Antonio Herrera, *Historia general de los hechos de los Castellanos en las Islas y tierra firme del Mar oceano* [1601], French translation, Beräs (1633).

Agustin de Zarate, *Historia del descubrimiento y conquista de la provincia del Perú* (Antwerp, 1555; Madrid, 1972). Zarate was one of the major historians of the history of the civil wars in Peru. He arrived in Peru in 1543.

José de Acosta, *Historia natural y moral de las Indias* (Seville, 1590).

Juan de Betanzos, *Suma y naración de los Incas* [1551] (Madrid, 1968).

Cieza de León, *Crónica del Perú* [1553] (2 vols., Madrid, 1984).

Martin de Murua, Historia general del Perú [1590–1611] (Madrid, 1987).

Pedro de Bamboa Sarmiento, *Historia de los Incas* [1572] (Buenos Aires, 1943).

Pedro Gutierrez de Santa Clara, *Historia de las guerras civiles del Perú* [1544–1548] (6 vols., Madrid, 1904–1905).

Las Casas, *Historia de las Indias* ed. L. Hanke and L. Millares (3 vols., Mexico, 1951), and *Breve historia de la destrucción de las Indias* [1552], French translation, Maspero (1979).

In putting this work together, I have essentially stayed with the sources. But some modern or contemporary works have also been extremely useful. As a general introduction: Pierre Chaunu, *Conquête et exploitation des nouveaux mondes* (PUF, 1969), bibliography of 1,560 titles on the conquest of the Americas by the Spaniards. The classic works of W. H. Prescott, although written in the last century, remain a monument: *History of the Conquest of Mexico* and *History of the Conquest of Peru* [1847] (New York, 1940). More recently, on Peru: John Hemming, *The Conquest of the Incas* (New York, 1970), French translation, Stock, 1971. Nathan Wachtel, *La Vision des vaincus. Les Indiens du Pérou devant la conquête espagnole 1520–1570* (Gallimard, 1971).

On the Aztecs: the work of Jacques Soustelle, perhaps complemented by the works of Christian Duverger. On the Spaniards present at Cajamarca: James Lockhart, *The Men of Cajamarca* (University of Texas, 1973). Finally, on the military aspects, A. M. Salas, *Las Armas de la Conquista* (Buenos Aires, 1950).

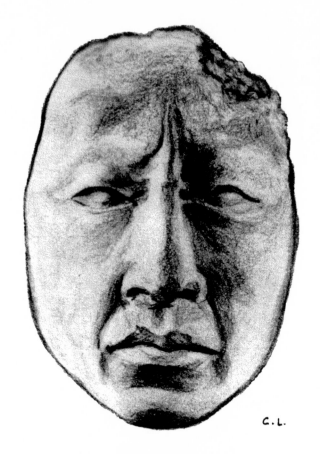

Mayan mask (Museum of Mexico)
Drawing by Carole Laporte

CHRONOLOGY

Mid Fifteenth century	Establishment of the Aztec empire.
1438–1471	Reign of Pachacuti Inca Yupanqui.
1471–1493	Reign of Topa Inca Yupanqui. Formation of the Inca empire.
1493–1527(?)	Reign of Huayna Capac.
1492	Christopher Columbus's first voyage. Reconnaissance of Greater Antilles.
1493	Columbus's second voyage. Reconnaissance of Jamaica and Lesser Antilles.
1498	Columbus's third voyage. Reconnaissance of Trinidad and coast of Venezuela.
1499	Juan Diaz de Solis sails along the coast of Honduras. Juan de la Casa and Alonzo de Ojeda reconnoiter the coast of Venezuela.
1501	Amerigo Vespucci sails along the Atlantic coast of South America as far as southern Brazil.
1502	Columbus's fourth voyage. He sails along the coast of Panama.
	Montezuma heads the Aztec empire.
1510	Cuba and Santo Domingo are thoroughly occupied. The first *Audiencia* is established in Santo Domingo (Hispaniola). The two islands serve as bases for the conquest of Mexico and Central America.
1513	Vasco Nuñez de Balboa crosses the isthmus of Panama (Darien) and reaches the Pacific Ocean.
1517	Hernando de Cordoba sails along the coast of Yucatan.
1518	Juan de Grivalja sails along the coast of Mexico.
Feb. 18, 1519	Cortes leaves for Mexico.
Nov. 8, 1519	Cortes enters the city of Mexico.

May 1520	Battle between Cortes and Narvaez (sent by the governor of Cuba).
June 30, 1520	The *Noche triste*.
July 7, 1520	Battle of Otumba.
May 28, 1521	Beginning of the siege of the city of Mexico.
1522	Conquest of Nicaragua by Gil Gonzalez Davila. Nicaragua becomes, with Panama, the jumping-off point for the conquest of Peru.
1523	Pedro de Alvarado reconnoiters Guatemala.
1524–1525	Pizarro's first voyage.
1526	Pizarro, Almagro, and Luque agree together in Panama. Francisco de Montejo reconnoiters Yucatan.
1526–1527	Pizarro's second voyage.
1527	Creation of the *Audiencia* of Mexico.
1528–1532	Civil war between Huascar and his half-brother, Atahualpa.
Dec. 27, 1530	Pizarro leaves for his third voyage.
May 16, 1532	Tumbez. Pizarro sets out with some 167 men.
Nov. 16, 1532	Cajamarca. Capture of Inca Atahualpa.
Jan. 6–Apr. 25, 1533	Hernando Pizarro's expedition to Pachacamac.
Aug. 29, 1533	Execution of Atahualpa after payment of ransom.
Nov. 15, 1533	Spaniards enter Cuzco.
Dec. 1533	Coronation of Manco Inca.
1534	Pedro de Alvarado lands in Ecuador.
June 1534	Benalcazar enters Quito.
Jan. 6, 1535	Pizarro founds Lima, the "City of the Kings."
July 1535	Almagro embarks on the disastrous expedition to Chile.
1536	Revolt by Manco and siege of Cuzco.
Aug. 1536	Indian failure before Lima.
Apr. 1537	Almagro takes Cuzco and imprisons Pizarro's brothers.
1537	Manco takes refuge in the mountains of Vilcabamba. He is hunted to Vitcos by Rodrigo Orgoñez.
1538	Foundation of the *Audiencia* of Panama.
Apr. 26, 1538	Battle of Las Salinas. Hernando Pizarro defeats Almagro.
Apr.–July 1539	Vilcabamba is taken by Gonzalo Pizarro. Manco manages to flee.
Oct.–Nov. 1539	The second revolt is virtually ended.
1540	Valdivia enters Chile.

	Beginning of the conquest of the Mayas by Francisco de Montejo the younger.
July 26, 1541	Francisco Pizarro is murdered by Almagro's men.
Sept. 1542	Vaca de Castro defeats Diego Almagro the younger.
Nov. 15, 1542	The "New Laws" are promulgated.
1542	Creation of the *Audiencias* of Guatemala and Lima. Orellana sails down the Amazon.
	Beginning of civil wars in Peru.
May 1544	Blasco de Nuñez de Vela named viceroy of Peru.
June–July 1544	Manco murdered by Spanish renegades at Vitcos. Sayri-Tupac succeeds him.
Oct. 1544	Gonzalo Pizarro enters Lima.
Apr. 1545	Discovery of silver mines at Potosi.
Jan. 13, 1546	Gonzalo Pizarro defeats and kills the viceroy Blasco de Nuñez de Vela.
Apr. 9, 1548	Pedro de la Gasca defeats Gonzalo Pizarro, who is executed.
Aug. 1550	Debate at Valladolid between Las Casas and Sepulveda.
1533–1534	Last rebellion of Spanish "colonizers" led by Francisco Hernandez Giron.
Jan. 1556	Charles V abdicates. Philip II crowned.
Oct. 1557	Sayri-Tupac leaves Vilcabamba and goes to Lima.
1559	Mercury mines at Huancavelica discovered.
1560	Death of Sayri-Tupac. Titu Cusi named Inca at Vilcabamba.
May 1561	Hernando Pizarro, imprisoned for twenty years, is released and returns to Trujillo (Estremadura).
1563	Foundation of the *Audiencia* of Quito.
1566	Treaty between Titu Cusi and the Spaniards.
1567	Titu Cusi is baptized.
Nov. 1569	Viceroy Francisco de Toledo arrives.
Oct. 1570	A special commission endorses forced labor in the mines.
Nov. 1570–Mar. 1571	Toledo's *informaciones* on the history of the Incas.
May 1571	Death of Titu Cusi. Tupac Amaru Inca.
Apr. 14, 1572	War declared on Tupac Amaru.
June 1, 1572	Tupac Amaru's forces defeated.
June 24, 1572	Vilcabamba besieged.
Sept. 24, 1572	Tupac Amaru executed at Cuzco.

INDEX